PROCUREMENT WITH PURPOSE

'The decisions we make this decade are the most important in human history.'
Sir David Attenborough

PROCUREMENT WITH PURPOSE

How organisations can change the way they spend money **NOW** to protect the planet and its people

PETER SMITH with MARK PERERA

First published 2021

Published under licence by Brown Dog Books and
The Self-Publishing Partnership Ltd, 10b Greenway Farm, Bath Rd,
Wick, nr. Bath BS30 5RL

www.selfpublishingpartnership.co.uk

ISBN printed book: 978-1-83952-371-7
ISBN e-book: 978-1-83952-372-4

Cover design by Kevin Rylands
Internal design by Andrew Easton

Printed and bound in the UK

This book is printed on FSC certified paper

CONTENTS

SECTION 3 – The Issues and Options

SECTION 4 – A Directory of Procurement with Purpose Topics

Acknowledgements

Many thanks to everyone who contributed to this book in some way. Starting at the beginning, Samia Calvet at software firm SAP Ariba commissioned me to write a "thought leadership" paper on the topic back in 2018. While I was already very interested in the whole area, that really got me thinking about producing a book , so thanks to her for that inspiration .

Mark Perera and I then discovered our common interest in the topic, and we interviewed many interesting people, initially for our website. Many of those folks now appear in this book, so our sincere thanks to them for giving their time and wisdom to the cause of Procurement with Purpose.

Thanks also to those who read the proof and provided testimonials and reviews for us to use, and also to Sarah Clarke, Nancy Clinton, my wife Jane and daughter Ginny, who all provided input to the book in terms of content, design or both.

Finally, thanks to Douglas, Frances and the team at the Self-Publishing Partnership. We decided to self-publish so we could control the pricing of the book and make sure as much of the revenue as possible goes to good causes. But I also knew from past experience that the team at SPP would make the experience pleasant and straightforward, as it proved.

About the Authors

Peter Smith

Peter was born in Sunderland and after graduating from St. John's College, Cambridge, he started his procurement career at Mars Confectionery. He was then Procurement Director for Dun & Bradstreet Europe, the Department of Social Security, and the NatWest Group. He is a Fellow and was 2003 President of the Chartered Institute of Purchasing and Supply, acted as a Senior Adviser to the UK National Audit Office and has served as a non-executive director of two large public sector organisations and a growing private firm.

He founded his consulting firm, Procurement Excellence Ltd. in 2004 and from 2010-18 was Managing Editor of the Spend Matters Europe website, read by thousands of procurement professionals every day. His first co-authored book, (with Fiona Czerniawska), *"Buying Professional Services"* was published by The Economist Books in 2010. A second book, *"A Procurement Compendium"* was published in 2019, and in October 2020, Penguin Business published his latest book, *"Bad Buying – How Organisations Waste Billions Through Failures, Frauds and F*ck-ups"*!

Mark Perera

Mark graduated from Southampton University with a degree in Biology, and after a few years of corporate life moved into the entrepreneurial space, co-founding Procurement Leaders in 2004. That organisation grew into the leading global membership, events, and intelligence network for procurement across major businesses. In 2014, Mark stepped back from Procurement Leaders and founded Vizibl, a leading cloud technology platform that enables organisations to drive growth through supplier collaboration and innovation. He also has an interest in a number of other start-ups and growing businesses, and is a recognised thought leader in the procurement and technology worlds. Mark lives in south-west London with his wife and two teenage daughters.

For more information on procurement with purpose topics, and regular new articles, please see the website at:
https://www.procurementwithpurpose.com/

Introduction

Procurement with purpose as an expression is relatively new. Procurement professionals have talked about the purpose of procurement for many years, but it is only relatively recently that we have used the newer phrase to indicate the aspect of responsible and purposeful business that relates to how organisations spend money with suppliers.

Software firm SAP Ariba started including the expression in promotional material in 2017, and I wrote a briefing paper for the firm in 2018 titled "Procurement with a Purpose – Making a Positive Impact on Organisations, Human Rights and Communities".

In simple terms, procurement with purpose aims to use corporate and public sector spend with suppliers to drive wider benefits, environmental, social and economic, rather than simply support the spending organisations' short-term, internal goals. And in the last few years, it has assumed greater importance and priority across many organisations and become of real interest to millions of people around the world.

Mark Perera and I launched the Procurement with Purpose website in late 2019, and I started writing this book in the 2019/20 New Year holiday period. We were looking forward to skiing holidays, music festivals, major corporate events and conferences through that year. The global economy looked in pretty good shape, although Brexit and the 2020 Presidential election in the USA loomed ahead of us. By late March around half the book was in first draft form. And then, everything changed.

The coronavirus pandemic swept the globe, with countries including the US, UK and much of Europe severely affected. Hundreds of thousands died, businesses were put into suspended animation or closed forever. People lost their jobs, whilst those in the medical sector and other critical service areas ended up working flat out for months to try and save lives, sometimes sacrificing their own. One friend who was at the front line of PPE supply (personal protective equipment) into the UK National Health Service talked of working 100-hour weeks.

I stopped work on the book for a couple of months. It was hard to think logically about deforestation or diversity in the supply chain when you're not sure how to get food to a 92-year-old mother "shielding" at the other end of the country, or whether flights to Singapore would ever resume (my daughter and son-in-law flew out on a two-year assignment to the city just two weeks before the virus really hit).

But even in the worst of the first lockdowns, there were some unexpected benefits of the industrial shutdown – not that anyone wanted that to continue for long. But dolphins swam in the usually polluted canals of Venice, and wild goats roamed the streets of Llandudno in Wales.[1] The air became magically cleaner, and that sparked renewed discussion around how to address climate change, reduce emissions and further address pollution.[2]

As you can see, the book was completed, but with further interviews over Zoom taking the place of discussions in pleasant pubs, more's the pity! Writing this now in the summer of 2021, the picture is still mixed. In some places, the third (or fourth) wave is still killing thousands daily. But vaccines are being delivered to millions of people every day, and in some countries, we can see that life might return to something closer to normal

---

1 https://www.youtube.com/watch?v=bMUlppJbbI8

2 https://www.theguardian.com/environment/2020/apr/11/positively-alpine-disbelief-air-pollution-falls-lockdown-coronavirus

by the end of 2021. However, it will be a "new normal" everywhere, and it is not clear what COVID will do for the whole sustainable business and procurement with purpose movements. It could go either way; but we will come back to those implications at greater length in Chapter 14.

The "moving target" challenge has also been an obvious issue in writing the book. As the text goes off for layout and printing, we are weeks away from the COP26 climate summit, which might have major implications for the planet. Technology, politics and economic issues all move fast, so some comments here may seem outdated by the time you read the book. I apologise for that, but it is inevitable, and maybe we will look at regular updates if there proves to be enough interest in procurement with purpose.

Back to COVID. Whatever changes it brings, procurement with purpose has the potential to benefit critical environmental issues such as climate change, pollution, plastics, and deforestation. It can also help to address social and economic challenges including modern slavery, human rights, and the encouragement of innovation and diversity. These are issues that will define the future of our planet and everyone who lives on it.

That potential benefit from procurement with purpose arises because businesses and public sector organisations can use the money they spend with third parties to influence the behaviour of those suppliers. That can have an impact on the whole range of purpose-related environmental, social and economic issues. In most cases, the impact organisations can have by working with and through their supply chain is far greater than they can achieve by purely internal actions.

Organisations globally spend over $50 TRILLION every year with the businesses that provide the goods and services they require to operate. Of course, most businesses are suppliers themselves, as well as buyers, so we can look at this as a huge network of trading organisations, with vast sums of money flowing in exchange for everything needed to keep economies running. That scale and the network effect are what give the procurement with purpose movement its power and potential to do good.

The concept of organisations acting in a responsible and purposeful manner is not new, and the pressure for more action has been building for many years. But the urgency with which these issues are being addressed has undoubtedly quickened in the last ten years or so, and that has been driven by five groups exerting increased pressure:

- Governments, which have increasingly legislated to drive certain business behaviour, arguably driven by the expectations of citizens (the voters).
- Organisations' customers and clients who are demanding change, whether customers are public sector bodies, other businesses or individual consumers.
- Business owners, whether individuals or institutions such as pension funds and insurance companies, who are acting based on their own beliefs, customer pressure or both.
- Staff themselves within organisations, from CEOs and Boards to the grass roots workers, who want to drive change and bring that desire for "purpose" into their own workplace.
- Charities, lobby groups and the media, who have picked up on various causes, providing knowledge and insight, and helping to publicise issues and bring them to wider attention.

But why have these various groups – all made up ultimately of individual people, we should say – driven the "purpose" agenda up the priority list? What has caused this groundswell of opinion, from the public but also from bastions of capitalism, that has made these ideas about creating a more sustainable world more prevalent? And if procurement with purpose does provide us with a major opportunity to change the world, how can we make that happen as quickly and successfully as possible?

These are questions this book attempts to answer, although of course it cannot provide all the solutions. Many of the topics, such as climate change, use of plastics, or human rights, are vast and have inspired entire libraries of more specific books. But the major issues and ideas are covered here, with supporting case studies and interviews, particularly where procurement activities can lead to positive change in vital areas.

Section 1 covers the background to procurement with purpose. That starts with how businesses have developed greater awareness of their potential impact on issues wider than their own short-term success and profit. Procurement with purpose is a subset – a very important one, for reasons we'll examine – of a wider movement, which encompasses a range of issues identified as "corporate social responsibility" or "sustainable and purposeful business". The chapters look at exactly why the pace of change is accelerating, and how key stakeholder groups are driving that.

Section 2 moves onto procurement with purpose issues, and how organisations are taking action. What works – and what doesn't? There are practical suggestions and ideas in terms of how your organisation can understand the issues and contribute to the procurement with purpose movement. That includes aspects such as how to incorporate this thinking into supplier selection processes and contracting, or what needs to be done if you are driving significant change that requires supplier collaboration. Through sections 1 and 2, you will also find the "Top Ten Take-Aways", aimed at highlighting the most important core messages that everyone should bear in mind when implementing procurement with purpose.

Then Section 3 looks more closely at eight key procurement with purpose topics. Although these huge topics can't be covered in every detail, issues are explained with examples of how organisations are addressing them, and suggestions as to how you can make any of these central to your own efforts.

Finally, in Section 4, a standard template format summarises the key points for no less than 25 different procurement with purpose issues, to help you understand each and decide which might be appropriate for your organisation focus. As well as briefly describing the key aspects for each, the section suggests which type of organisation might see each as a priority, and explains potential barriers, as well as some success measures.

Throughout the book, I have drawn on my and Mark's own experiences, other published work, "roundtable" discussions, and around twenty major interviews conducted with key players in this field. That has enabled us to bring stories of good practice, success (and the odd failure) from people who are involved in procurement with purpose. Many are genuinely passionate about what they are doing and hope to achieve, and we hope that comes across and inspires readers.

We have not hesitated to comment on poor practice, issues such as "greenwashing" and the like, but the main purpose of the book is to be positive: to help readers understand the issues, identify and implement good ideas that can help their own organisations. So we make no apology for taking a "glass half full" approach in most cases.

But speed is now of the essence, as Sir David Attenborough, Greta Thunberg and others have reminded us. Change is essential now, in this decade, not at some vague moment in the future. There are huge and urgent problems to be faced, but we think there are enough inspiring and innovative people out there to move us in the right direction. Let's all hope so, anyway.

Procurement with Purpose –

A PERSONAL PERSPECTIVE FROM MARK PERERA

Everyone has a different journey in terms of developing their own priorities and sense of purpose. I was lucky enough to spend most of my childhood by the ocean. My family lived in Australia for ten years, and then I lived in Wales on the beautiful Gower Peninsula in my teenage years. The Gower was the first nominated Area of Outstanding Natural Beauty in the UK, and my grandparents owned a small farm there, which is still in the family today.

But swimming and surfing had a downside, even in those idyllic situations. In the case of the Gower in the 1990s, that was the raw sewage discharged into the Atlantic. I joined Surfers Against Sewage, and campaigned for a cleaner ocean. One of my school friends joined the council, and his work included putting dye down the toilets of various houses in order to try and work out which water treatment systems were not working properly!

My father was Sri Lankan, and I also travelled to that country as a child. There are happy memories, but the poverty and inequality I saw there also made an impact, and like many of my generation, I was moved by stories of famine in Ethiopia. I was also a big fan of the nature documentaries we started to see from David Attenborough and others.

My passion for the natural world led to a degree in Biology, with an emphasis on ecology and the environment, and the first start-up I was involved with after university looked to use technology to help homeowners model how they could apply environmentally friendly solutions to their property. We were probably ahead of our time!

Then my passion for procurement developed, and in 2003 I founded Procurement Leaders alongside two good friends. We saw that suppliers could help businesses drive growth, and procurement could be truly strategic, not just about saving money. Hundreds of leading firms agreed, participating in the PL network. In only our second year of operation, we started a sustainable sourcing website, some time before this became such a hot topic.

Moving forwards, in 2019, the three founders sold Procurement Leaders, and I decided that I wanted to try and "make a difference" in the next stage of my career and life. Help light a few fires, as it were. I want to look back in twenty years' time and feel I have contributed something to the greater good. So I contacted Peter Smith, an old friend I've known since he chaired one of the very first Procurement Leaders conferences, with ideas about a procurement with purpose website and book. "That's funny," he said. "I've just been working on an outline for exactly that book." It was clearly meant to happen!

We quickly agreed on our collaboration, and that's how the process started that led to the website and now publication of this book. We looked to interview people who had interesting views and ideas around purpose, or were already into implementation mode, and as well as providing articles for the website, those interviews feature heavily in these pages.

How Procurement with Purpose Developed

I have been inspired through my journey by many companies and individuals. Unilever is an obvious example. Paul Polman took a risk when he announced sustainability targets and a new focus for the firm in 2010. But through the last decade, firms like his have led the way, looking to use their sustainability actions and their sense of purpose to build premium consumer brands. They moved away from a short-term bottom line-driven culture and started looking at the bigger picture. And it is not just the environment – if you pay your own staff fairly, why would you not expect or want your suppliers to do the same with their own people? Suppliers play strategic roles and are often seen as an extension of our organisation, so shouldn't they behave properly? We need to show as much respect to them and their people as we do within our own four walls. We would not tolerate human rights abuses in our own factories or offices: why would we turn a blind eye to that in companies supplying us?

Organisations have also seen the value of collaboration, with suppliers and also more widely across sectors or industries, and that theme will re-emerge regularly through the chapters here. The vision for Vizibl, the software company I founded in 2015, was and still is very much around collaboration between businesses. But recently, we have seen our clients becoming focused on collaboration to support their purpose goals as well as to drive innovation, revenue and profit.

Our clients also want to apply the principles to smaller suppliers as well as large – small suppliers can both bring innovation and be the source of purpose-related opportunities and issues. We initially worked with early adopters, but now clients include dozens of leading firms in consumer goods, pharma, chemicals and more. They use our tool to support strategic programmes, with cross-functional teams focused on action to drive business growth and their sense of purpose.

The Developing Role of Procurement

The development of sustainable and purposeful business thinking has proved to be a great opportunity for procurement functions and people to get closer to the Board, support the business and contribute to growth. Opportunities have emerged upstream and downstream, with the circular economy and related thinking around that now on many agendas.

Procurement can and should support strategic programmes, as long as it aligns closely with the business. Think about issues such as packaging, where long-term collaboration between buyers and sellers has driven technological innovation. Getting to grips with Scope 3 emissions is another critical issue where procurement has to play a leading role. This is no longer just about monitoring compliance and ticking boxes – it is about real action. And procurement has to step up. For most organisations, suppliers will account for something between 50 and 80% of total emissions, so getting to grips with your supply chain is an essential, not a nice-to-have.

However, procurement people and functions have not always recognised what is possible if we unleash the full potential of procurement with purpose. We need to raise the bar and see every category manager involved, unleashing the abilities of our suppliers, looking for innovation and harnessing what new technology can bring. Boards are now expecting this of procurement, and awareness is growing. Every procurement function in any organisation can contribute – if you haven't got started yet, do it now.

In all of this, procurement has to work with the business. And this involves change management, which we all know isn't easy and is a skill in itself. But I truly believe this is an exciting time for procurement and a great opportunity. Often, we will need to look at end-to-end processes – the principles of circularity, for instance, are fascinating but need whole new ways of looking at business models, and developing the circular economy will need backing from entire industries as well as consumers and governments.

When we started the movement, I felt the "procurement with purpose" term was important because it does go beyond what is sometimes thought of as "sustainability", which tends to be heavily focused on the environment. Important though that is, "purpose" covers all the ESG (environmental, social, and governance) definitions and supports the goals of the United Nations Sustainable Development Goals. It has been very positive to see leading firms such as Vodafone and bp badging their internal programmes and initiatives of this nature as "procurement with purpose", and we hope this will continue. (I should say we have no commercial interest in the terminology!)

But we shouldn't think that everything is on the right track. It is vital that we have a quantifiable impact, with hard targets. Big goals are fine, but we need robust reporting and verification to gain credibility. Greenwashing is always a danger. And a survey by Procurious and Ivalua of 470 procurement executives in early 2021 reported that 23% have not yet started on the supply chain sustainability journey; 39% said they were just starting out, 22% had an established programme, and just 15% reported an advanced programme. There is a long way to go.

The Future and Getting Started

"The natural world today is greatly diminished. That is undeniable. Our climate is warming fast. That is beyond doubt. Our societies and nations are unequal and that sadly is plain to see. But the question science forces us to address specifically in 2021 is whether as a result of these intertwined facts we are on the verge of destabilising the entire planet? If that is so, then the decisions we make this decade – in particular the decisions made by the most economically advanced nations – are the most important in human history."

(Sir David Attenborough, environmentalist and COP26 People's Champion)

We still have an opportunity to solve the big environmental issues before it is too late, as Sir David tells us, but this is the decade of our lives to make a difference, to bring it back in terms of emissions, deforestation, plastics and more. That needs action now. There are bold targets for reducing emissions by 2030, for example, with the UK committing to net zero by 2050. But that means every 5 weeks, another 1% of the available days up to that target date have gone. There is no time to waste and individuals, governments and businesses have to step up now.

If we don't turn this around, I fear we won't leave much of a world for our children and children's children. I have two teenage daughters, and much as we all still love the Gower, the plastic pollution in the sea, on beaches, everywhere, is terrible. We have turned off the sewage discharges since my childhood, but there are new types of waste everywhere.

One positive, though, is that firms are realising that it is better to get onto the front foot rather than wait until they are forced into action. I suspect Shell was shocked to lose the recent court case in the Netherlands relating to their preparations for net zero. Whether that verdict sticks on appeal or not, it is a sign that if firms don't take the initiative, they may be pushed into actions anyway. Responding to that, some firms are making big commitments, including some such as bp that must make massive changes to their whole business in order to reflect climate change issues. If bp can take that initiative, then there is no excuse for any organisation to think that this is too difficult.

What also inspires me now, and should encourage all of us, is how governments and firms are increasingly working together. The G7 group of countries made important commitments on coal-fired power stations in Cornwall in June 2021 (although China continues to build new plants). In the business world, the 100+ Accelerator initiative is a great example of collaboration, not competition, with AB InBev, Unilever, Coca-Cola and Colgate-Palmolive championing start-ups that have innovative solutions to sustainability challenges.

On a more personal note, one question Peter Smith and I often ask those we interview is: "how do procurement teams or individuals get started on this journey?" I would suggest initially reading your organisation's annual report, or sustainability report if one exists. Talk to colleagues who are in a sustainability role already – ask how procurement can contribute. Look at what the competition in your industry is doing (or similar organisations if you are in the public sector). Then work out what the biggest opportunity might be and start with that. Don't try to boil the ocean, but look to gain early success in one area, find people to collaborate with internally or externally, then expand.

If there is no sustainability function or executives yet, then you can take the lead. Build awareness, communicate with suppliers, maybe organise supplier events to talk about opportunities. And what if your organisation has no interest in these issues? Well, networks such as the Sustainable Procurement Pledge provide support for those who may feel somewhat alone.

But ultimately, if your organisation is not interested in developing a sense of purpose, or in contributing to making the world a better place for those who come after us, then you always have a choice. Good luck!

Section 1 –
Purposeful Business

Chapter 1 – The Origins of Sustainability and Business Purpose

"I do truly believe that, together, we can make a better future. I might not be here to see it, but if we make the right decisions at this critical moment, we can safeguard our planet's ecosystem."

(David Attenborough, from "Extinction: The Facts", BBC, September 2020)

My grandfather worked underground as a coal miner for 50 years, from 1903 to 1953, in a small County Durham village in the north-east of England. The village was dominated by a huge "slag heap" made up of the black waste material from the mining. The health and safety issues of life as a pitman were horrendous, let alone the animal welfare issues around the "pit ponies", and pollution to the land and waterways was significant.

Burning coal, as almost everyone in that area did to heat their homes, also contributed of course to emissions and climate change. But the pit also provided a sense of community for the village, and reasonably well-paid jobs compared to other largely manual roles at the time.

When the Durham mines closed in the 1960s and 70s, there was a palpable economic effect, with towns and villages becoming run-down and seriously deprived. There was also a tangible loss of community coherence. But the slag heap also disappeared, slowly converted into green spaces and woodland. Today, you would have no idea that Sherburn Hill ever hosted a huge coal mine. But the residents in the main all commute by car into Durham or Sunderland, contributing to emissions.

The issues around sustainable business are not new, and are often complex. From the days of the Industrial Revolution, business organisations have always provided both positives and negatives to their own local communities and workforces, as well as presenting a mixed picture in terms of their impact on the wider world.

Quakers, Carnegie and Chocolate – The Pioneers of Purposeful Business

It may feel that issues related to corporate responsibility and business purpose have only hit the headlines relatively recently. But the idea that people involved in business and the businesses themselves should pursue more than just short-term profit is not at all new, even if the topic has gained vastly increased attention in recent years.

There wasn't too much concern about global warming and other environmental issues until the 1960s (indeed, there were more scientists warning about a new "ice age"),[3] but we can trace other issues that are currently hot topics back to the 1800s. In that century, a range of "caring capitalists" came to the fore, men[4] who combined successful business with wider activities that aimed to fulfil social purposes.

The Quakers, for instance, are a historically Christian group of religious movements formally known as the Religious Society of Friends, Society of Friends or Friends Church. Members of the various

3 https://www.iceagenow.com/Scientists_worried_about_new_ice_age.htm

4 It was pretty much all men, a reflection of the times.

Quaker movements generally believe in the ability of each human being to experience and make use of the "light within", and "that of God in everyone". This sense that every individual is important led early Quaker business owners to show concern for the health and well-being of staff to a greater extent than the average industrialist.

Successful Quakers included the founders of banking and financial firms such as Barclays, Lloyds and Friends Provident; manufacturing companies, including shoe retailer C. & J. Clark and the big three British confectionery makers Cadbury, Rowntree and Fry. Famously, George Cadbury of the chocolate dynasty built the model village of Bournville in the 1890s, on the outskirts of Birmingham in Central England, to house his factory workers. Houses were spacious, with gardens, and the village incorporated park and recreation areas, encouraging swimming, walking and outdoor sport, all designed with the workers' health in mind. Bournville is still today a highly desirable place to live.

In the United States, some of the 19th century's most prominent and wealthy businessmen became great philanthropists, supporting causes that might fit under today's "sustainability" headings. Ironically, or perhaps inevitably, those who gave the most money, such as John D. Rockefeller, Calouste Gulbenkian and Andrew Carnegie, did so at the end of careers that often demonstrated a high degree of ruthlessness and aggressive corporate behaviour.

Rockefeller's life was driven by religion. In his first job as a clerk, at age 16, he gave six per cent of his earnings to charity, as recorded in his personal ledger. By the time he was twenty, his charitable giving exceeded ten per cent of his income. Rockefeller and his advisers invented the conditional grant, which required the recipient to "root the institution in the affections of as many people as possible who, as contributors, become personally concerned, and thereafter may be counted on to give to the institution their watchful interest and cooperation".

Biographer Ron Chernow[5] wrote of him: "What makes him problematic – and why he continues to inspire ambivalent reactions – is that his good side was every bit as good as his bad side was bad. Seldom has history produced such a contradictory figure."

Carnegie argued that the life of a wealthy industrialist should comprise two parts. The first part was the gathering and the accumulation of wealth. The second part was for the subsequent distribution of this wealth to benevolent causes. Philanthropy was key to making life worthwhile.

Whilst some still follow that two-stage approach, many of their modern-day equivalents look to do good in parallel to their business careers. Microsoft founder Bill Gates is an example, having gone from being seen by many as a brattish, young, aggressive billionaire to being one of the most admired people on earth (along with his soon-to-be ex-wife Melinda) for their work to alleviate poverty, disease and misery globally. That started when he was still involved with the firm, although he did step back in 2008 to focus on philanthropy.

Other firms have long pursued approaches that recognised more nuanced values than simply maximising profit. The Mars family made its fortune from chocolate, but with a somewhat different approach from the Quakers. Mars was less paternalistic, but focused on the concept of mutuality – everyone connected with the business should benefit in some way. That drove actions ranging from a sense of loyalty to suppliers, to supporting local community events in Slough where the UK factory was situated.

5 https://en.wikipedia.org/wiki/John_D._Rockefeller#CITEREFChernow1998

Where Have All the Flowers Gone?

For millions of years, humankind struggled against the environment and the natural world. We were at the mercy of the weather or wild animals. We spent considerable energy and lost lives trying to subjugate wild terrain for farming or commerce. But gradually, we won those battles, to the point where today it is the environment that needs protecting against humans if we are to carry on for a few more million (or even hundred) years.

That realisation has slowly grown over the last two centuries. There was legislation to protect waterways and some agricultural systems as far back as the 19th century – the US Rivers and Harbors Act, for instance. Theodore Roosevelt was the first US President (1901–09) to be interested in conservation, placing 230 million acres (930,000 km^2) under federal protection, establishing the US Forest Service and creating five National Parks. The famous mass trespass on Kinder Scout in 1932 led to greater public access to the hills of the UK and led to the creation of National Parks and long-distance footpaths.

But environmental awareness amongst the wider public really took off in the 1950s. As populations and economies grew after the Second World War, problems became evident. The Great Smog of London in December 1952 blanketed the capital with a dense layer of smog, formed largely from airborne pollutants. It lasted just 5 days, but killed 4,000 people according to statistical estimates, and brought the city to a standstill. Eventually legislation, such as the City of London (Various Powers) Act 1954 and the Clean Air Acts of 1956 and 1968, led to a reduction in air pollution, as citizens were encouraged (or forced by legislation) to burn less coal, and industries gradually became more regulated, too.

The growth of incomes and leisure time also led to a boom in outdoor hobbies such as fell walking and recreational cycling. The Peak District became the first UK National Park in 1951, and more quickly followed. But other aspects of environmental awareness did not emerge until later.

Whilst the Conservation Foundation, a precursor to the World Wildlife Fund (now known as WWF), was founded in 1948, these issues were not widely understood.

It is fascinating to see old clips of nature films and TV shows, such as the BBC "Zoo Quest" films of the early 1960s. Here, a young David Attenborough and others roamed jungles and plains, capturing animals and birds almost randomly to bring them back to Western zoos. The aim of the programmes appeared to be largely entertainment, with just a touch of education, rather than focusing on the conservation goals that most reputable zoos now respect. We are now in the middle of the "great extinction", but the idea that humans were in the process of driving other species to extinction on a huge scale was rarely considered before the 1960s.

In that decade, environmental issues became truly mainstream, and even fashionable. Rachel Carson's prophetic and influential book, *Silent Spring*, identified the damage that agricultural chemicals such as pesticides were doing to natural life. Pollution in rivers started to be addressed in many countries: the Cuyahoga River in Ohio became so polluted it "caught fire" some 13 times. A *Time* magazine article in 1969[6] after one of those fires grabbed the nation's attention, as the magazine reported that someone falling in the river "does not drown but decays".

Concerns about wildlife and the natural world also grew gradually but steadily. The hippy culture that emerged from California in the mid-1960s promoted greater environmental awareness. Songs such as "Where Have All the Flowers Gone?" (written in 1955 by Pete Seeger but a 1960s hit), "Big Yellow Taxi" (Joni Mitchell) and even The Kinks' "Apeman" brought issues to the general public in an easily understood manner. The photographs and videos taken from spacecraft in the late

---

6 https://time.com/3921976/cuyahoga-fire/

60s, showing earth as a beautiful yet somehow fragile planet, spinning in boundless space, caught the imagination of millions, and inspired more focus on these issues.

Since then, organisations such as WWF and Greenpeace have continued to draw attention to the effects of climate change, deforestation, pollution, and the growth in human population. Television programmes such as The Blue Planet have brought home the issues, showing, for instance, marine life dying because of the effects of plastic waste.

Slavery, Unions and the UN

The beginnings of what can be recognised as wider social awareness also go back many years. The "abolition" of slavery in the US Northern States dates to 1804, and Britain abolished slavery throughout its empire in 1833, except in India. Anti-Slavery International was founded in 1839 and still plays a major role today, which is vital because slavery has unfortunately not been "abolished". Incredibly, experts estimate that there are more people on earth today suffering some sort of modern slavery than there were people captured and sold as slaves between the 15th and 19th centuries. More about that later.

Trade unions grew through the 19th century in many countries, representing the rights of workers. In many countries, political parties such as the Labour Party in the UK grew out of the union movements. These institutions provided checks and balances against the harder edges of capitalism and business, as they campaigned for better and safer working conditions, shorter hours, paid holidays, and other benefits.

Human rights movements also emerged, and in 1948, the United Nations in just its third session adopted the Universal Declaration of Human Rights. It laid down 30 articles affirming an individual's rights, from the basic concepts of dignity, liberty and equality to more specific points such as the prohibition of slavery and freedom to peaceful assembly and to own property. The Declaration formed the basis of the International Bill of Human Rights, which eventually came into force in 1976.

> "We were ahead of the game in employing and supporting female staff, and in 1899, Richard MacGregor was IBM's first black employee. In 1953, a decade before the Civil Rights Act, IBM took a stand in favour of Equal Opportunity. In terms of our manufacturing heritage, we were always a firm that cleaned up after itself in terms of pollution. We're in 170 countries now, many in the developing world, and it is important that we can show appropriate stewardship".
>
> *(Alison Smith, IBM)*

Some firms took the lead in terms of diversity, and the 1960s saw the civil rights movement in the US addressing the rights of non-white people with leaders such as Martin Luther King Jr at the fore. As well as the focus on issues within individual countries, organisations such as Amnesty International, formed in London in 1961, worked to address global issues of human rights, building on the UN work.

From the 1960s onwards, there has also been a growing realisation that public sector expenditure can be used as a tool to promote various social policy initiatives: for example, to help businesses owned by minority groups, or to promote employment of diverse or disadvantaged groups and people, or to encourage better corporate behaviour.

Various ways of achieving this were developed. Government contracts could be reserved for certain types of business, such as small firms or those owned by military veterans. Quotas could be agreed whereby a defined percentage of contracts or expenditure would be directed towards these firms. Or companies bidding for government work could be asked to show they were doing the right things in terms of anything from health and safety issues, to reducing energy use, to supporting equal opportunities. That could be taken into account when choosing suppliers.

In the UK, the Social Value Act of 2012 required public bodies to consider these issues when they bought services, and gradually this sort of approach has become more regular practice in public procurement generally. We'll come back to current thinking and practice around social value later in Section 3. In the private sector, some firms have followed a similar line. We will also discuss examples such as Accenture's focus on supporting minority-owned and local suppliers globally, and we have seen welcome moves by many larger businesses to support more vulnerable firms in their supply base during the pandemic-related economic crisis.

There are many key historical events and movements that lie behind today's focus on sustainable business and procurement with purpose. But in recent years, it is clear that the momentum has increased significantly.

Chapter 2 – The Rise of Sustainability and Purpose

"Every business will benefit from operating in a more equitable, resilient world if we achieve the UN SDGs. We have an opportunity to unlock trillions of dollars through new markets, investments and innovation. But to do so, we must challenge our current practices and address poverty, inequality and environmental challenges".

(Paul Polman, Unilever CEO, 2016)

We have explained how the elements of what we see today in the sustainable business movement are not new in any sense. In fact, pioneers from Rachel Carson to those who fought against slavery can lay claim to be the real originators of wider business purpose. However, it is also clear that in the last twenty years or so, the focus on these issues, and the pressure for business to respond, have grown and accelerated. So what are the key drivers behind that increased pace of development and change in the purposeful business movement?

The UN 2030 Agenda and the SDGs

The United Nations adopted the Universal Declaration of Human Rights in 1948 and has considered issues such as the environment since the 1972 UN Conference on Human Environment (the Stockholm Conference), which was called to tackle the pollution caused by global industrialisation during the 1960s and 70s. In more recent years, the organisation has increased its efforts in terms of greater scope and more activity.

A significant development came in 2015, when world leaders signed up to the 2030 ***Agenda for Sustainable Development***. 17 global Sustainable Development Goals (SDGs) for a better world were agreed, under the auspices of the United Nations. The SDGs, set by the United Nations General Assembly and intended to be achieved by the year 2030, are listed in summary on the next page.

Sitting underneath those goals are no less than 169 targets. So, for example, under the first poverty-related goal, targets include reducing by at least half the number of people living in poverty by 2030 and eradicating extreme poverty (people living on less than $1.25 a day) by that date, too.

There are many critics of the goals, and some weaknesses are apparent. Some are very broad and general, and 17 goals may be too many to communicate easily to the general population. The complexity of some might also not help when it comes to getting clear messages across. Then there is a huge question of affordability – or, at least, where the money is going to come from to achieve many of the goals.

The goals aren't prioritised, either; some have lobbied that the climate "emergency" should take preference over everything else in the short-term, for instance. Others have criticised the SDGs for assuming a "business as usual" approach, placing a central emphasis on economic growth (the "development") which does not sit well with many of the environmental issues we see, even if those are captured in the "sustainable" aspect of the SDGs.

Reducing consumption by the world's wealthiest nations and individuals is seen by many experts as the only real solution, but the SDGs don't tackle this. As Jason Hickel said in a 2015 LSE (London School of Economics) article:

"And yet the core of the SDG programme for development and poverty reduction relies precisely on the old model of industrial growth – ever-increasing levels of extraction, production, and consumption. Goal 8 calls for 7% annual GDP growth in least developed countries and higher levels of economic productivity across the board..."[7]

Hickel points out that we are producing and consuming some 50% more than the planet's "capacity" every year at the moment, driven by consumer capitalism. Yet the SDGs only propose what he calls "superficial" responses such as reducing food waste, more efficient resource use, and encouraging companies to adopt sustainable practices.

The United Nations Sustainable Development Goals

1. End poverty in all its forms everywhere
2. End hunger, achieve food security and improved nutrition, and promote sustainable agriculture
3. Ensure healthy lives and promote wellbeing for all at all ages
4. Ensure inclusive and equitable quality education and promote lifelong learning opportunities for all
5. Achieve gender equality and empower all women and girls
6. Ensure availability and sustainable management of water and sanitation for all
7. Ensure access to affordable, reliable, sustainable and modern energy for all
8. Promote sustained, inclusive and sustainable economic growth, full and productive employment, and decent work for all
9. Build resilient infrastructure, promote inclusive and sustainable industrialisation, and foster innovation
10. Reduce inequality within and among countries

7 https://blogs.lse.ac.uk/africaatlse/2015/09/23/five-reasons-to-think-twice-about-the-uns-sustainable-development-goals/

11. Make cities and human settlements inclusive, safe, resilient and sustainable
12. Ensure sustainable consumption and production patterns
13. Take urgent action to combat climate change and its impacts (taking note of agreements made by the UNFCCC forum)
14. Conserve and sustainably use the oceans, seas and marine resources for sustainable development
15. Protect, restore and promote sustainable use of terrestrial ecosystems, sustainably manage forests, combat desertification and halt and reverse land degradation, and halt biodiversity loss
16. Promote peaceful and inclusive societies for sustainable development, provide access to justice for all and build effective, accountable and inclusive institutions at all levels
17. Strengthen the means of implementation and revitalise the global partnership for sustainable development

Why Now? "Purpose" in the 21st Century

The focus on responsible and purposeful business is not new. But what has caused so many people, from private citizens to the bastions of business and capitalism, to become more interested in these issues over the last decade? Where has the groundswell of opinion come from, a movement that has made ideas and initiatives around creating a more sustainable world more pressing, public and prevalent? In the very recent history of humankind, since the Millennium, we would suggest there have been several key factors that have accelerated the move towards sustainable business.

a. *The "crisis of capitalism"*

"Rampant capitalism is capable of destroying the world. We shouldn't let the private sector run untrammelled – we need sound public policy to guide people and firms to do the right things".

(Russell Picot, Pension Fund Chair, Honorary Professor at Durham University and co-author of the Sustainable Development Goals Disclosure (SDGD) Recommendations

---

For many years, young people in the developed world grew up with the expectation that they would be better off than their parents, and would benefit economically from new inventions and productivity gains. They believed the world was basically becoming a better place in which to live. Now, even pre-pandemic, factors such as climate change, globalisation, property price inflation, the growth of casual working and zero-hours contracts, have led to a decline in the confidence that young people hold in "the system". The feeling of discontent was magnified by the 2008/09 financial crash, and the behaviour of bankers, and a feeling that capitalism was benefitting the few rather than the many (whether that is true or not).

Writing this in 2020/21, we cannot say exactly how the pandemic and its consequences will play out. But the world may be entering an economic crisis even greater than that of 2008/09. There will no doubt be many debates about how the world recovers and the role of capitalism in that. But that decline in confidence, along with concerns about issues such as wealth (and health) inequalities, is unlikely to disappear quickly.

It is not just the economic situation that has led many young people to feel negative about their own futures. The negative aspects of social media and the culture around it, for instance, have contributed to poor mental health amongst too many youngsters. But it is not surprising that they also worry about the mega-issues around climate change, plastics pollution, and the extinction of thousands of the earth's living species. They see capitalism as having contributed negatively in many of those areas.

That crisis of confidence in capitalism has been reflected by businesses. In 2019, the Business Roundtable put out a radical statement signed by 181 CEOs[8] which defined the "purpose of a corporation". But before it got onto shareholder value, it talked about creating "value for customers", "investing in employees", fostering "diversity and inclusion", "dealing fairly and ethically with suppliers", "supporting the communities in which we work" and "protecting the environment".

Some CEOs are starting to sound like left-wing firebrands. Russell Picot, a senior finance man with a lifetime in the banking industry, is now a leader in how sustainability issues are incorporated into company reporting. Despite his establishment background and credentials, he is now passionate about addressing climate change and says, "rampant capitalism is capable of destroying the world". He is not alone, as many top businesspeople are similarly speaking out.

However, cynics argue this is about self-preservation for big corporations rather than a true change in belief systems. To prosper, and keep stakeholders happy, firms want to be perceived as more caring and less overtly ruthless and capitalistic. It is also worth highlighting that despite the supposed crisis, electors in developed countries have tended so far to reject most of the more left-wing solutions proposed by politicians, as in the case of the UK Labour Party's crushing defeat in the 2019 general election, and Bernie Sanders' failure to achieve the Democratic nomination in the 2020 US Presidential election.

But whatever the motivation, firms are taking action to reflect the mood of their customers and citizens more generally. They are looking beyond their traditional goals of growing revenue and maximising profit and the old definitions of "shareholder value".

---

8 https://www.businessroundtable.org/business-roundtable-redefines-the-purpose-of-a-corporation-to-promote-an-economy-that-serves-all-americans

b. *The increased pace of the environmental crisis*

The planet is getting hotter. The last six years have represented the earth's hottest period on record, and July 2019 was the hottest month ever recorded.[9] Some may still question whether that is man-made, or whether we can do much about it, but the outcome in terms of extreme weather seems undeniable. It is interesting to see how the absolute deniers have gone quiet in the last couple of years, as the weather globally has broken record after record. July 25th, 2019, was the hottest ever day in the UK (38.7 °C or 101.7 °F in Cambridge).[10] Nashville reached 97 °F on October 1st, 2019, making it the warmest October day in the city's history. The extreme weather is not just about heat either. "This has never happened, ever," said Ray Greely,[11] a meteorologist with the National Weather Service in Great Falls, Montana, when 9.7 inches of snow fell on September 28, 2019 – the highest one-day September snow amount in the city's history. Extreme rainfall in many parts of Europe appears to be more common in recent years, as seen in the German floods during the summer of 2021. But it is heat that tends to bring the biggest issues. In December 2019, the worst ever bushfires in Australia claimed lives and caused billions of dollars' worth of damage, as the country had its hottest ever temperatures of almost 50 °C. Southern Europe suffered too from similar fires in 2021.

No one had heard of Greta Thunberg before 2018. But by the end of 2019, the 16-year-old Swedish girl was named Time magazine "Person of the Year", reflecting both her own success in highlighting climate issues and also the growing realisation that the climate crisis is having

9 https://www.independent.co.uk/environment/july-weather-hottest-month-ever-climate-change-heatwave-global-warming-wmo-a9035356.html

10 https://www.bbc.co.uk/news/uk-49157898

11 https://edition.cnn.com/2019/09/29/us/september-snow-rockies-sunday-wxc/index.html

a major impact on human and animal life, an impact that could become catastrophic if more serious action is not taken quickly. Similarly, deforestation, the loss of natural species, and the problems of plastics and waste disposal have all become so serious that few people can now miss them.

Maybe the COVID-19 pandemic will also be seen as an example of how humans have abused the natural world, increasing the need for urgent action. We may see even more focus on PwP issues post-pandemic, or it could lead to a world where survival becomes everything and there is less time and fewer resources available to think about these wider issues. We will see. But certainly, more people are aware of "wet markets" and interspecies viruses than ever before.

c. *Communication and information*

One of the more positive aspects of better mass communications (from radio through to social media) is a greater public awareness of what is happening all over the world. Through history, there have always been wars, famines, floods, and fires. But only in the last generation or two have we seen them in our living rooms, often live and in distressing detail.

Businesses, rulers and governments have always discriminated against or victimised individuals for different reasons. But now in many countries those people have a voice, through Facebook or Twitter, although governments are fighting back with repressive tactics themselves to silence inconvenient voices.

So, whilst there are many negatives about the Internet, it is performing a crucial function in allowing knowledge and information to be spread more quickly. A factory collapsing in Bangladesh, or a drought in Australia, is now instant, global news, to be discussed and examined on both traditional and social media. Issues such as working conditions in factories have become better understood, which has built pressure for firms to act.

In 2017, a BBC TV programme achieved more in terms of the fight against plastic waste with a few minutes of film than many years of lobbying from pressure groups had managed. When David Attenborough looked at the problem of plastic in the ocean in The Blue Planet, the reverberations were instant and virtually global. One day the crisis was just one of a whole host of important environmental issues, the next a few struggling marine creatures had sent it right to the top of the agenda, and firms using plastic were expected to respond. Similarly, Greta Thunberg could not have become an international sensation with her messages about the climate crisis and the necessity for action without the media and communication tools that now abound.

Ethical Business Pays Off!

There have been other factors, but those three have led to a global population, particularly the younger and better educated, that is better informed and more concerned than ever before about issues such as climate change, modern slavery or species extinction.

This accelerating bottom-up groundswell has also been accompanied by more activity from the top, as national and international government legislation has played a part in many of these areas, from human rights to pollution and climate change. Such activity has sometimes generated more heat than light, but as well as involvement from political leaders, there has also been increased focus on how companies communicate these issues to shareholders and regulators, with reporting and accounting rules gradually developing to reflect this drive.

Business writer John Elkington coined the phrase the *triple bottom line* (TBL or 3BL) in 1994, referring to an accounting framework with three parts: social, environmental (or ecological) and financial. It was developed with the concept that organisations should adopt TBL to evaluate and report on their performance more broadly, rather than simply focusing on financial metrics such as profit. The firms' contribution to social and environmental benefit would also be part of the reporting, giving a more rounded picture of value created.

However, until recently many players in the financial and investment markets believed that ethically directed investments were likely to produce poorer financial returns than traditional businesses. Then assumptions started to be challenged. *The Fortune 100 Best Companies to Work For,*[12] initially a listing in the business magazine *Fortune*, then a book, started in 1998 to look at US firms based on corporate social responsibility as well as financial performance. ESG (environmental, social, and governance) criteria began to be talked about more frequently in terms of assessing company performance and potential.

Of the three areas of concern that ESG represents, the environmental aspect initially received most public and media attention, because of the growing fears concerning climate change. And the Fortune list led to an important piece of research in 2011. Alex Edmans, a finance professor at Wharton, published a paper in the *Journal of Financial Economics* showing that the *100 Best Companies to Work For* outperformed their peers in terms of stock market returns by 2–3% a year over 1984–2009. They also delivered earnings that systematically exceeded analyst expectations.[13]

Now the importance of ESG criteria is generally accepted, and increasingly investors are looking at this wider picture when making decisions. That has been reflected in several initiatives to develop standards and consistency in company reporting. These developments also help to direct capital and investment to the areas that might prove useful (and profitable) in terms of combatting climate change and other ESG priority areas.

---

12 https://fortune.com/best-companies/

13 https://papers.ssrn.com/sol3/papers.cfm?abstract_id=985735

TOP TEN TAKE-AWAY

Understand why you are embracing procurement with purpose. Look at developing purposeful and sustainable business approaches as a potential source of competitive advantage, not just as risk mitigation activities that come with a cost.

However, it would be foolish to think all businesses are fully aligned to the sustainability and purpose movement. Alison Smith, a senior manager at IBM, told us that when she attended the Conservation Optimism Summit in Oxford in 2019, as someone with a deep personal interest in conservation, she was shocked to find herself the only business person amongst the 400 delegates! The rest were conservationists plus a few policymakers, media folk and academics, and yet *"business can contribute so much more to these debates, and this is where the money is"*, as she puts it. Business must get more involved.

The Regulators and Accountants Take an Interest

Russell Picot was until his retirement the Group Chief Accounting Officer for one of the world's largest banks, and still chairs a huge pension fund. He is now a leader, an evangelist even, in an area that could lead to profound changes in how businesses globally think, act and report.

Picot was a Council member of the IIRC (the International Integrated Reporting Council), co-chair of the Financial Stability Board's Enhanced Disclosure Task Force (EDTF), and is a Special Advisor to the FSB Task Force on Climate-related Financial Disclosures (TCFD), chaired by Michael Bloomberg. He is also Honorary Professor at Durham University, and was one of three authors (along with Carol Adams, Professor of Accounting at Durham, and Paul Druckman) of the *Sustainable Development Goals Disclosure (SDGD) Recommendations*. This is how he sees the issue for investors:

"As the chair of a large pension fund, I know that achieving good outcomes for our pensioners and future pensioners will rely on the market, and returns will obviously be better into the future if we have a functioning system. Firms that are healthy and think about the long term, who see the SDGs as both risks and opportunities, are those that are likely to prosper."

Indeed, global stability could be threatened by climate change, which would do nothing for business or all of us as individual savers, investors or citizens. So, the idea of these reporting rules and guidelines is that companies will have to demonstrate in annual reports how they are facing wider sustainability issues. That means informing investors what steps the firm is taking to manage its own risks (related to climate, for example), and how it is improving its performance in the areas that link to the SDGs.

Picot also explains how influence works in the financial world, where pressure on fund managers is potentially a powerful lever. *"Winning mandates – from pension funds and the like – is the lifeblood of the fund management industry"*. Investors can therefore reward good behaviour, all through what we might call the "ownership chain", which runs (for example) from individual pensioners to pension funds, to investment managers, to the businesses themselves that rely on that capital provided by shareholders.

Various groups are addressing these issues now. **The International Integrated Reporting Council** (IIRC)[14] is a global coalition of regulators, investors, companies, standard setters, the accounting profession and NGOs. Together, this coalition shares the view that communication

14 https://integratedreporting.org/

about value creation should be the next step in the evolution of corporate reporting. The International <IR> Framework has been developed to meet this need. Its purpose is to "establish Guiding Principles and Content Elements that govern the overall content of an integrated report, and to explain the fundamental concepts that underpin them".[15] The aim is to provide a foundation for the future of corporate reporting.[16]

The **Financial Stability Board** (FSB)[17] is an international body that monitors and makes recommendations about the global financial system. The FSB Task Force on Climate-related Financial Disclosures (TCFD), chaired by Michael Bloomberg, was formed in December 2015 to "develop voluntary, consistent climate-related financial risk disclosures for use by companies in providing information to investors, lenders, insurers, and other stakeholders".

The mission statement continues: "The Task Force will consider the physical, liability and transition risks associated with climate change and what constitutes effective financial disclosures across industries. The work and recommendations of the Task Force will help companies understand what financial markets want from disclosure in order to measure and respond to climate change risks, and encourage firms to align their disclosures with investors' needs."

15 https://integratedreporting.org/resource/international-ir-framework/

16 https://integratedreporting.org/wp-content/uploads/2015/03/13-12-08-THE-INTERNATIONAL-IR-FRAMEWORK-2-1.pdf

17 https://www.fsb.org/

"Compounding the effect on longer-term returns is the risk that present valuations do not adequately factor in climate-related risks because of insufficient information. As such, investors need better information on how companies – across a wide range of sectors – have prepared or are preparing for a lower-carbon economy; and those companies that meet this need may have a competitive advantage over others."
(TCFD 2019 Status Report)

In 2017 the Task Force issued recommendations aimed at helping companies disclose relevant information to enable markets to better understand financial risks and opportunities. The voluntary recommendations are designed to help companies identify and disclose the potential financial impacts of climate-related risks and opportunities on their businesses, which in turn will help lenders, insurers, and investors to better assess and price those risks and opportunities. Ultimately, this disclosure can help drive capital towards sustainable investments, building a resilient economy.

The Sustainable Development Goals Disclosure recommendations of 2019, mentioned earlier,[18] offer a new approach for businesses and other organisations to address sustainable development issues, and align to all the major initiatives – the IIRC Framework, Task Force on Climate-related Financial Disclosures, and the Global Reporting Initiative. They attempt to establish a best practice for corporate reporting on the SDGs and enable more effective and standardised reporting and transparency on climate change, and social and other environmental impacts.

But there is still much to be done and Russell Picot acknowledges this: *"It is the Wild West out there in terms of disclosure – there is no framework, for example, for mapping the SDGs to company reporting"*. The guidance he

---

18 https://integratedreporting.org/wp-content/uploads/2020/01/Adams_Druckman_Picot_2020_Final_SDGD_Recommendations.pdf

produced with Adams and Druckman is certainly useful and well worth examining, but he acknowledges it is quite high-level – *"it is not a detailed industry guide and doesn't get into suggested metrics"*.

Where does this all this leave the "traditional" focus on shareholder value? Isn't that still what really matters for business? *"There's a growing recognition that shareholder value is not necessarily the right lens for looking at companies,"* Picot suggests. It parallels the debate about whether GDP is the right measure at national level, or whether issues such as happiness and health matter at least as much to the nation's overall position. He is also clear that consumer pressure is good, but not enough. There needs to be a regulatory policy framework to drive the right behaviours.

However, these rapidly developing initiatives are leading to a situation where Boards, CEOs, CFOs, and procurement and supply chain leaders really must take an interest in these issues and how they are reported. For most, it is no longer just an option. Whether it is regulators, investors, or customers, the number of stakeholder groups driving purposeful business is increasing, and their reach is becoming broader and deeper.

Chapter 3 – Understanding the Stakeholders

"Plenish is a fantastic addition to Britvic's stable of market-leading products, and I am delighted to welcome them to our business. In only a short time, Plenish has built a hugely impressive brand offering a fantastic range of products that cater to the growing demand for healthy and nutritious juices and plant-based milks ... we see tremendous potential in Plenish that we look forward to realising in the years ahead."
(Simon Litherland, CEO of Britvic, May 2021)

External and macro-level factors have built over the years and have led to acquisitions such as Britvic's and more generally the interest in corporate purpose, responsibility, and sustainability. These issues have risen up the business, political and consumer agendas, and the pace at which organisations are responding has quickened in recent years.

As we move into the present tense, rather than the past, it is vital that organisations understand the distinct (but overlapping) stakeholder groups that are driving the agenda. If sustainable business and procurement with purpose are going to be beneficial to the world and positive for individual organisations, this awareness of who is interested in these issues, and how they might perceive the actions firms take, will be key.

The Key Stakeholders for Sustainable Business

There are five key stakeholder groups in terms of the sustainable and purposeful business movement. Some of the players drive change; some are reactive and simply respond to change. There is some overlap, too. Many of us will personally fall into several groups, perhaps as customers, employees and probably investors, too, directly or through pension funds or savings schemes.

These groups share some interests, but can also have different outlooks on the key issues. That is true of us as individuals, as we have our own internal conflicts. We can see the benefits of cycling and perhaps love doing it ourselves, yet get frustrated by the behaviour of some cyclists when we are driving! We want to buy products manufactured or farmed in a sustainable and thoughtful manner; but the 3 for 2 offer on cheap chicken or chocolate biscuits catches our eye. Flying to the Alps for a skiing holiday is not a very sustainable activity; but after a tough year, don't we deserve our break?

Those examples may seem trivial, but they highlight the complexities within the sustainable and purposeful business agenda. Similarly, our viewpoint as an investor might be somewhat different from that we hold as a customer of a firm. Those conflicts have to be managed at corporate level, and balancing different interests will continue to be a key role for politicians, Boards, and senior corporate executives.

Let's examine the five key stakeholder groups in more detail. They are:

- The ***customers*** of organisations, whether those customers are individual consumers, public sector bodies, or other businesses. Ultimately, we can argue that most business change is driven by customer wants, needs and behaviours, and pretty much everyone in the world fits into this group in some way.
- ***Business owners***, whether individuals (owners of private firms and shareholders in public companies) or institutions

such as pension funds, investment managers and insurance companies. Owners may be driven by their own beliefs, customer pressure or both.

- ***Staff*** within organisations, from CEOs and Boards to the grass roots "shop-floor" workers, who want to drive change and bring that imperative into their workplace. Staff are also customers and consumers (and they may be business owners, too), but working within organisations to promote change can bring an added dimension to the picture.
- ***Governments, and regulatory bodies*** linked to government, that have increasingly legislated to drive certain business behaviour, arguably in turn driven by the expectations of citizens (the voters).
- ***Other interested and expert parties***, including the media, academics, charities and lobby groups who have raised awareness of issues generally or specifically. Whilst such individuals and organisations would probably not achieve much if the general public were not showing an interest in these topics, many provide valuable information and act as an amplifying force as the sustainable business movement develops.

All these groups are made up ultimately of people, but their interests and viewpoints on any particular issue can be different. They therefore have somewhat different roles when it comes to influencing sustainable business thinking and practice.

a. The Customer and Consumer Demand

Back in the 1950s, food packaging was usually paper-based. The butcher wrapped meat in paper, the vegetables from the greengrocer were placed in paper bags, and takeaway fish and chips came in old newspaper. Buying a coffee on the High Street meant finding a cafe and being served a cup of muddy brown liquid in a chipped china cup, that would be "washed" and then reused a few thousand times.

Then, the 1970s and 80s saw a boom in supermarkets, pre-packaged products and the ubiquitous fast food. I remember as a student passing McDonald's in the Strand in 1978 as the anti-Nazi march left Trafalgar Square – the first modern fast-food joint I'd ever seen.[19] Starbucks and a million other coffee shops appeared. And now, almost everything we buy comes with its ubiquitous plastic packaging. Our whole way of consuming, and our use of plastics, changed totally over 20 years or so.

To begin with, this all seemed very positive. Food kept for longer, and was more easily sourced. Again, exploring the recesses of my memory, I remember 1960s bed and breakfast holidays with my parents, where we literally could not find anything to buy for a picnic lunch in small towns in Scotland or the Lake District, except maybe chocolate from the newsagent. Or maybe the butcher's shop sold a few meat pies (no segregation of cooked and uncooked food there either...) Certainly there was a total absence of the ubiquitous "savoury snacks", pre-packaged sandwiches, or Ginsters pasties, let alone a Starbucks or McDonald's.

As things changed, few people thought about the packaging surrounding products bought at the convenient supermarket. It all went in the one and only bin each house possessed. Gradually, recycling was introduced, and consumers started thinking at least about which colour receptacle the chocolate bar wrapper or ready-meal tray should go in.

But scroll forward and now an increasing number of consumers really do think about packaging when it comes to their buying decisions. They may reject products that use too much packaging or material that

---

19 Strangely, he remembers X-Ray Spex's performance at the gig in Victoria Park at the end of the march better than that of The Clash, more's the pity.

can't be recycled. In June 2019, Waitrose launched a packaging-free trial at its store in Oxford. Morrisons has been doing similar experiments in two of its stores.[20] Whether some of these initiatives survive the COVID-19 constraints on handling products remains to be seen, of course. Unfortunately, it feels like we may move backwards in terms of packaging use because of the pandemic.

It's also clear that some people don't care about these issues. We all know someone who just hasn't signed up to the green / blue / brown / grey bin system, even after years of recycling education. However, it doesn't have to be every consumer changing their views in order to make firms consider their approach. This is a key point to note: change occurs at a tipping point at which businesses realise that they are in danger of losing a significant number of customers – or realise that there is an opportunity to grow business by taking purposeful actions. When that point is reached, which might be at 10% of customers, or 20%, but certainly doesn't need to be anywhere near 100%, then there will be change.

It is not just packaging we're talking about here either. Few people 30 years ago worried about human rights in terms of the factories where our goods were being made. That was in part because more production was close to home, so people knew local factories, the conditions in them and the folk who worked there. We didn't all own smartphones made on the other side of the world, and our TV sets were probably made in our own country. All this has changed, and gradually we have become aware of downsides of globalisation, as the drive for cheaper and cheaper production has led to human rights violations, poor employment practices and worse.

Some people have worried about nature conservation for decades, but going back 50 years, the rainforest still seemed something mythical and

20 https://www.theguardian.com/business/2019/jun/04/waitrose-launches-packaging-free-trial

vast, not a source of concern in terms of its devastation to make room for soya or cattle. And moving through today's various sustainable business causes, considering whether to support minority-owned businesses, or promoting the idea of better employment opportunities for autistic or people with disabilities – these were very niche concerns until recently, to say the least.

So, these issues have developed very rapidly and become more critical in the last few decades. Our understanding of these concerns and issues is very new and, in many cases, rather underdeveloped. As we get into discussions about what works and what doesn't in procurement with purpose terms, remember that much of this is emerging thinking. It is only in recent years that organisations have seen their customers taking such an interest in these wider issues and have responded accordingly.

Customer reaction post-pandemic is also an unknown at this moment. Will a deep recession force people into survival mode, with economic issues taking centre-stage? Or will issues such as "provenance" of foodstuffs and animal welfare be more topical given the source of the virus? Perhaps seeing the benefits of lower emissions and pollution during lockdown will encourage us to pursue those goals more strongly, too.

In any case, many businesses have already moved quickly to reflect the growing interest in these issues. Indeed, some businesses such as outdoor clothing firm Patagonia have built their entire consumer marketing strategy around purpose.[21]

Other firms such as Unilever, Mars and Bayer crop up through this book as examples of businesses that have put these issues at the heart of what they do. And the customer factor does not just apply where considering the final consumer. The whole business to business (B2B) world is subject to the same customer drivers. At corporate level, many

---

21 https://www.patagonia.com.au/pages/the-activist-company

organisations now expect their suppliers to work and behave in certain ways that reflect these wider purpose issues. Indeed, this is at the heart of our discussion throughout the book.

> "At Patagonia, the protection and preservation of the environment isn't what we do after hours. It's the reason we're in business and every day's work." That extends to the firm's supply chain and also through initiatives such as their "Worn Wear" website – some worn clothing can be returned for merchandise credits, and the firm has won awards for its "circular economy" approach.
>
> *(https://www.patagonia.com.au/pages/the-activist-company)*

Public bodies as customers are also playing their part in driving this movement. Any firm which bids for government work in many countries (including in the EU, the US and elsewhere) will be familiar with tendering processes that require a lot more than simply a description of the product or service's quality and price. Buyers may ask about their environmental performance; employment of apprentices; what "social value" they will provide; or how they are supporting smaller or minority-owned firms in their own supply chains.

b. Business Leaders and Owners

If customers are taking a serious interest in these issues, it won't come as a surprise to learn that business owners and those who run businesses are also concerned. Whilst capitalism has its faults, one of its strongest points is its flexibility. In most cases, if firms are not meeting the needs and expectations of their customers, whether because of shoddy products or poor environmental practices, then other firms, perhaps totally new ones, will spring up and usurp the existing order.

So smart business owners, from private individuals through to pension funds, investment trusts and insurance companies, know they must adapt and reflect what customers expect – which is that the firms they buy from reflect their own concerns about climate change, plastics, or social issues such as inequality or homelessness.

But it is not just customers driving behaviour change from business leaders. The allocation of capital, the funding that is the lifeblood for new and existing businesses, is increasingly being directed towards firms that are (as a minimum) taking note of the United Nations SDGs, or are actively involved in developing products and services to help achieve those goals. Investment firms are setting up funds that are specifically aimed at sustainable businesses, or are divesting from firms seen as high risk because of their ESG approach.

In October 2019, the Governor of the Bank of England told *The Guardian*[22] newspaper that firms which didn't move towards a zero-carbon emission position *"will be punished by investors and go bankrupt"*. It is remarkable really that such a pillar of the financial establishment was prepared to give such a stark warning.

Paul Polizzotto, founder of Givewith, puts it like this: *"Firms realise that their ESG (environmental, social, governance) ratings play into investment and capital allocation decisions today – that may be just as important as the consumer push on companies. There are trillions of dollars being invested in socially responsible businesses and ideas."*

In May 2020, in the midst of the pandemic, a report from investment firm BlackRock,[23] which managed $6.5tn (£5.3tn) in assets at the end of March 2020, claimed that investing in companies with better records on social issues and good governance pays. Those investments proved

22 https://www.theguardian.com/environment/2019/oct/13/firms-ignoring-climate-crisis-bankrupt-mark-carney-bank-england-governor

23 https://www.blackrock.com/corporate/about-us/sustainability-resilience-research

to be more financially resilient during the initial coronavirus market crash. Investment funds tracking the performance of companies with better ratings on environmental, social and governance (ESG) issues lost less money than others in 94% of cases during the crisis, according to the analysis.

> "Companies with strong profiles on material sustainability issues have potential to outperform those with poor profiles", the report said. "In particular, we believe companies managed with a focus on sustainability should be better positioned versus their less sustainable peers to weather adverse conditions while still benefiting from positive market environments."
>
> *(Blackrock report, May 2020)*

So, investors and business owners are seeing that paying attention to these issues is not just good for the soul; it may well be positive for the wallet, too.

c. Staff

There is a story, apparently from John F. Kennedy, relating to a visit he made to NASA, the space centre, in the early 1960s. He saw a janitor mopping the floor, and JFK asked him what his job was at NASA. The guy paused from his work and said, "I'm helping send a man to the moon." That was a great example of someone truly understanding the strategic purpose of their own organisation and how their work contributed to it. Studies have shown that people are happier and work more effectively when they have this alignment.[24]

---

24 https://www.mckinsey.com/~/media/McKinsey/Business%20Functions/Operations/Our%20Insights/The%20aligned%20organization/20141218_the_aligned_organization_lean_comp.ashx

People want to feel they are contributing to something above and beyond the organisation's own immediate objectives. That is perhaps even more relevant if the organisation is not doing anything quite as exciting as NASA, or as obviously worthwhile as a hospital. If you work for an accounting firm, or build car seats, you might struggle to find the same intrinsic motivation and sense of self-worth as our janitor. That's one reason why many organisations are looking to wider issues around purpose to help motivate and attract staff.

So an employee of a firm making vegetarian food products to sell in supermarkets may see themselves as helping to reduce meat consumption. That is arguably good for both consumer health and the fight against global warming (given the methane emitted by cattle). Now the food company may simply see vegetarian products as a good market sector to be in, for purely financial reasons. But increasingly we see business adopting wider "purpose", driven both by the marketing opportunity and by genuine pressure from staff to make changes for the greater good.

Dave Ingram (the Chief Procurement Officer) and Stephanie Schmid of Unilever describe how Unilever's industry leading position on purpose-related issues is mentioned by almost every job applicant as a key reason why they want to join the firm. In the proverbial "war for talent", being seen as a worthwhile, responsible business that cares about wider issues such as climate, pollution and human rights is without a doubt a positive factor. There is a positive self-reinforcement here, too. As more people join who believe in this stance, the organisation gains more internal strength and focus in terms of that positioning.

Bernhard Raschke was a partner at recruitment firm Korn Ferry for seven years. He was also a partner with PWC, so has worked with thousands of top executives over the years as a recruiter and adviser. He talks about the importance of senior executives having a sense of purpose above and beyond simply doing a good job. *"While everyone is motivated by different issues, desires and experiences, most people like to think they are doing something useful in their lives and their jobs"*.

In the procurement profession, 2020 has seen great enthusiasm for the Sustainable Procurement Pledge,[25] created by Thomas Udesen of Bayer and Bertrand Conquéret of Henkel. Already, thousands of individuals who work in procurement and supply chain management have signed up, committing to acting in a manner that is aligned with the principles of sustainable and purposeful business. Some work for firms where wider purpose is already embedded; others don't. But all want to participate in this movement.

d. Government and Regulators

Governments are making high-level commitments around climate change and are taking direct action that drives business behaviour. For instance, the UK government has a commitment to reduce UK greenhouse gas emissions by 50% on 1990 levels by 2025 and by 80% by 2050. In 2019, that was made more ambitious when a target to reach net zero on emissions by 2050 was agreed. Various government investment programmes and initiatives are in place or planned to contribute towards this goal.

For many purpose-related issues, there is also direct legislation that informs, directs or mandates organisations' behaviour. That includes the obvious, such as laws making firms liable for direct pollution of rivers or the atmosphere, or laws against human trafficking and modern slavery. The UK and other countries now have legislation that requires executives to act against modern slavery in their organisations or supply chains. Or pressure might be less direct but still influential – perhaps tax

25 https://spp.earth/

advantages for firms that switch to renewable energy sources, or legal requirements to provide access for disabled staff or customers.

That is now flowing into requirements for company reporting, as we discussed in the previous chapter. Work carried out by various groups is leading to ESG factors featuring more regularly in reports and AGMs, which encourages the focus on these issues in Boardrooms, and helps regulators scrutinise company behaviour.

Governments can have a huge impact through both their own direct actions and via their procurement spend. The public sector is directly responsible for a significant proportion of carbon emission, but trillions are also spent globally by the public sector buying goods and services from suppliers who also create emissions. Over recent years, that has driven growing interest in how this spend can be leveraged to support sustainable and purposeful business.

e. Charity and Lobby Groups, Media and Academia

The fifth category of influential people and organisations is something of a catch-all, including many who help bring wider issues onto the corporate and governmental agenda – charities, lobby and campaign groups, the media and academia. Some are perceived as irritants or even enemies of business, as they pursue their own causes or ideas. Others seek to be helpful to organisations that are looking to act in a more sustainable and purposeful manner.

Specific charities and lobby groups have been active in most sectors, from promoting the employment of disadvantaged people to campaigning against pollution and threats to the natural world. Some take a measured and thoughtful approach to the issues, whilst others believe in more direct action.

The Coalition for Rainforest Nations is an intergovernmental organisation of over 50 rainforest nations, from Ecuador to Bangladesh to Fiji. It was formed in 2005, and partners directly with governments and communities to protect their rainforests. It developed the Reducing Emissions from Deforestation and Forest Degradation (REDD+) mechanism. That ensures developing countries get paid if they can show that they have prevented deforestation, which has many environmental benefits.

Founders Pledge is an organisation that works to increase the effectiveness of purposeful business-type activities. It assesses the effectiveness of charities, and its model suggests that a donation of just 12 cents to the Coalition will avert approximately a metric tonne of CO2 (or the equivalent in other greenhouse gases). So, a $100 donation averts around 857 metric tonnes of CO2, an impressive return.

In the UK, controversy has arisen over the actions of Extinction Rebellion. The group blockaded parts of London and dug up the lawns at Trinity College, Cambridge, for instance, in protest against the college's investments in fossil fuel companies. They have certainly brought climate issues into the spotlight; but it is hard to say whether their overall effect is positive or their methods effective. They may alienate more people than they motivate.

The media has often provided a platform for these bodies to promote their causes, and for promoting sustainability and related issues. Despite the efforts of some political leaders,[26] academics have also provided valuable insight into issues such as climate change or species loss. In virtually every one of the topics we discuss here, from monitoring the effects of climate change and mitigating actions, to how to increase

---

26 https://www.newyorker.com/news/news-desk/trumps-cuts-in-climate-change-research-spark-a-global-scramble-for-funds

employment amongst people with disabilities, there are academics carrying out useful research, increasing our understanding.

These disparate groups have brought influence to bear on businesses, and increased the pressure for action. There are also useful resources available from academia, charities and special interest groups that can help organisations looking to implement change and pursue sustainable approaches.

TOP TEN TAKE-AWAY

Analyse which of your organisation's stakeholder groups (customers, staff, investors, regulators and others) are interested in this agenda and why. Understand exactly who they are, why are they interested in how you develop "purpose", and which potential aspects of the agenda they most care about.

From Sustainable Business to Procurement with Purpose

This first section has discussed the concept that businesses benefit from focusing on wider issues (social, environmental, and economic), going beyond short-term goals such as revenue and profit. While this isn't a new idea, growing pressures have led to today's position, where we see most significant businesses being well aware of these issues. They are committed to behaving in a certain manner to reflect the concerns of customers, staff, regulators and others.

It's worth stressing again that businesses and business owners are following this strategy for solid business reasons, not just out of the goodness of their hearts. A study from Boston Consulting Group conducted in 2017[27] found that companies that do well in delivering

27 https://www.bcg.com/publications/2017/total-societal-impact-new-lens-strategy.aspx

total societal impact (TSI – the aggregate of their impact on society) boast higher margins and valuations.

All our discussion so far applies to business generally, and to all aspects of activity through the value chain, from buying, through manufacturing to sales and marketing – as well as taking in support functions such as technology or human resources. But now it's time to look at our core topic. How can organisations use the money they spend with third-party suppliers to contribute towards some of the challenges the world faces?

"**Procurement with purpose**" as we call it (abbreviated to PwP) is becoming a major movement and is potentially a huge force for good, but only if organisations and individuals understand what it is, and how it can be successfully implemented. Those are the core topics for Section 2.

Section 2 –
Procurement with Purpose

Chapter 4 – Procurement with Purpose Today

"At one of our recent Procurement Leaders events, we calculated we had firms in the room together whose total third-party spend was a trillion dollars a year! Research we conducted also shows that 60% of the average firm's environmental footprint sits in the supply chain, along with 62% of its human rights impact. For certain sectors such as consumer goods it is far higher. That explains why there is so much interest in the agenda, particularly from the more advanced members of the community."
(Nandini Basuthakur, CEO, Procurement Leaders)

Shifting the Focus – Internal to External

Through the 20th century, as more businesses considered wider issues, they focused initially on internal actions and policies. Pollution created by their factories, or policies on recruiting from ethnic minority groups, came under the spotlight. But it wasn't long before they realised there was another dimension of opportunity and challenge.

Leaders understood they could also use the money spent with third-party suppliers to influence behaviour and impact a range of wider social, environmental and economic issues. The effect they could have by working through their supply chain was far greater than from purely internal actions. That is, in summary, what we mean by "procurement with purpose".

Of course, there is alternative terminology, in particular "sustainable procurement". That is widely used to describe very similar ideas and activities, and in most cases, we assume the terms are interchangeable. Sustainable procurement does perhaps sound like it is focusing on environmental issues in particular, although it is often used to include social and economic elements, too.

The topics and areas of interest that can be addressed by procurement with purpose activities are varied and extensive. They can be categorised in various ways, but perhaps the most straightforward is to use the "environmental, social, economic" taxonomy, and that is our preference. A full list of topics is provided at the beginning of section 4, but some of the most important are;

Environment – including emissions and climate change; use of natural resources; species extinction; waste, recycling and circularity.

Social – including human rights and modern slavery; supply chain diversity; addressing discrimination and inequality; helping disadvantaged people and groups.

Economic – including promoting employment; localism; fair treatment of suppliers.

It is worth noting that some initiatives can address more than one high-level area. For example, developing a more diverse supply chain, perhaps including more minority-owned or local businesses, may well have both wider "social" *and* "economic" benefits.

So procurement with purpose in our context means ***taking action through the money spent with suppliers to influence wider social, environmental and economic issues*** – expressed, for instance, in the United Nations sustainable development goals.

But businesses must focus on surviving, growing, and thriving. They meet customer needs and provide employment as well as profit for their owners. If businesses are not successful, then they will not be able to contribute to wider issues anyway. So procurement with purpose must *not* be seen as having a major cost to business or standing in the way of good business performance. In fact, it has the potential to contribute positively to a business in terms of profit, growth, and revenue, as well as supporting those important wider goals.

We would also stress that talking about "procurement with purpose" does not suggest "traditional" procurement has been *without* purpose. Effective procurement has always been a critical success factor for public and private sector organisations. Choosing, contracting with and managing suppliers who can help an organisation create competitive advantage is about as "purposeful" as any activity can be. Good procurement and supply chain management is essential for pretty much every organisation to run operations efficiently, and to thrive in the longer term.

What we really mean when we discuss this topic is ***wider*** purpose. In other words, purpose that goes beyond the organisation's short-term goals and the immediate drive for profit and revenue – or beyond the direct actions taken to meet a public sector organisation's own policy goals.

The Power of Procurement with Purpose

It is desirable for organisations to act within their own four walls in the spirit of sustainable and purposeful business. They can look to minimise emissions or pollution from their own factories, warehouses or offices. If they use natural resources, they can do so in a sustainable fashion. They should treat staff properly, and ensure that modern slavery, discrimination and human rights abuses are not happening internally. They can look to recruit from disadvantaged or minority groups, and promote diversity, education, health and happiness amongst their own staff.

But when we compare the scope for internal action with what can be done through procurement spend, we see the multiplicative and network effect of procurement with purpose. The impact generated by working with and through suppliers and supply chains makes this approach attractive for purposeful organisations, and usually far outweighs what can be done purely by internal actions.

Let's take an example. A large firm might spend 50 or 60% of its revenue with suppliers (in one study, the average was as much as 69% for the firms involved). So, consider "Procurement with Purpose Corporation" or PWPC – a firm with a $1b annual turnover. It spends around $600m with other businesses.

That will follow a Pareto profile in most cases, so the 20% largest suppliers to PWPC might represent 80% of the total spend. That could mean (simplifying the profile) perhaps 50 firms as key suppliers, each of which is receiving on average $10m a year from PWPC.

That makes PWPC a pretty important customer for these suppliers. Even further down the pecking order, there will be smaller firms, perhaps local businesses, for whom PWPC's $100,000 or even $10,000 a year spent as a customer is important.

Now consider the influence PWPC has over those suppliers. If it takes steps described in detail later, it can affect the behaviour of 50, 100 or maybe even 1000 other firms. If it works with some of those key vendors to address human rights issues in countries where they have factories, plantations or mines, it can make a real difference. Closer to home, if it looks to spend some of that $600m every year with social enterprises, or minority-owned businesses, it can directly and positively affect thousands of individual lives.

Then consider the power that a group of large firms can have in a particular industry or location. Look at firms that are substantial cocoa buyers, or have major manufacturing subcontractors in Thailand. Again, Pareto tends to apply, so for any raw material, for instance, there will be a relatively small number of buyers with huge market influence. More than 50% of the total output of the world's cocoa market finds its way to a handful of firms, including Mars, Nestlé, Hershey, Mondelez, Suchard, and Ferrero.

If those businesses work in a coordinated manner, they can impact issues in the cocoa supply chain, from human rights to land use and sustainable agricultural practices. The same principle applies in most sectors, industries and markets. That provides an opportunity for firms to make a real difference by working both with their fellow buyers and with suppliers and supply chains.

Suppliers are Buyers are Suppliers ...

Most businesses are not just buyers. Our imaginary firm, PWPC, is almost certainly a *supplier* in its own right, as well as a buyer. It has customers, whether consumers or other businesses. They may well put pressure on PWPC to work in a sustainable and purposeful manner. That's good news again; it means ideas will be shared and spread around vast supply chains and business networks across geographies, sectors and industries.

For instance, while Mars and Nestlé can influence their major suppliers in markets from cocoa to packaging, energy to technology services, they are also suppliers themselves to large retailers. They see buyers in firms like Walmart, Carrefour or Tesco looking to influence how they work and behave as suppliers. Indeed, at a recent conference, a senior Mars procurement leader spoke about the pressure from large retailers for the firm to use more recyclable packaging. This all reinforces that multiplicative, network effect for PwP, emphasising why it is arguably more important than purely internal actions firms can take.

Nandini Basuthakur is one of the best-connected individual in the global procurement world. She is CEO of Procurement Leaders (PL), which became part of executive membership business World 50 in 2019. Procurement Leaders has around 800 leading global businesses as members, representing an amazing $6 trillion in annual procurement spend, and serves over 33,000 senior procurement practitioners. *"We help our members make faster, more informed decisions to progress and transform their organisations – I like to think of it as identifying 'next practice' rather than best practice"*, is how Basuthakur describes the overarching goal.

"It's clear that people care," she says. *"Procurement has a unique 360-degree view of the organisation – and its suppliers – so is well placed to drive the sustainability agenda and make it a central part of decision-making."* PL helps firms build their programmes, providing opportunities to collaborate and learn from each other, through research reports, case studies, tools, and networking in various forums.

Basuthakur believes the move towards a wider view of procurement is accelerating. *"It was at our World Procurement Week in 2019 that we really saw the big change, from firms having savings still as their top priority, to sustainable and purposeful procurement really being important."*

She also observes that there is a considerable correlation between overall procurement sophistication, in areas such as capturing supplier innovation and collaboration, and "procurement with purpose" maturity. *"Unilever, Ikea, Patagonia – these are firms who are leaders in how they work with their supply chain generally as well as in this area"*.

So imagine the spending power that large (and not so large) firms control, literally trillions of dollars' worth, used in a structured, coherent and intelligent manner to support desirable and purposeful outcomes. If we can move towards that situation, then the procurement with purpose movement truly can make a huge difference.

Taking Action – Four Procurement with Purpose Options

We've explained the power of the procurement with purpose movement and the scope for organisations to have an impact through suppliers and supply chains. That is fine in theory, but how do you actually make things happen? What are the steps that should be taken, from initial strategy formulation to implementation of detailed actions?

It's important first of all to understand the four categories of actions and initiatives that organisations can undertake with a "purposeful" or sustainability goal in mind. Being clear about these options is key, as some require more commitment than others and all require appropriate action and activity from the organisation. They are:

a. Internal actions within the (buying) organisation that do not impact suppliers.
b. Principally internal actions by the buyer that have an impact on suppliers or the supply chain – but don't involve them actively.
c. Actions that are taken principally by suppliers that are encouraged, facilitated or mandated by the buying organisation.
d. Actions that require collaboration between the buying organisation and suppliers / supply chain.

a. Internal actions within the (buying) organisation

In this first case, the organisation's suppliers and supply chain are not involved at all. The initiative is purely within the organisation and does not even have an impact on suppliers. For instance, actions might include encouraging staff to recycle their lunchtime food waste into compost bins; ensuring that staff from minority groups are treated fairly; or inviting local schools in for careers workshops or other relevant sessions.

It also covers work within the organisation on diversity and inclusiveness, such as ensuring that recruitment and promotion decisions are made in an unbiased fashion, or even implementing positive actions to right imbalances; setting targets for female or BME staff at senior levels, for instance. Clearly, organisations would also wish to assure themselves that they are not abusing human rights or being involved directly in modern slavery.

As well as having merit in their own right, it is important that organisations set a good internal example if they wish to have significant influence on their suppliers, as we'll describe shortly. Clearly, there could be allegations of hypocrisy if (for example) the buyer was trying to push suppliers into looking at workforce diversity, or employing more apprentices, but the procurement team in the buying organisation was made up entirely of white, straight, middle-aged men!

b. Principally internal actions that have an impact on suppliers and the supply chain – but don't involve them actively

These initiatives are driven purely by the buying organisation, but the results have some impact on suppliers or supply chain. However, that is in a largely passive sense and no real effort, contribution or collaboration is required from the supply side.

For instance, a manufacturing organisation that implements an energy reduction programme will look to spend less with their electricity suppliers. But the firm does not necessarily need any input from those energy firms. Those suppliers would purely observe the outcomes of the exercise and be affected by them in some way. A total move away from plastic packaging to paper – whether in terms of coffee cups, packaging or even components – may not need any involvement from the supplier of the plastic product. However, as soon as the steps taken by buyers involve in some way what is being bought, and therefore involves suppliers, the actions fall into the two remaining categories.

c. Actions that are taken principally by suppliers that are encouraged, facilitated or mandated by the buying organisation

In such cases, the buyer generally does not take any direct action itself but encourages, persuades or even legally obliges actions to be taken by the supplier or suppliers. A London-based public sector organisation might insist that all its suppliers pay the London Living Wage to their own staff (see pages 181–84). Or a buyer might seek an energy supplier that guarantees that a minimum percentage of its power is generated from sustainable sources, or require a timber supplier to show it is actively supporting reforestation.

Suppliers might be encouraged to bring more diverse firms into its own supply base, or the buyer might include legal conditions in the contract around modern slavery or other human rights issues. The buying organisation does not necessarily take any action in terms of how it runs its own business, although as we pointed out earlier, it could be accused of hypocrisy if it does not "walk the walk" in terms of what it is doing internally.

The ability to introduce initiatives of this type does depend to some extent on the relative power balance between the buyer and supplier. In negotiation terms, the buyer needs to consider what it will do if the supplier refuses to comply with the request or demand. If a firm refuses to sign up to your human rights statement or charter, will you remove them as an approved source of supply? Thomas Udesen gives an example of Bayer taking that approach (see page 102) but smaller firms may not be able to afford such actions, or have alternative suppliers to use. For many large buyers, this route may well be feasible, but for smaller firms or those in a less powerful market position, caution may be needed.

That power is linked to how much you are spending, but that is not the only factor. Spending a million a year with Microsoft does not in all truth make you very influential or important in their eyes. Spending a million with a local facilities management firm may well make you their most important customer, and they will certainly want to be responsive and keep you happy.

d. Actions that require collaboration between the buying organisation and suppliers / supply chain

These initiatives require genuine *collaboration* in order to deliver change and success, which can be challenging; but equally success can lead to significant positives in terms of procurement with purpose outcomes.

For instance, looking at how factory equipment can be made more energy-efficient will almost certainly require collaboration with the manufacturers of the equipment or other external technical experts. A desire to use smaller or local firms, or charities and social enterprises as suppliers might affect some current suppliers negatively but will require identifying, verifying and onboarding new suppliers – this might be described as collaboration with the market.

Another example of broad collaboration is in the design of more environmentally friendly plastic packaging. Many changes to packaging will be driven by both buyer and seller working together to find alternatives to reduce plastics volume or increase recyclability. In some cases, work can take several years to come to fruition, and may involve multiple players on both supply and buy-side. Eliminating human rights abuses in the supply chain will again require collaborative working and the cooperation of suppliers.

Focusing on Collaboration

Our focus in the book is primarily on ideas and initiatives that fall into those last two categories, although we may touch on some in category b. We are less interested in those purely internal initiatives in the first category. Valuable though they can be, they do not really qualify as "procurement" and therefore cannot really fall into our "procurement with purpose" definition.

This categorisation is helpful when we come to talk about actions that can be taken. Category c issues take us into questions of regulation and compliance, and which mechanisms you can use to drive supplier behaviour. Do you use evaluation techniques in the supplier selection stage to drive the desired goals? Do you contractualise the requirements, perhaps with penalties / incentives? And how do you manage compliance as part of a contract management regime?

In our fourth and final category, actions are about collaboration and working together and have a link to supplier relationship management and innovation capture. Implementing such actions can be challenging, but many of the most impressive and powerful examples of procurement with purpose fall under this heading, as described in later chapters.

Chapter 5 – Prioritisation and Focus: Developing a Strategy for PwP

"Prioritisation is vital; even the largest global organisations such as Unilever or Microsoft can't hope to address every possible procurement with purpose issue to a maximum extent. There are many worthwhile options, so every organisation must think strategically and prioritise to direct their resources and achieve meaningful results."

(Mark Perera, CEO, Vizibl)

Some organisations are already well down the path towards considering or implementing procurement with purpose (PwP) activities. But as Nandini Basuthakur, CEO of Procurement Leaders, says, even amongst the large firms she works with, there are both "cheetahs and tortoises".

While some organisations have yet to really get started with this agenda, even those that have made progress have not always developed a clear strategy to direct and structure their activities. In other cases, tortoises may not even have considered how best to start developing their approach to procurement with purpose. But for any organisation, effective implementation of these ideas starts with the development of that appropriate, robust and intelligent strategy.

Why Procurement with Purpose?

Thinking about the strategy should always start with the organisation considering why it wants to implement procurement with purpose actions and approaches. It can be useful to think about this in terms of both risk and opportunity.

Smart organisations use these ideas to build reputation and performance by "doing the right things" in terms of sustainable business, including procurement and supply chain activities. That builds a position of strength with customers, staff and other stakeholders. So organisations should consider the ***benefits*** that can be driven through PwP activities. Many have built strong, credible brands in part through being seen as supporting wider purpose. There is also emerging evidence that companies operating with purpose simply perform better, and are valued more highly by investors.

Equally, organisations should consider the ***strategic risks*** that they face, and for most firms, much of their risk exposure today is generated from the supply chain and suppliers, rather than internally. A thoughtful PwP approach can counter many of those risks, reputational damage in particular, because risk issues such as pollution, human rights or provenance of raw materials often occur via supply chain activities. There are many examples where supply chain risks connected with these issues have had a serious impact on businesses, from negative publicity connected with the treatment of workers in the apparel supply chain, to the "horsemeat in burgers" scandal.

So this initial strategy step must consider PwP options and analyse how different specific activities could bring benefit and mitigate risk. That initial step is vital, because there are literally dozens of different issues and hundreds of specific activities that organisations can consider. Beyond doing whatever is mandatory because of regulations, organisations must think carefully about where they want to put in effort.

Prioritisation is vital; no organisation can do everything to a maximum level. That is one reason why collaboration is another key theme of the PwP movement, and crops up regularly here. Working with others greatly increases the potential for any one firm to contribute.

Think About Stakeholders – and Where You Can Succeed

We identified different stakeholders in Chapter 3, and choosing which initiatives to pursue should relate to what those groups care about, as well as the opportunity for the organisation to genuinely have a positive effect.

Ideally, an organisation should focus on topics where there is real interest from key stakeholders (particularly customers), and where it can also make a real impact. The chance of making an impact in itself is made up of two components – the size of the prize, in terms of how much could be gained if the work is successful, and the ease (or difficulty) of implementing the initiative.

A drastic reduction in water use might have a major potential benefit to the planet, but be very difficult to achieve for a firm in an industry that intrinsically needs a lot of water. Developing more suppliers owned by disadvantaged groups might be a worthwhile but lesser goal in terms of benefits, but be much more easily achievable.

If a firm's core business uses a large amount of plastic packaging, which is a high-profile issue for consumers, then focusing on work with suppliers to develop more recyclable and sustainable packaging materials would be sensible. It would be more relevant for that firm than campaigning to stop deforestation in Indonesia. But if the firm is a food manufacturer, then deforestation for palm oil production is a relevant issue.

A regional construction business might focus on how it can help local young people, by offering apprenticeships or jobs for disadvantaged individuals, and encouraging its own suppliers to do the same. For that business, deforestation would not have much relevance, but plastic use might be an issue, as such materials are increasingly used in some areas of the construction industry. In any case, choosing areas of focus carefully will increase the chance of making a real difference.

The size of the prize can be estimated by looking at what the organisation might be able to achieve and converting that in some way to a quantified wider benefit where possible. If an organisation decided to reduce plastic packaging use by 50%, that can be estimated in terms of tonnes of plastic "saved", and what might that represent in terms of reduced emissions (as well as the reduced waste)?

In some cases, tools such as the National Social Value Measurement Framework,[28] offered by the Social Value Portal, can be useful to help quantify options. That provides estimates for benefits arising from different types of social value offered in bids to the UK public sector. Whilst this is not a precise science, it does provide estimates of everything from the value of taking on an apprentice, to the value of reduced emissions.

When it comes to the analysis of how difficult it will be to achieve potential procurement with purpose targets, the organisation needs to be optimistic and positive, but also pragmatic and reasonable. There is no point announcing to the world that you will stop buying vegetable oil from any supplier operating in a rainforest country, if that means you can't meet your needs and will have to stop making half your products. No one will thank you for that, certainly not investors, customers or staff.

Equally, we have seen examples where firms announced ambitious targets without being totally clear how they would achieve them. Unilever was the classic example. When Paul Polman announced the Unilever Sustainable Living Plan in 2010, there were some "sharp intakes of breath" amongst his senior management community, according to people who worked there at the time. Much work was then needed to

---

28 https://socialvalueportal.com/national-toms/

work out how the target might be achieved, and even then, one of the targets was later changed when it became clear that the original aim was indeed unachievable. But there is no doubt that the ambitious target stimulated activity and motivated the whole company.

Prioritising the Initiatives

It can be useful to look at the options in a graphical manner, to help decide where the organisation wants to focus its efforts. There are different ways this can be done, but in this example (Figure 1), one axis of the chart shows the enthusiasm with which the organisation's key stakeholders (customers in particular) are likely to receive various different initiatives.

The other axis then represents the ease or difficulty of achieving significant results in this area. And finally, the size of the "ball" represents the size of the impact the organisation believes it can have in that area. That can highlight, for instance, that one initiative might be both easier to achieve and matter more to customers than another, which might make it a preferred option. But if another initiative has a huge potential for benefit, you might accept a little more difficulty.

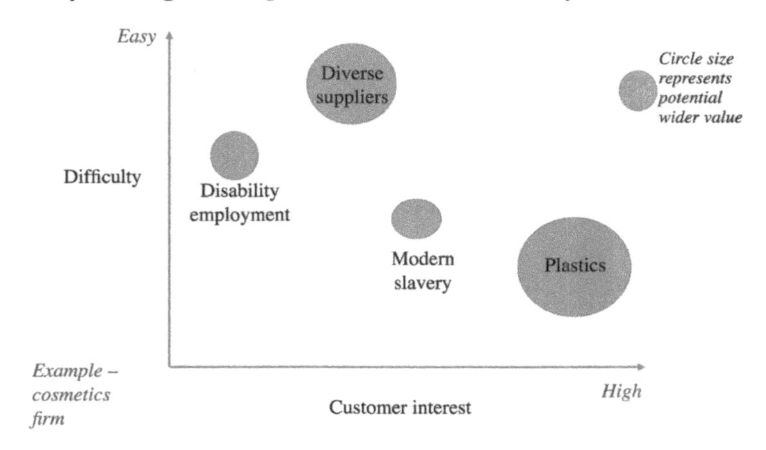

Fig. 1 – Determining Priorities

Our example shows just a handful of options out of the dozens that exist for an imaginary cosmetics firm. The firm assesses a number of potential areas of interest (there are more) and considers on the x-axis how strongly their consumer base, relatively young women in the main, feels about each.

So, customers perhaps currently care about plastics more than they care about seeing a diverse supply chain for the firm, or more even than modern slavery. That's not for a moment to suggest customers don't care at all about these issues, but this is a relative ranking.

On the y-axis, the firm considers how difficult it would be to meet the aspirations of those customers. So, moving towards a more diverse supply base is relatively easier than addressing the use of plastic in the business, as the material is vital for packaging and even to some of the products themselves. The size of the circle then represents the potential "prize" – in other words, how much benefit the firm could deliver if it does address the issue. So as a big user of plastics, the firm could have a real impact here, even though making it happen might be tricky.

We can see that this analysis could help the firm make decisions. Should it focus on relatively easy targets, even if customers don't care that much and the benefit might be small? Or does it go for those big, hairy challenges? Eliminating single-use plastic or, in a different market, guaranteeing to use only sustainable palm oil, might be tough but could bring a huge pay-off for the world and benefit the firm in terms of customer perception.

Figure 2 summarises the strategic process we have described in this section.

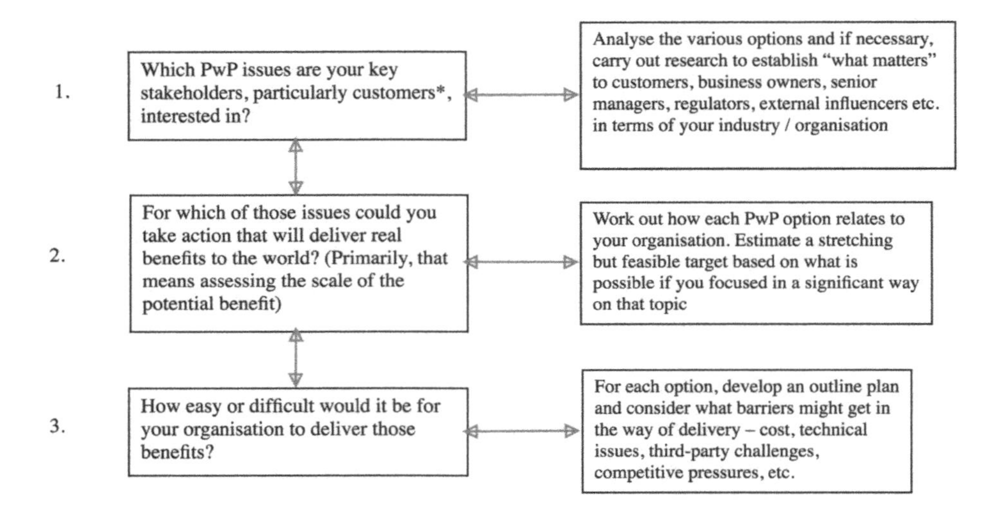

* *may be elected officials, voters, or service users in the case of the public sector*

Fig. 2 – Three Questions to Help Determine Procurement with Purpose Priorities

---

TOP TEN TAKE-AWAY

Develop a clear procurement with purpose strategy, focused on the areas where your organisation can have real influence, the "size of the prize" (the potential benefits for you and the world), and what your stakeholders care most about.

Turning Strategy into Plans

Once the organisation has determined which procurement with purpose initiatives and areas of interest it wants to address, it needs to get into specifics. This brings another dimension to the process. It is not only which *issues* you want to focus on, but which *categories* of spend will be addressed as priorities.

That might be obvious. If the centrepiece of your commitment is around plastics, the major activity for a consumer goods firm is probably going to centre on the packaging buying area. In a different sort of business, where plastic items form components for manufacturing, a number of different product or category spend areas may need to be involved to address the issue.

In the case of the imaginary construction firm mentioned earlier, let's assume that a focus on local employment issues, such as supporting apprenticeships, appeals to their public sector customers, so has been prioritised. Not only will the firm make sure it is taking on apprentices itself, but it will look to persuade its own key suppliers to do the same.

In this case, focusing on suppliers of subcontracted services (such as demolition or electrical contracting) might be a great place to start. You might move on to trying to get suppliers of steel or indeed of enterprise software to participate in your initiative, but frankly they may well have less scope to help you achieve your goals. And the Italian supplier of high-quality granite work surfaces probably isn't going to employ many apprentices in your locality.

The strategy should then look at setting the goals and objectives of the programme. It is vital to look at this as a long-term commitment, not a short-term tactical activity. That's because (as will become obvious when we consider specific cases), almost anything worthwhile will take time. However, don't rule out the opportunity to seek quick wins along the way. As always, in any change or transformation programme, that balance is key. You need persistence, to drive towards a long-term vision, combined with energy to achieve more rapid successes.

As well as objectives, consider up-front what success will look like and how it can be measured. It is always better to think about this when setting up a programme rather than later, because in most cases the baseline (starting point) will be an important element in the measurement of success. So, if you want to reduce emissions, increase the number of minority-owned firms in your supplier base, or reduce use of non-recyclable material, then you must know where you started from. That enables you to report back on progress with credibility.

Frank Omare of SAP Ariba, who works with many different large businesses, sees that the aspirational strategies we read in annual reports *"are too often not backed up with a clear plan at operational level – what will actually be done"*. So more organisations are being called out for their actions (or lack of actions) and investors look for firms to have appropriate strategies, realistic plans. Often, Omare says, change is driven by new leadership. *"We've seen clients where what seemed impossible, suddenly becomes possible"* when a passionate CEO arrives.

But, as we know, objectives, measures and plans in themselves don't guarantee success.

Chapter 6 – Moving into Implementation

> "It ought to be remembered that there is nothing more difficult to take in hand, more perilous to conduct, or more uncertain in its success, than to take the lead in the introduction of a new order of things. Because the innovator has for enemies all those who have done well under the old conditions, and lukewarm defenders in those who may do well under the new. This coolness arises partly from fear of the opponents, who have the laws on their side, and partly from the incredulity of men, who do not readily believe in new things until they have had a long experience of them."
>
> *(Machiavelli, The Prince)*

As Machiavelli pointed out some centuries ago, *delivering* change is a lot harder than making hopeful statements about strategies, aims and targets. Having thought carefully about a procurement with purpose (PwP) strategy, decided which topics to focus on, and which spend areas are most relevant to the programme, we must turn that strategy into reality. The proof as always is in the ability to convert ideas and aims into operational activity, with successful results and outcomes. So in this chapter, critical success factors that contribute to successful delivery are discussed.

Data and Technology

As a vital starting point for PwP, an organisation requires a robust understanding of how money is being spent. That means having appropriate data and information regarding what is being bought (the product or service), who is buying it, where, when and with which suppliers. This knowledge is of course necessary for all aspects of good procurement, not just purpose-related initiatives.

Then you need to have the right information about suppliers, at an appropriate level of detail depending on how important they are for your organisation. That means basic factual information – vendor master data, as it is sometimes called – but also performance data, and information related to any PwP initiatives being pursued.

It is impossible to consider whether firms in your supply base have appropriate human rights policies in place or act ethically in other ways if the buyer does not even know who key suppliers are, where they operate, or who owns them. How can you take action against plastic waste if you don't really understand how the packaging product you buy is made, or it isn't specified clearly?

Understanding the internal dimensions of spend is vital, too. You need to know what the organisation is buying from each supplier; how it is used; how much is being spent and by whom; and the internal budget holders, specifiers, or contract managers. Having the right data concerning all of these factors, data that can be turned into actionable intelligence, is absolutely key.

Today, there are many technology options that support this sort of information management. For a start, all the "traditional" types of procurement technology can assist here. That includes purchase-to-pay or source-to-pay platforms, spend analysis systems, and contract and supplier management platforms. Supplier management tools are incorporated into the suites provided by the major software players, and more specialist firms major on areas such as master vendor data management, or supplier collaboration. Spend analytics is another dynamic sector within the solutions market; in all these areas, Spend Matters and other research firms provide considerable market information, both free and commercially.

As procurement and supply chain leaders understand, having a *sustainable* supply chain is closely related to risk management and having a resilient supply chain. For both of these objectives, you need to understand suppliers, and the markets they operate in. You need to know about the provenance of what you are buying, and need to be alerted if anything changes that might affect the risk profile or PwP issues.

This relationship between purposeful, sustainable procurement and the wider issues around supply chain data and risk is clear. But obtaining, verifying, managing, and utilising supply chain risk and purpose data requires technological assistance, just as it also requires human skills and knowledge. Because of that, and the growing focus in recent years on risk and sustainability, this is currently one of the most active areas within supply chain technology development.

Increasingly, technology will support multitier visibility of the supply chain, too, not just at prime contractor level. It is not enough to know about your suppliers; you need to understand their suppliers and maybe even their suppliers' suppliers. Witness how Unilever, Mars or Nestlé want to go right back to the small farmers and growers who produce the basic commodity, whether cocoa, palm oil or beef. And this can't be static information either; rapid availability of new data and intelligence will become the norm.

So, the major procurement technology firms such as SAP Ariba, Coupa, Jaggaer or Ivalua have all put considerable effort into both the core supplier management aspects of their platforms, as well as looking at additional risk management capability. Specialist firms such as

EcoVadis and riskmethods also provide valuable options in areas related to risk and sustainability; we will talk further about those in Chapter 12.

TOP TEN TAKE-AWAY

Understand your suppliers and supply chains. If you don't know the basics around your organisation's suppliers, who and where they are, what they do, and what you buy from them, then you cannot possibly address complex and challenging issues such as emissions or human rights in the supply chain.

Gaining Senior Support

Implementing a serious procurement with purpose initiative or programme is not a simple matter. As well as having the right tools, it requires focus on change management, as with any other new business innovation or strategy.

Experts on corporate change management tell us that major change almost always requires top-level support if it is to succeed. Whilst there are no doubt examples of change that has been initiated and driven in a more bottom-up manner, in most cases it needs senior-level corporate sponsors because making it happen is tough – as the 400-year-old quote at the beginning of this chapter from Machiavelli highlights.

When we look at organisations that have progressed successfully with PwP, there is almost always that top-level drive, energy or passion behind it. Sometimes that comes from the ultimate owner of the business. In the case of Patagonia, it has been the founder Yvon Chouinard who personally committed the firm both to be both a great place to work and to create a "resource for environmental activism".

UK construction company Wates is still family-owned and has been a leading supporter of the Social Enterprise UK challenge, putting as much of their third-party spend as possible through social enterprises. The firm defines their key area of focus here as "building sustainable local economies through our trade and investment with SMEs and the social enterprise sector". With leadership from Chairman Sir James Wates and effort from many in the firm, by December 2019 it had surpassed its target of spending £20m through social enterprises in its supply chain, a goal set in 2015.

As well as these privately owned businesses, many publicly quoted corporations have also embraced these ideas thanks to one or more top managers who had the vision and passion to drive this work. Paul Polman at Unilever is the classic example, but there are many others.

Sometimes a procurement or supply chain leader has provided the senior impetus, although the most successful have also tended to get Board level colleagues behind the programme, to widen top-level commitment. In some cases, we have seen procurement leaders working closely with a sustainability champion – perhaps designated as the "Chief Sustainability Officer". Their remit may be broader than procurement, but given the importance of the supply chain in determining overall business sustainability and purpose, they should be natural allies.

But what does a procurement executive do if Board-level colleagues don't seem interested in these issues? Firstly, they can look for external support. The Sustainable Procurement Pledge, aimed at all procurement professionals, can help anyone learn from peers and perhaps develop a route to bringing top management on-board. Similarly, the Contracting for Change initiative has provided a forum for UK public sector people (and some from the private sector, too) to join together, develop good practice and share experiences.

Secondly, the procurement sponsor can work to build a compelling business case internally that can persuade top management to take action.

In subsequent chapters, specific initiatives and how they can bring real business benefits are covered – but the case needs to be made persuasively and professionally if you are starting with a sceptical internal audience. Referring back to the key stakeholders and why they are interested in these initiatives (see Chapter 3) can also be useful in terms of persuading senior colleagues to support business and procurement purpose.

The Two Sides of Targets

In 2010,[29] Paul Polman, the new CEO of global consumer products giant Unilever, launched the Unilever Sustainable Living Plan. Whilst committing to double revenues by 2020, he also targeted the firm to "reduce environmental impact by half". The other two legs of the Plan were to "improve health and well-being for more than 1 billion people" and "enhancing livelihood for millions".

It is clear that the targets set by Polman were not the result of detailed analysis and clever projections into the future. Few within the firm knew quite how they would achieve the sustainability goals when they were announced. But having the clear target, which was put into the public domain, increasing public pressure on the firm to take action, certainly mobilised internal effort.

Initial activities might not have been as well planned, structured and managed as the project management textbooks would suggest, but the clarity of the goals and obvious commitment from the top motivated and inspired staff. The detail of the programme followed. There is always the danger that targets, if made public, will become a stick to beat the organisation with if it fails to achieve them, but equally it is hard to gain real commitment and buy-in without clear goals.

Microsoft has now set itself a similarly challenging target. By 2030 the

29 https://www.bbc.co.uk/news/business-11755672

tech firm aims to be carbon negative, and by 2050 it aims to remove from the environment all the carbon it has emitted either directly or by electrical consumption since it was founded in 1975.[30] There is some scepticism as to whether this is achievable; but we imagine that it has energised people internally and made staff focus on how to make that happen.

However, sometimes a target can be counterproductive. The UK government has consistently failed to hit its target for central government expenditure with smaller suppliers (SMEs), because it is basically unrealistic. Because of that, it tends to announce the annual figures very late, and in a low-key manner. Arguably the scrutiny of the target has also meant there is less focus on what government could actually do to promote a more diverse and dynamic supply base. Effort has gone into massaging the data and finding ways of presenting it as a "success", instead of focusing on the changes that would lead to more SMEs winning contracts, or indeed examining whether that is the right target at all.

That particular failure also reflects the need for targets to be realistic – stretching, yes, but impossible, no. Expecting the Ministry of Defence to buy major weapons programmes from small firms, or a family construction firm to build a new motorway, was always a far-fetched idea in terms of this particular target.

TOP TEN TAKE-AWAY

Focus and concentrate; don't think you can do everything and address every purpose-related issue to the maximum. It is better to achieve significant and meaningful success in one area than dabble in many, delivering little of value.

---

30 https://news.microsoft.com/2020/01/16/microsoft-announces-it-will-be-carbon-negative-by-2030/

Skills and "Soft" Issues

Implementing PwP usually requires action from a wide range of internal staff, not just the procurement department. It also needs additional skills and knowledge to those we traditionally see in the procurement and supply chain community. Others, such as contract managers who are closely involved with suppliers, also need to play their part. All this has implications for recruitment and training of relevant staff.

For organisations that have gone some way along the road towards PwP, there have been interesting results in terms of people issues, in a generally positive manner. At firms such as Unilever, which have emphasised their sustainable business credentials, the profile of applicants has changed to reflect that.

> "Once you start promoting the idea that, as a firm, you are committed to sustainability and purpose, then you start seeing a different sort of person applying for jobs. People for whom these issues really matter are drawn to work for firms that reflect that – within a few years, we found that our workforce was increasingly positive about our commitments, and people were taking on the challenge themselves and really driving progress."
> *(David Ingram, Chief Procurement Officer, Unilever)*

Timo Worrall, the Director for Supplier Social Responsibility at Johnson & Johnson, in a 2018 interview for the Spend Matters website, said that *"millennial talent wants to work for a technology-enabled procurement function that delivers value in different ways, not just through cost-cutting"*.[31]

No doubt there are cynics around who either don't align themselves with these wider issues, don't see them as important, or maybe are just

31 https://spendmatters.com/uk/procurement-with-purpose-jj-and-wildhearts-take-centre-stage-at-sap-ariba-summit/

doubtful about the motives of their organisation if it has declared itself part of the PwP movement. But most people want to feel that their job is purposeful, rather than just a way to earn a crust.

However, that doesn't mean positive motivation is enough in terms of staff skills and behaviours. Applying the principles requires different approaches, and many procurement and supply chain professionals do find the change quite challenging. Traditionally, procurement has been very cost-focused. Whether or not that should be the primary procurement objective, it has been for most procurement organisations. That has led to many professionals acting in a manner that appears tough, controlling, cautious about disclosing information, not particularly collaborative by nature, even a little ruthless.

Now, the same people are being asked to consider a range of sustainability issues when selecting a supplier, or become more proactive in finding more diverse suppliers, or get used to interrogating a whole supply chain carefully to examine human rights abuse. They may well need to engage in deep collaboration with suppliers or even with competitors to drive the more innovative PwP initiatives.

"Traditional" procurement traits	**"Collaborative" traits**
Tough	Empathetic
Controlling	Listening
Cautious	Innovative
Cost-focused	Collaborative
Closed	Open
Ruthless	Considerate
Analytical	Imaginative
Organised	Creative

Even though many staff may embrace the new approaches happily and comfortably, some people who were well suited to beating price reductions out of suppliers may not be able to handle the new world of purposeful procurement. Others will need considerable education and perhaps re-skilling, so these issues must be considered if you are implementing a PwP programme.

The formal goals and objectives of procurement people and teams need to be addressed, too. Giant global technology firm Accenture has removed cost reduction and savings totally from the procurement function's objectives. That is a bold move, but one that reflects what that organisation and its procurement team are trying to achieve in terms of putting issues such as carbon neutrality and support for a more diverse supplier base at the top of its priority list.

The Sustainable Procurement Pledge

Generally, the procurement and supply chain profession has embraced the sustainability and purposeful agenda enthusiastically. That has been demonstrated by the success of the Sustainable Procurement Pledge.

In 2019, two high-profile Chief Procurement Officers, Thomas Udesen of Bayer and Bertrand Conquéret of Henkel, started the initiative to enrol procurement professionals to support these causes in 2019. As Udesen explains, *"we wanted to help the thousands of procurement professionals who don't work for the firms who really care about these issues – but who believe personally in the agenda"*. Individuals can take the Sustainable Procurement Pledge and align themselves as "ambassadors" for the movement, whatever their own organisation's enthusiasm or otherwise.

"The large corporates, NGOs and governments are pushing this agenda from the top down – we thought this was a way of developing a bottom-up approach with our procurement ambassadors, who can help to drive and preserve this legacy for the next generations," Udesen says.

The community is increasing, "there is a passion to learn and share", and there are well over 5000 ambassadors now. But many, particularly in smaller firms, *"just aren't sure how to get going, how to start slicing the elephant of procurement with purpose"*, as it were. Many who have signed up aren't getting support from their own CEOs or even CPOs (which is disappointing), but they want to make a difference personally, and see the wider community as a way of learning and getting involved. *"They are thinking of the impact they can have, giving back to society and what they can do for the next generation."*

He believes that some people lack the mandate to drive action, whilst others are afraid to step into the unknown, so the idea with the Pledge is to create a collaborative platform, with smaller "communities" forming around particular topics such as use of palm oil. He hopes to bring together practitioners, NGOs, academics, service providers – anyone with an interest in the subject. *"If we can feature and promote success stories then that will help people build confidence,"* he explains.

He wants to "unleash the passion" he sees in many young professionals. But there is a generational challenge in Germany (and probably elsewhere). In the "Mittelstand", the layer of successful mid-sized firms that powers the economy, he believes there are *"a lot of middle-aged men with a narrow view of what procurement should be doing"*. They can be blockers of the next generation, too, so we need to find a way of persuading them to follow the cause.

As we move into 2021, the Pledge and the leaders behind it – a much wider group now rather than just Udesen and Conquéret – have further plans to help their ambassadors create more impact. As an international and grass-roots movement, that is an exciting prospect.

Taking Stakeholders With You

Even if senior support has been generated early on in the programme, enthusiasm and commitment needs to be built amongst a range of internal and external stakeholders. Whilst it may be the procurement or supply chain function who takes a lead on this, there are usually a range of internal staff who will need to play their part in a successful initiative.

Procurement staff are of course key stakeholders, and even some of those professionals may need convincing of the benefits of this approach. However, there are some powerful arguments. Procurement and supply chain teams that have embraced PwP have often seen their credibility and visibility grow within the organisation. In one huge global healthcare firm that is supporting social enterprises in their supply chain, a senior category manager told us about the personal benefits the initiative had brought. It had given him and his team more exposure at a senior level than he'd ever had previously in 10 years with the firm. *"I might occasionally speak to factory management or equivalent about usual procurement issues; but I got to present our social enterprise programme to the global President of the business,"* he said.

These issues are significant for many organisations today, so those who are active, innovative and energetic internally in pursuing the right approaches can benefit from the personal kudos that can bring (as well as contributing to the wider good).

Other stakeholders may include the Chief Sustainability Officer (CSO) or equivalent and their team, if it exists. They should be great allies for procurement and indeed, more and more firms are combining the roles of CSO and CPO (Chief Procurement Officer). Organisations including Mars, Babcock and Diageo have taken that to the logical point of having a single "Chief Procurement and Sustainability Officer".

Nandini Basuthakur of Procurement Leaders explains the development like this: *"Both roles report to the CFO in many organisations. Given that the supply chain is such a major element of the sustainability picture, and the CPO can have real impact, then it's not surprising that often we are seeing that dual role. Post-pandemic, I think that might increase further as Boards question whether they need a separate CSO who doesn't have a P&L – even if they do have a critical monitoring and sensing role."*

The reaction of other internal stakeholders to PwP can be mixed. We've seen budget holders pushing back, if the more sustainable option or the supplier with the better human rights record is going to cost them more than their previous less admirable supplier. That tension will always be there, so, as well as having that senior sponsorship in reserve in case things get difficult, education and communication are key.

Make sure all stakeholders understand what the issues are, the risks and opportunities, and why the organisation is getting behind this programme. Where collaborative working with suppliers is necessary to move forward on more complex initiatives, involve key internal colleagues in that work, too, from the early stages. Communicating good practice, and, in time, your own success stories and outcomes should reinforce the commitment to procurement with purpose across the organisation.

Educating the Market

In the following chapters, we look at how procurement with purpose can be addressed through the various stages of the procurement process, from initial supplier selection to ongoing contract and supplier management. But useful work can also be done outside the core process, on an ongoing basis or before a particular contracting process starts. Organisations can engage with suppliers and potential suppliers with two main aims in mind: communication and education.

At its most basic, a communication programme may simply look to explain what the buying organisation is doing in terms of sustainable and purposeful business and procurement in particular. That may overlap with more general communication, PR or even advertising activities which are designed to get positive messages across to wider stakeholder groups, such as customers.

Communication can be designed to tell external firms what the organisation is doing and how it expects suppliers to behave. That will help them understand what is expected if they do win business. But this has a number of benefits beyond simply informing suppliers of policies or processes. It can stimulate the market and perhaps make other firms think that they want to be a supplier to a forward-thinking business or public organisation.

When a firm such as Unilever holds a session to engage with hundreds of its suppliers around a sustainable procurement agenda, it has a direct purpose of communicating to those firms. But it also reflects well on the wider corporate programme for sustainable business, and reinforces the view amongst the public, consumers and opinion-formers that Unilever is a leader in this context.

Work can also go beyond simply communication. Buyers can look to train or educate suppliers and potential suppliers in relevant areas. In Chapter 9 we look at collaboration with existing suppliers, which can include an element of education, but here we are considering applying that to a wider universe, including firms that are not and may never be suppliers.

This might be as simple as including some useful content and resource about sustainability and purpose issues on the organisation's website. Material might be useful and educational to other businesses, whether or not they are suppliers. Or the activity could be more focused – running a workshop within a particular supply market to help participants develop better practice in managing emissions or improving human rights, perhaps.

Some public sector organisations have run workshops for local firms to help them understand what is expected of them when they bid for work, including issues such as the requirement for "social value" and how the firm might address that in their proposal. All of this spreads the desired messages and should develop the universe of potential effective suppliers.

Chapter 7 – Driving Action Through Supplier Selection

"South Africa used to punch above its weight and was a genuine participant in the global economy. We produced things of value. Sophisticated things. Technologically advanced things. Then came BEE, and it changed the rules of the game by skewing the playing field in favour of those whose only attribute was that they were politically connected. It actively discriminated against anyone who was creative and nimble in the field of science, engineering and technology."
(Professor Anthony Turton, University of the Free State, South Africa)

In Chapter 4, the four types of purposeful action that organisations can take were discussed, and the two of most interest were identified. They are situations where buyers want to *push or persuade suppliers* into acting in a particular manner, and those where buyers *collaborate with suppliers* to deliver procurement with purpose (PwP)-related benefits.

Many organisations now look to reflect their PwP-related goals when they choose suppliers. They want to identify firms to work with that will support those objectives. So the supplier evaluation and selection process can take into account key PwP issues in terms of the current situation and actions of the potential supplier, or it can look to assess what the supplier will promise or contract to do in the future if they win the business.

In this chapter, how the supplier selection process can drive suppliers into acting in a certain way is discussed. Later chapters cover more collaborative actions that can be undertaken with your suppliers and supply base once contracts are up and running. But this and the following chapter major on how your actions and approaches during the supplier selection and contracting stages of the end-to-end procurement cycle can incentivise and promote the behaviours you want from suppliers.

There are three primary approaches to incorporating purpose-type issues into the assessment methodology used to select a supplier. Any combination of the three may be used in a particular procurement exercise.

Using Binary "Qualification" Factors

In this first option, one or more aspects of PwP are used to sift suppliers on a basic "in or out" basis, depending on whether they have achieved something or promise to achieve it. For example, you might simply ask whether the bidder has an equalities policy in place, explaining that if a bidder answers "no" they will be excluded from consideration. (You may or may not actually choose to check out every word of the full, glorious policy document!)

The question could be based on compliance with a legal requirement or a standard, perhaps "can you confirm you are compliant with the Modern Slavery Act?" It could go further and ask for supporting material as well to back up a simple assertion. Or it could be a "performance obligation" – the supplier accepts a requirement that they will perform a specified task or activity once they have won the contract. "Will you agree to employing 12 apprentices on this project if you win the contract?" Sometimes I wonder if anyone ever says "no" to this sort of question. It can be somewhat similar to the declaration travellers make on entering the United States – "can you confirm you aren't a Nazi / have never plotted to overthrow a democratic government ...?" Would anyone ever tick the box on a pre-qualification questionnaire to say they don't adhere to the law, or even that they don't believe in diversity and equality?

That means there is a danger that these selection questions become a purely box-ticking exercise. But if the buyer *doesn't* cover these issues, and something then goes wrong, they will get criticised later. That's a strong driver for public sector organisations in particular, where the criticism could be public and might affect senior executives or even elected politicians. So in reality this exercise probably protects the buying organisation more than it really drives better supplier behaviour from a purpose standpoint.

However, it can be worthwhile if used sensibly with appropriate follow-up. Thomas Udesen, Chief Procurement Officer at Bayer, has examples of success stories:

"We are seeing good collaboration in the pharmaceutical supply chain, with firms working together on assessments and audits in the industry. And more specifically in Bayer, we are at the point now where, for example, I have just written to the CEO of a major shipping firm to say we will drop them as a supplier because they won't sign up to our code of conduct. We would not have done that a few years ago." He suspects once the shipping boss sees that letter, the intransigence lower down their organisation will be resolved quickly.

So, this in/out approach has some value, and it is worth including (within reason) such approaches during a procurement process. But be aware that in terms of genuinely mitigating the risk that suppliers might behave in a manner which is not aligned with your aims, it has limited effectiveness.

There is also a danger that introducing such qualification hurdles can be a barrier to entry. For smaller firms or start-ups, having to prove that they have a plethora of policies in place, or that they have gone through a certification process, or committing to some future actions, can be a real burden. Large firms can more easily make sure they know how to jump through those hoops. So be careful that you are not creating significant barriers that might rule out promising potential suppliers.

Introducing Bias into Supplier Selection

Another fundamental issue at this stage is whether you want to tilt explicitly the playing field in the direction of the type of supplier you want to promote or support. For example, if you want to support social enterprises, do you simply hope they come through the evaluation process – allowing for the fact that you might ask questions to help choose the "right" sort of bidders, as we will describe in the next section? Or do you want to give social enterprises a clear and overt advantage in the process?

That could go to the extreme of saying "only social enterprises can bid for this work" (or local firms, or minority-owned businesses). In countries including the USA some government contracts are reserved for particular supplier groups. The US has targets for work going to female- and veteran-owned businesses and "small, disadvantaged businesses", too. The US General Services Administration website says this:[32]

"The federal government establishes formal goals to ensure small businesses get their fair share of work. Every federal government purchase between $10,000 and $250,000 is automatically set aside for small businesses, as long as there are at least two companies that can provide the product or service at a fair and reasonable price."

Instead of going as far as reserving contracts for certain types of supplier, it is also possible to build some advantage into the selection process, without guaranteeing work for such firms. That could perhaps take the form of saying "we are prepared to pay up to 5% more to support

---

32 https://www.gsa.gov/small-business/-become-a-gsa-vendor/explore-business-models/-setasides-and-special-interest-groups#WOSB

a favoured firm", or it could rely on a complex formula.

South Africa has taken that approach in order to favour businesses owned by non-whites. The "Broad-based Black Economic Empowerment" programme has attempted to support the black community since the end of apartheid. The B-BBEE Act contains formulas that calculate a "B-BBEE score", which is then used when selecting suppliers in tendering situations. In effect, the playing field is tilted by an amount proportionate to the level of black involvement in the bidding firm.

Whilst the approach in South Africa is totally understandable, what has happened in practice demonstrates the potential for problems with this whole approach. In some cases, firms have bent the rules to score more highly by concealing the real ownership of the firm. In other cases, talented individuals and good businesses that are not favoured may have given up trying to win work in South Africa – there has certainly been a "brain drain" evident at the individual level.

Perhaps most seriously, once supplier selection decisions become less objective and are based on more than simply the best value for money product or service, then the door is opened to corruption. BEE is sometimes disparagingly referred to as "Black Elite Enrichment" and the measures taken are perceived to have helped a small elite become extraordinarily rich through corruption in government and private sector organisations, as suggested by Professor Anthony Turton in the quote that starts this chapter.

There is also an economic argument which suggests firms who need help to win contracts may simply be not good enough. Giving a new or disadvantaged business the chance to prove itself – an initial "leg up" – is a concept most might support. But if a business goes on year after year winning contracts only because of the race or gender of its owner, you have to wonder whether it really deserves to do so. It is certainly unlikely to thrive in the free market, so should it be supported in a way that might freeze out genuinely innovative and effective new businesses?

The issue is somewhat different if the organisation is delivering additional social value – by employing staff with disabilities, for instance. In such cases, you might justify paying a little over the odds because of the wider benefit to society and perhaps the economy. But careful consideration is needed before introducing overt bias into the supplier selection process.

Assessing PwP Status and Proposals as Part of the Selection Process

The third and perhaps most interesting option in terms of embedding purpose into the supplier selection process relates to scoring and ranking prospective suppliers based partially on PwP issues. That means their current or promised future performance in the PwP areas chosen by the buyer can contribute to the selection decision.

Rather than introducing bias in terms of favouring certain suppliers, buyers can pursue the procurement with purpose (or social value) agenda by including relevant factors in the structured evaluation process. Suppliers can be assessed against their proposals through that lens, as well as considering price, quality and other key evaluation criteria. This approach could also be combined with some overall bias in terms of certain types of suppliers, as explained above – it is not an either/or situation.

Using this approach means what is put to bidders is not just a "pass / fail" question. Rather, questions are asked where bidders can show themselves to be stronger than others in the relevant area or areas of interest. That is taken into account in terms of their chance of winning the work.

This approach has become increasingly common in public sector bodies in many countries, including the UK, where that has been driven by the Social Value Act of 2012 and its updates (see Chapter 15). But it is also being used in the private sector. For instance, telecommunications giant Vodafone announced in 2020 that they would be assessing potential suppliers on purpose-related issues as part of the selection process. "From October 2020, a supplier's 'purpose' will account for 20% of the evaluation criteria for a 'Request For Quotation' (RFQ) to provide Vodafone with products or services", the firm announced.[33]

There are different ways of approaching this process. We might ask a very general question, such as ***"tell us how you will deliver purpose and sustainability, supporting the UN SDGs and social value?"***

Whatever the precise wording, each supplier then has a chance to talk about anything, from reducing emissions to employing people with disabilities. Or we could ask the potential suppliers to complete a template that lays out a number of PwP-related options, perhaps using a notional financial value for each option that can be used in assessing the proposals.

However, there are issues with both these approaches. The first can lead to proposals from bidders that are very difficult to compare as part of the selection process. The second can become a box-ticking exercise, and both can lead to offers from bidders that are not strategically aligned with what the buying organisation really wants or needs.

A better approach is for the buyer, through the strategy process described already, to ask bidders to focus on a small number of key PwP areas. Those are chosen as the most important in that spend category for that buying organisation – and note that they may be different for different categories. The bidders may be allowed some flexibility, in terms of which areas they will focus on and in the creativity they show in terms of how they will deliver. But some direction seems sensible rather than a totally blank canvas.

33 https://www.vodafone.com/news/press-release/vodafone-embeds-purpose-commitments-in-its-supply-chain

---

"We estimate that there are currently 15,000 local residents who are actively seeking work or receiving employment support from the Department for Work and Pensions. Bidders are required to maximise work opportunities for the following groups of people: long-term unemployed individuals, people from BME communities, and disabled people. Please demonstrate how you would assist the local authority in addressing this matter."
(Suggested question to bidders, VODG social value toolkit)

The aim is to ensure bidders focus on relevant aspects for the buyer within the PwP universe. You might ask how they will support local employment creation for a contract with a city council. Or the supplier could describe what they are doing to reduce carbon use in their business (and supply chain, perhaps) if your organisation has made a commitment to carbon neutrality.

In the UK public sector, the *VODG social value toolkit*[34] is a useful document produced by the Voluntary Organisations Disability Group. It gives examples of questions that bodies such as local councils are using to assess suppliers, combining clear focus with the potential for creative and supplier-specific ideas.

In terms of scoring, many organisations use something like the matrix shown below. This could apply to the social value or sustainability offering from the supplier, just as it can to quality, service or other criteria.

34 https://www.vodg.org.uk/wp-content/uploads/2016-VODG-Social-value-toolkit.pdf

Score	Description
5	An excellent answer, indicating a response to this question that fully meets our needs and requirements with no weaknesses or issues
4	A good answer, indicating a response to this question that generally meets our needs and requirements, with only very minor weaknesses or issues
3	A satisfactory answer, indicating a response to this question that meets our basic needs and requirements, but which demonstrates tangible weaknesses or requires some minor compromises from us
2	A poor answer, indicating a response to this question that fails to meet some of our basic needs and requirements, and which demonstrates significant weaknesses or requires major compromises from us
1	A very poor answer, indicating a response to the question that fails to meet our basic needs and requirements, or requires an unacceptable compromise
0	No answer or totally irrelevant response

Fig. 3 – Scoring guidance

The selection process can also incorporate more forward-looking proposals on how the supplier and buyer might work together, linking with "collaborative" actions, described in Chapter 9. So, if you are appointing a supplier of plastic packaging, you might ask how they will fulfil current needs, and what they are currently doing to increase the proportion of their products that are recyclable and reusable. But you could also ask how they propose to work in the future specifically on your key products to reduce plastics use or increase recycling.

However, if you are going to assess suppliers based on proposals, ideas and commitments made at bidding stage, you must have mechanisms for follow-up. You must make sure that what is promised gets delivered. The VODG document is again useful, giving this example of how such an issue can be addressed at bidding stage, by requiring bidders to explain how they will be able to provide evidence of delivery:

"Outline your evidencing, verification and evaluation methodology to demonstrate that the social value outcomes have been achieved".

More on this critical issue later when the contract and supplier management phase of the end-to-end process is discussed.

Selecting Based on Wider Value

When evaluating bids or proposals, buyers often find it a challenge to assess hard costs against more subjective or hard-to-measure factors, such as quality, service levels, how innovative the supplier will be, and so on. That is not easy, even before the wider factors are considered, which introduce more potential subjectivity.

There are two ways of handling this. The buyer can simply give a score for the elements of purpose or "social value" (the public sector terminology here), as they probably do for quality or service factors. The scores can be weighted, based on how important each factor is, then combined with the score given for the costs to obtain a final total for each bid.[35]

For example, you might see something like the table below (Figure 4). A basic method for scoring cost is used here, giving the lowest bid full marks and the other bid, which is 10% higher, 10% fewer marks. (I am not recommending that methodology, incidentally: it is just used for simplicity's sake here.)

The weightings for the different selection criteria are quite typical for recent UK public sector procurement exercises: the 2020 Cabinet Office guidance in the UK calls for a minimum of 10% of the marks in evaluation to be given to "social value" factors. Fifteen per cent is used here, along with weightings for quality, service and cost making up the total.

35 How costs are translated into scores that can be compared to and combined with quality or service scores is another interesting issue – I will leave that for another day!

This example highlights both the power and the risks around using social value or PwP factors to select suppliers and bids. You might well feel positive about choosing supplier A, whose offering in the social value area was clearly far superior to that of supplier B, scoring five out of five rather than a meagre two.

However, looking at the results, supplier B is £250,000 cheaper and has a slightly superior offering in terms of quality. Yet supplier A has won, based on the total score, because they rated so highly on social value.

		Supplier A		**Supplier B**	
Evaluation criteria	*Weighting*	*Raw Score*	*Weighted score*	*Raw Score*	*Weighted score*
Cost	50%	£2.75M	45	£2.5M	50
Service	20%	4/5	16	4/5	16
Quality	15%	3/5	9	4/5	12
Social Value	15%	5/5	15	2/5	6
TOTAL			**85**		**84**

Fig. 4 – Example Scoring Table

The question is: are you really happy about paying that premium and obtaining a lower-quality product in return for extra "social value", which you may not be able to describe in terms of quantifiable benefits, and cannot absolutely guarantee will be delivered once the contract is underway? And can you be sure that the marking was fair, and not tainted perhaps by a well-meaning desire to see supplier A triumph because of their excellent environmental or social value credentials?

Those questions apply whether or not the additional cost from supplier A is caused by the social value that is being offered. The firm might have built in another £250K specifically to cover the costs of the social value initiatives proposed, and that has led to the additional bill. Or it may be that supplier A would have been more expensive even if social value had not been included. It is hard to establish those underlying assumptions simply from analysing the bids.

Some buyers have claimed that social value does not drive additional costs. No doubt, in some cases, that is true. Transport for London argued that pushing suppliers into paying the London Living Wage did not drive increased prices, and that may be valid. But it would be naïve to think that *all* social value / PwP commitments from suppliers are *always* "free" to the buyer, even if, as Paul Polizzotto of Givewith argues, these programmes can generate value rather than costs for all parties.

No doubt he is right in many cases; but certainly suppliers will sometimes increase prices to cover actions that support their response to purpose or social value requirements. Smart buyers need to be aware of these risks and be prepared to dig into just how suppliers are constructing their proposals and bids.

So, it is vital that organisations understand how much they are paying for additional social value, if indeed they are actually paying a premium. Local citizens might, for instance, be happy that another £10,000, 10,000 or $10,000 of their taxes is supporting a construction firm that has offered to train apprentices, recruit more from disadvantaged groups, and buy 50% of their material from local firms. But they might be less happy if that cost was a million pounds, euros or dollars. That also comes back to how social value, sustainability or purpose is assessed and weighted in the evaluation process.

One useful approach is to model the likely results of the evaluation process ahead of issuing bid documents to the market. Take some theoretical examples of responses from suppliers on cost, other non-cost factors and the purpose/social value criteria, and work through what this might mean in the evaluation process. As in our example, think about how much extra you are *really* prepared to pay for different levels of wider value. If the answer does not seem reasonable, you need to change elements of the evaluation methodology – the criteria, weightings, or scoring system.

Turning "Purpose" into Financial Benefit

Instead of giving proposals that relate to social value / purpose-related goals a score, as just described, some buyers look to convert the bidders' proposals into a hard monetary value. That could then be applied as a benefit to the financial side of the proposal and rolled into the cost scoring when assessing bids.

This approach has both potential advantages and problems. On the positive side, it gets over the subjectivity problem in scoring competing bids. Which bidder gets the higher mark – the proposal to employ 10 apprentices, or the one that commits to using green energy in delivering their contract?

Putting benefits in financial terms using some transparent methodology makes the decisions somewhat simpler. You can convert those factors (employing apprentices and using green energy) into financial benefit values which can be incorporated into the assessment. In the public sector, that structure and apparent objectivity give some protection against the risk of corruption or political interference, which is increasing as social value becomes a major element in selecting suppliers. Those financial values can then be combined with the actual cost proposal from suppliers to arrive at a "net cost" which can be evaluated alongside quality, service, and so on.

However, attaching financial numbers to social value or PwP actions is not a precise science. It may be based on expertise and understanding, but often it is also somewhat subjective itself. For example, it is not easy to estimate the financial benefits of getting a disabled person into work, or of actions to reduce deforestation. Using "hard" numbers in the supplier assessment process might give the *impression* of fairness and objectivity, but it cannot be 100% accurate.

Giving bidders a broad "shopping list" of potential actions, with values attached, might also lead to potential suppliers offering benefits that are not strategically aligned with the buyer's organisation, as we pointed out earlier. Suppliers who win work by promising action on climate change might not be what the local town council really wants, just as for a large food firm, a supplier committing to employ disabled staff might not resonate strategically. Another supplier offering great ideas for addressing plastic packaging waste might have far more relevance and impact for that buyer.

Having said that, putting a financial value on suppliers' proposals in these purpose areas is not always the wrong thing to do. But this methodology must be used with care, and combined with strategic focus. Suppliers need to understand which PwP aspects the buyer is most interested in and therefore will be most strongly considered in the selection process.

TOP TEN TAKE-AWAY

Including purpose-related issues in basic supplier qualification processes is often sensible but the tick box approach is rarely enough in itself to drive supplier and supply chain change and improvement. Including the issues as a central part of supplier evaluation process and selection decisions when awarding contracts is often more powerful, but must be handled carefully.

Using PwP Factors in Supplier Selection – Recommendations

We've seen that the PwP agenda can be driven by using the supplier selection process to choose firms that satisfy our purpose-related objectives. That can be done through direct bias, or by using selection mechanisms to incorporate analysis of the wider value the prospective suppliers can offer.

This is a really fundamental topic in terms of how organisations can implement practical PwP actions and initiatives. So, before we move on to the next stage of the process, it is worth highlighting some key points that should help organisations successfully navigate what is a tricky element of the overall process.

a. Using yes / no qualification questions or requirements can be useful: for instance, insisting that suppliers sign up to standards or reach levels of certification before they can be considered as potential suppliers. However, be aware that this can become a "box-ticking" exercise.
b. Introducing straightforward bias into the process in favour of certain firms is effective in helping them win contracts. But it can have unforeseen consequences, including corruption, misrepresentation of supplier ownership, and even squeezing other good firms out of a market.
c. Remember, there are other ways to help businesses that are disadvantaged in some sense – for instance, offering them training or support so they can build their own genuine capability.
d. If you want to favour bids and suppliers with a strong "wider value" offering, be cautious about the percentage weighting given to social value / PwP in formal bid evaluations. Understand that if you use too high a weighting, it might lead to

you paying a substantial premium over other bids for "purpose". That is fine if you are prepared to do that; but do understand the consequences.

e. If you are scoring potential suppliers in terms of their current or proposed purpose-related activities, ensure that the proposed value in bids that wins good "marks" is linked and aligned to your own strategic goals. Also work to ensure it is as tangible as possible, and that it can be properly tracked (i.e. so that suppliers do as they promised) and measured if at all possible. Effective contract management is, as always, important in this regard.
f. However you introduce procurement with purpose into the evaluation process, ensure that any supplier that wins really does have the basic capability to deliver the contract efficiently and effectively.
g. Also be aware of the dangers that you might introduce barriers to entry accidentally. Larger firms are more likely to be able to tell a good story about purpose or social value than smaller or younger businesses. It would be ironic if this agenda led to the most powerful firms and suppliers becoming even more so!

Chapter 8 – Driving Action Through the Contract

> "Poor contract management is a long-standing issue… Our work started to highlight widespread problems with contract management... We highlighted poor risk management, inadequate performance measurement and limited use of performance incentives. Since then, we have reported on many contracts with weak contract management. These weaknesses have far-reaching consequences …."
> *(UK National Audit Office report, 2015)*

Another way of encouraging suppliers to behave in a certain manner or carry out particular tasks is to make their agreed actions part of the contractual terms and conditions. That may follow on from offers made in the supplier selection and evaluation phase discussed in the previous chapter, or it may be issues that are covered during the negotiations and final agreement of the contract.

Using Contractual Terms and Conditions to Drive Purpose

Some contractual conditions relevant to these issues may simply reflect an overarching legal obligation that the supplier must accept, whatever the unique commitment to a particular buyer. It may be that the supplier is bound by the law even if it is not mentioned specifically, as in the case of the Modern Slavery Act in the UK or the US Foreign Corrupt Practices

Act. However, the buyer may wish to reinforce how important an issue is by including some reference to it in their specific contract.

Or the contract may reflect specific codes of conduct, standards or equivalent that the buying organisation wants the supplier to recognise and agree to meet. Such standards may be developed by the buying organisation itself, or they could be sector-, industry- or geographically related. For instance, the UK government's standard "short-form" contractual terms and conditions published by the Cabinet Office[36] contain this section:

> 13.1 The Supplier must, in connection with provision of the Deliverables, use reasonable endeavours to:
>
> (a) comply and procure that its subcontractors comply with the Supplier Code of Conduct appearing at (https://assets.publishing.service.gov.uk/government/uploads/system/uploads/attachment_data/file/779660/20190220-Supplier_Code_of_Conduct.pdf)
>
> (b) and such other corporate social responsibility requirements as the Buyer may notify to the Supplier from time to time;
>
> (c) support the Buyer in fulfilling its Public Sector Equality duty under S149 of the Equality Act 2010;
>
> (d) not use nor allow its subcontractors to use modern slavery, child labour or inhumane treatment;
>
> (e) meet the applicable Government Buying Standards applicable to Deliverables which can be found online at: https://www.gov.uk/government/collections/sustainable-procurement-the-government-buying-standards-gbs

36 https://www.gov.uk/government/publications/short-form-terms-and-conditions

In this case, the terms cover both a general legal requirement – the Equality Act – and something more specific to government suppliers (the Code of Conduct).

It is also worth noting here that the modern slavery clause covers not just the supplier but their subcontractors, too, although "subcontractor" does not appear to be defined. So it could apply to all the supplier's suppliers – which is tough, as it is hard to see realistically how any firm can guarantee every supplier acts in a certain manner. In reality, it probably relates to a much narrower cohort of subcontractors, those who carry out specific work that clearly relates to that particular contract or buyer.

In any case, this type of clause is worth considering for private sector organisations as well as public. But often a buyer will want to include contractual details beyond standard wording or simply adherence to a code of conduct. Those more specific contract elements will relate to the purpose-related actions that have been agreed during the supplier selection and negotiation process.

Getting into the Detail

If the supplier has committed in their tender, bid or proposal to employ 20 local apprentices as part of winning a construction contract, that can be incorporated into the contract. It doesn't have to be, of course – some buyers might wish to handle that commitment as part of ongoing relationship management, rather than "contractualise" it formally. But generally, if you want a supplier to do something, including it in the contract does focus their attention. It can also provide levers or sanctions if the supplier does not meet its promises.

That leads on to the question of penalties (and incentives). What happens if the supplier doesn't recruit those apprentices? They are then in breach of contract, so does that give the buyer, at the extreme, the right to terminate the contact? Or should the buyer invoke penalties of some sort? This can be covered in the contract, too.

If there are no real sanctions against a supplier that does not perform, then there is less motivation for them to keep their promises. In the public sector, where social value proposals being made in bids often now form an important element of the selection process, it is particularly vital that suppliers do deliver. Otherwise, bidders will start promising the world in order to score more points in the evaluation, knowing that the chance of being held to account is low.

The contract can also be supported by service level agreements (SLAs) and/or sets of KPIs (key performance indicators) relating to PwP issues. So, if a supplier has agreed to a range of activities around promoting employment opportunities, KPIs could be set with targets relating to apprenticeships, employment diversity, bringing long-term unemployed back into the workforce, and so on. The contract could then refer to a commitment to achieve the targets on the KPIs, with an explanation of the process for measurement, feedback and review, and details of any sanctions, penalties or incentives that might be actioned depending on those KPIs.

TOP TEN TAKE-AWAY

Performance and outcomes must be tracked and measured to ensure suppliers are following through on promises made in the selection process and in terms of contractual requirements. That is not always easy, but it is vital.

Contract and Supplier Management

Once the contractual terms are agreed, and the champagne is flowing following the contract signing ceremony (it is nice to dream), then we have to manage that contract.

In the context of procurement with purpose (PwP), we're talking here about the situation post-contract award, where a buyer has asked or insisted that the supplier takes certain actions, or behaves in a certain manner to reflect the agreed goals. This applies less to forward-looking, collaborative actions, which may not be defined in the contract, and will be covered in the next chapter.

But in the case of core contract management, you generally want to:

- check that the supplier is doing what the contract said they would;
- make changes to contract terms and conditions in order to reflect new or different requirements;
- encourage the right behaviour to continue;
- reward or penalise the supplier where appropriate; and
- take corrective action if the agreed things aren't happening.

Laying out key tasks in that manner shows immediately that handling PwP issues in this phase of the end-to-end process has much in common with what we would call "supplier performance management" in conventional procurement and contract management terms.

Even if you just want to check a supplier is meeting quality and delivery requirements for a basic product or raw material, you need to check what you're getting, have some way of measuring that performance, compare that against what is contractually agreed, and either thank the supplier for good performance or implement corrective actions. That might range from the "quiet chat" with the account manager, through to kicking them out or even taking legal action.

PwP requirements can be considered in exactly the same way. There must be a route to understand whether suppliers are meeting promises and measure performance if objective measures are defined. That should be mapped against desired outcomes or outputs, and action taken where necessary requirements are not being met.

That all seems obvious. And yet, it often doesn't happen, in either day-to-day contract and supplier management or when it comes to PwP issues. How many organisations have a robust way of establishing that suppliers are complying with the Modern Slavery Act? Or understanding provenance of agricultural products, rare metals or minerals? How many suppliers have promised (perhaps as part of a "social value" commitment) to employ a certain number of disabled or long-term unemployed people, or take on a number of apprenticeships – yet can't provide any hard data to show what they have actually done? How many buyers follow up on that?

The level of management needs to be appropriate to the risk and opportunity for the buyer. If a construction supplier has agreed to take on apprentices as part of their contractual deliverables, you should check that they are doing what they promised. But it is hardly a matter of business life and death for the buyer, and that checking can be relatively light touch.

However, if a food company's whole *raison d'être* and brand positioning is around its vegan products, checking that raw material suppliers are not providing material contaminated with pigs' offal is extremely important. The effort going into managing those contracts and suppliers needs to be significant and robust.

Good contract management requires robust planning, appropriate resourcing, and the right people in terms of quantity and quality. Often contract and supplier management are tacked onto someone's main day job, and sink down the priority list over time.

Contract Management Recommendations

Whole books have been written about contract management (and my 2007 guidance written for the UK National Audit Office is still used in government circles),[37] and this one chapter does not claim to compete with those. But in the context of PwP, here are some key points to note if you want to ensure success. These are also relevant to successful contract and supplier management generally, but all certainly play a major role in managing PwP commitments:

1. Ensure you have a record of the agreed contract, and a full understanding of procurement with purpose terms, supplier commitments and activities.
2. Identify who is responsible for managing the contract – and who the contact points are on the supplier side. Resource levels and capability must be appropriate and sufficient for each contract.
3. Make sure all parties understand the measures that will be used to monitor and manage performance. Measures should be SMART.[38] In terms of reporting progress and achievement, it may be useful to consider a blend of self-reporting by the supplier and some independent verification (inspections, audits, etc.).
4. For more significant and strategic contracts, make sure that the right "governance" is in place – for example, reporting lines, roles to be played by executives on both sides, scheduled meetings, problem resolution and structured escalation processes.
5. Relationship management sits alongside governance. Contract management works best when both parties approach it in the spirit of mutual benefit and shared problem-solving, rather than as an adversarial contest. Building relationships can be an

37 https://www.nao.org.uk/report/good-practice-contract-management-framework-2-2/

38 Specific, Measurable, Achievable, Realistic, and Timely.

important part of that – but that doesn't mean a buyer should be afraid to take strong action in the case of supplier failure.

6. Incentives and (potential) penalties drive supplier behaviour, including in terms of PwP issues. Think carefully about this during the procurement process, as the contract is being negotiated and constructed, and then stay on top of these issues during the contract management phase.
7. Risk management is a key aspect of contract management for all but the least significant contract. Where procurement with purpose is an important aspect of the contract, risk is often closely aligned with PwP issues – for example, the reputational risk issues around many of the topics discussed here (human rights, pollution, etc). Remember, a sustainable supply chain is a low-risk and resilient supply chain – and vice versa.

Chapter 9 – Collaboration with Suppliers

Unilever announced its "Less, Better, No" plastics framework in 2017, and has pursued many innovative ideas since, working with and alongside a whole range of plastic industry firms. The firm has explored new ways of packaging and delivering products, such as concentrates, including its new Cif ecorefill which eliminates 75% of plastic, and new refill stations for shampoo and laundry detergent in shops, universities and mobile vending stations in Southeast Asia. "Better plastic" led to a new detectable pigment being used in Axe (Lynx) and TRESemmé containers, which allows black plastic to be seen and sorted by recycling plant scanners.

As well as building procurement with purpose (PwP) goals into supplier selection and contracting, there are often ways for buyers and suppliers to work together *collaboratively* to take forward initiatives, whether or not these are defined in the formal contract.

Indeed, such work includes many of the most exciting current initiatives in the business world, ranging from finding replacements for non-recyclable plastics to solving challenging social problems, from halting rainforest destruction to supporting dynamic minority-owned businesses.

Most of the ideas in this chapter are applicable not just to PwP activities but to supplier collaboration, whatever its motivation. Collaboration can drive more sustainable business, or faster innovation, or even greater efficiency and cost reduction. In all cases, though, there are techniques and approaches that can help organisations to collaborate more successfully across the traditional buyer / supplier divide.

Collaborate for Innovation

In many leading organisations, the major goal of collaboration with suppliers is to seek and implement innovation of some sort to drive competitive advantage. In the case of PwP goals, innovation from the supply side is often a key element in delivering the required benefits or outcomes. The buyer cannot achieve their goals alone. But whatever apparent power the buyer holds, they can rarely dictate exactly how a supplier behaves. It is extremely difficult to threaten or bully an individual, or an organisation, into being "creative" or "innovative" for your benefit.

In terms of purpose-related activities and goals, new thinking is often needed. Tough implementation challenges may need to be overcome, or at the extreme, totally new inventions or technology required. It is pointless specifying plastic packaging with incredible properties if it doesn't exist in the market! So, examples of PwP initiatives that are likely to involve collaboration and innovation include:

- Working with suppliers to develop more recyclable or compostable packaging materials.
- Working with farmers and agricultural firms to make sure cultivation of key crops is sustainable economically for the growers and environmentally sound, and respects workers' rights.
- Using new technology – from drones to AI – to analyse agricultural yields and develop recommendations for more effective and sustainable approaches.

- Public sector "social value" activities where suppliers work with a council (the buyer) to improve training opportunities for local disadvantaged youngsters.
- Developing a mentoring programme where the buyer and key suppliers provide experienced executives to help social enterprises, small or minority-owned businesses thrive.

In several of those examples, collaboration will be with more than just one supplier, and may involve multiple firms on the buy-side, too, as with many human rights and economic improvement initiatives. There are many cases where a broader approach is useful, even involving collaboration across an entire sector or industry.

But the point is that the buyer usually can't *demand* that a supplier acts in a certain way, in the manner the previous two chapters discussed. Positive collaboration and aligned behaviour are needed. Here, the parallel is with SRM (supplier relationship management) thinking and practice. SRM programmes have traditionally seen buyers looking to develop close relationships with key suppliers, so that benefits and competitive advantage can be delivered for the buying organisation.

Integration, Incentives, Innovation

Danish procurement executive Alis Sindbjerg Hemmingsen was an early supporter and advocate of responsible procurement going back a decade or more. But she always made it clear that she "is not a philanthropist". Sustainability and responsible procurement must be integrated into the business and should be seen as activities that are going to add value to the organisation; we don't do this just to feel good about ourselves.

Back in 2015, Spend Matters reported[39] on a conference presentation

39 https://spendmatters.com/uk/responsible-procurement-from-alis-sindbjerg-hemmingsen-at-the-trade-extensions-event/

where she talked about the journey that firms make, from seeing these activities as primarily about risk avoidance, then getting into the issues that surround life cycle efficiency, and finally using collaboration techniques to enable supplier innovation. *"Collaboration with suppliers on sustainability issues can foster product, service and technology innovation,"* she said. She then talked about the "three I's":

Integration – integrating responsibility for the actions connected with responsible procurement into and across the supply chain and making sure that it is seen as everyone's responsibility within the organisation, not just a job for procurement.

Incentives – there must be something in it for suppliers. So, a major branded goods firm ranks their suppliers (gold, silver, bronze, yellow, red) on sustainability issues, and the higher-ranked get priority on orders and the chance to work together with the buyer on innovation and developmental activities.

Innovation – ultimately, innovation is needed to drive better responsible procurement, but innovation will also arise from working with suppliers in this collaborative manner.

Whilst pursuing innovation in collaboration with suppliers requires more effort and skill than simply demanding that they sign up to a code of conduct on a PwP issue, the rewards can be significant. The leaders in purposeful procurement certainly recognise that they must work in this way to make significant progress. They also recognise you can't do this with every supplier; you have to be selective, as we described in Chapter 5 when we talked about setting your strategy. But great improvements, innovations and benefits are possible with collaboration.

Internal Stakeholders Matter, Too

Aligning internal stakeholders to these activities is often more challenging than developing collaboration with external suppliers, particularly if suppliers are strategically vital to the Chief Marketing Officer, IT VP or other top-level executives. Again, there are parallels in PwP with the development of supplier relationship management (SRM) over recent years.

David Atkinson is an expert in that field and has been writing, speaking and educating executives around the world for years on the topic. Writing for the Spend Matters website in 2016,[40] he said this:

"We've all learned that excellence in category management is, in part, based on securing the involvement of stakeholders in category teams. Such cross-functional teams bring expertise, deep knowledge of the varying business requirements of each function, and are more likely to collectively make wise sourcing decisions. Well, cross-functional SRM is no different, and success in managing supplier relationships is ultimately predicated on ensuring the key people are involved."

Any collaborative PwP activity with key suppliers is almost certain to impact key stakeholders. So how do we encourage them to become willing and enthusiastic partners? Atkinson says that first of all we must understand the needs and requirements of stakeholders, then we have to map potential improvement activities to their needs. It is all about *"finding ways to bring suppliers and stakeholders together to collaborate on idea generation and then implementation"*.

Whilst Atkinson was talking about SRM generally rather than specific PwP activities, his words apply exactly to the initiatives we're discussing here, and he identifies in those words a central imperative for successful PwP programmes. Significant success comes from people and groups working together – the suppliers, the sustainability and procurement functions (or whatever group is driving PwP within the buying organisation) AND the key internal stakeholders, such as budget

---

40 https://spendmatters.com/uk/srm-five-leadership-challenges-part-1/

holders, specifiers, users of services, and top management.

We are asking suppliers to behave differently or change in some way what or how they supply us. It is almost inevitable that such change will affect internal stakeholders who deal with, rely on, or have an interface with suppliers. Key stakeholders in particular need to be content with that.

At the PwP roundtable Mark Perera and I hosted in late 2019, one delegate told the story of procurement approaching a key supplier, a major logistics firm, to discuss a move to an electric-powered vehicle fleet. Sure, we can do that, said the supplier, but we'll have the charge you 20% more as such vehicles are expensive to purchase.

Now, whatever the logistics buyer's personal views, and how passionate they felt about climate change, it was not their budget to spend. And their internal budget holder was not too impressed with the idea of costs going up 20%, to say the least. That became another idea put into the "too difficult" bucket, although as the relative costs of electric vehicles reduce, its time may come.

But you could imagine a scenario where the logistics buyer engaged with the key budget holders up-front, perhaps setting up a task force to look at how logistics spend could be made greener and more sustainable. That team might work to understand its own priorities and issues, and then start bringing key suppliers into the discussion. Thoughts might turn to a business case with a gradual implementation of an electric fleet, or a longer-term contractual commitment that allowed suppliers to offset changeover costs over some years' income. Perhaps the immediate priority could be transport within towns and cities, where pollution issues are more urgent.

The positive side of that business case would include using this strategy as a selling point when bidding for new contracts, as well as a worthwhile health impact for staff, and reduced risk of bad publicity or regulatory action against diesel vehicles.

Whatever the potential solutions, the point is that involving internal colleagues as well as suppliers will always pay off. They must see the benefits, and certainly they must understand why the organisation is following a procurement with purpose approach.

Mutuality – the Suppliers' View

As well as understanding internal stakeholders' views, suppliers must be considered, too. Perhaps they share your or your organisation's outlook about how you want to "change the world". Or perhaps they don't. So, it is not enough to simply assume that they will cooperate in PwP initiatives because of aligned interests. There must be some benefit to them in working with the buyer on these activities.

That might be a direct gain. For example, there may be potential for more revenue or profit (or both) if the collaboration is successful, as Nestlé made explicit in 2020.[41] The food firm announced that it would be prepared to pay a premium for certain products to support its commitment to make 100% of its packaging recyclable or reusable by 2025. To create a market, Nestlé committed to sourcing up to 2 million metric tonnes of food-grade recycled plastics and allocating more than CHF 1.5 billion to pay a premium for these materials between now and 2025.

Generally, the scope for suppliers who develop innovative products or services that address challenging issues, including in the areas of plastics, energy efficiency or recycling, is considerable. Good ideas developed by working collaboratively with your organisation may allow the supplier to sell more or increase profit elsewhere with other customers, too.

A similar benefit can be seen in the public sector where suppliers might develop innovative and successful ways of delivering "social value". A

41 https://www.nestle.com/media/pressreleases/allpressreleases/nestle-market-food-grade-recycled-plastics-launch-fund-packaging-innovation

supplier who has particular success, for example, with a programme to employ disadvantaged local people for one contract might take that experience and use it to support bids for other public contracts.

Even if there aren't obvious opportunities for the supplier to drive revenue, there might be a threat, direct or implied, that they will lose business if they don't cooperate. Whilst the carrot is often a better way of working, sometimes the stick is a useful alternative. Explaining to a supplier that if they don't collaborate on PwP, they are likely to lose your business, can also be effective.

Collaboration and cooperation may also bring indirect benefits for the supplier. Just as successful actions can have a positive reputational effect for the buyer, they can also reflect well on the supplier. That can only help the firm win more business from different customers. As a buyer, you might agree to help your supplier promote the work you're doing together, bringing benefits to both parties.

But far too often we have seen organisations expecting suppliers to act collaboratively, sharing innovation and ideas, without any benefit. Organisations that believe that this will work in the medium and long term are arrogant, naïve, or both. In the 2016 State of Flux Global SRM survey,[42] no less than 47% of respondents said they "never" shared the benefits of supplier relationship management activities with their suppliers. Most of the others said they "occasionally" shared. When it comes to PwP initiatives, it is hard to see why suppliers should make much effort if there is nothing in it for them.

Mutually beneficial collaboration is at the heart of an initiative described by Mark Smith, a senior procurement executive at bp. "We're working closely with our cloud service providers such as AWS and Microsoft. Migrating to cloud brings some direct emissions benefits, as

42 https://www.stateofflux.co.uk/ideas-insights/reports-and-publications/2016-global-srm-research-report-digital-srm-suppli

we can close down some relatively inefficient infrastructure and buy more energy-efficient provision." In turn, AWS and Microsoft have committed to zero carbon in their own businesses, and have also signed up to renewable-generated power purchase agreements with bp.

As Smith explains: "That initiative brought together people from our technology, trading, operations, procurement and finance areas as well as a lot of involvement from procurement. It's a good example of corporate purpose and procurement with purpose being well aligned."

bp is starting to bring sustainability criteria into procurement strategies, supplier selection and contract award decisions. Circularity is yet another emerging area of collaborative interest. "We're working with a US university looking at development of a digital asset repurposing hub," says Smith. Getting longer life from equipment, whether it is a laptop, furniture or a phone is a simple but effective idea, and the thinking around total cost of ownership is changing to reflect that. Again, that will require a broad collaborative effort.

TOP TEN TAKE-AWAY

Collaboration between buyers and suppliers (or potential suppliers) to drive innovation and improvement is vital for success in many of these areas. To drive systemic and real change, collaboration often needs to be long-term, and also in many complex cases must go wider than just buyer/seller to cover whole markets, sectors or geographies.

Collaboration or Competition?

Implementing PwP successfully requires engagement from both suppliers and internal stakeholders. Procurement or sustainability leaders cannot drive change on their own.

But sometimes a third type of collaboration is sensible or even essential to make real change. Increasingly, different organisations, outside the buyer/seller paradigm, sometimes even competitors, are coming together to address these major issues. That has several benefits. It can reduce the costs for all participants; it enables sharing of ideas, knowledge and good practice; and the weight of multiple firms supports the network effect mentioned earlier. That also means the collaboration is more likely to carry influence with regulators, or when persuading other firms (including suppliers) or industries to act in the manner that the group wish to see.

In areas such as auditing suppliers and supply chains, this type of collaboration is not unusual. Mark Smith of bp explains that there has been a strong focus historically on safety in the energy sector supply chain, an area where "competing" firms have worked collaboratively for many years. That has fed across successfully into wider sustainability approaches. The use of shared audits, common standards and certifications helps and, he says, *"we are coming from a position of strength here – although we know there is more to do"*.

In 2016, Procter & Gamble's sustainable packaging expert Gian De Belder put together a coalition of companies to pioneer the "HolyGrail" initiative in Europe under the Ellen MacArthur Foundation's New Plastics Economy Pioneer Projects banner. The firms included many big names: L'Oréal, BASF, Danone, PepsiCo, Nestlé and more. Three years of innovation led to the improvement of post-consumer recycling, using chemical tracers and digital watermarks for packaging products, with the aim of moving closer to a circular economy. The project won the overall award at the 2019 "Sustainability Awards" ceremony.[43]

Competitors worked together as the initiative looked at how packaging can be made easier to recycle via tracers and watermarks

---

43 https://packagingeurope.com/holygrail-project-wins-top-prize-at-sustainability-awards-20/

embedded in the plastic. If used plastic items can be sorted more easily, there is a chance to improve the quality and quantity of recycled plastic material on the market, which would of course reduce waste. That collaborative effort sits alongside P&G's own internal Ambition 2030 programme, which aims to achieve 95% recyclable or reusable packaging by 2025.

As always, there are some issues with this approach. Principally, there is confusion in some sectors because of the plethora of collaboration-based bodies that have developed, all looking at similar issues. Oliver Hurrey, an experienced operator in the supply chain sustainability world, describes the complexity faced by buyers who may have to choose between several not-for-profit-type organisations, all focused on "eliminating modern slavery" or "supporting agriculture in the developing world". They all mean well, but the effort is dissipated and this situation can lead to unnecessary work through the supply chain – multiple inspections or onerous reporting requirements for suppliers, perhaps.

Another objection to collaboration comes from those who ask whether firms lose out on the chance of gaining competitive advantage by working together. But many perceive that the positives outweigh any potential negatives.

There is also the "cascade effect", which is driving awareness and action. For example, as the CEO of CSR ratings platform EcoVadis explained, *"clients invite their suppliers to join the platform, then suppliers invite suppliers… and so on. If we start with the biggest firms at the top of the supply chain, then the thinking flows down to the mid-sized firms and beyond."*

In most cases, it is customers (in both B2B and B2C worlds) that push a firm to take action on sustainability issues, and similarly to use the EcoVadis services.

"The benefits are just so great if firms collaborate. Of course, firms would like to share the risk and keep the opportunities for themselves! But they generally see that they can reduce the risks and the costs so much by collaborating, it is worth working with and sharing with others."
(Pierre-François Thaler, Founder and CEO, EcoVadis)

At the Chartered Institute of Procurement and Supply conference in late 2020, Emma Peacock from the Mars Food Group explained that the firm *did* see the opportunity to gain some advantage from their sustainability initiatives. But in terms of many underpinning activities, such as setting standards, data gathering, communication with supply markets and spreading core good practice, it was better to work together with others. The advantage would come, she suggested, from what you did in your own marketplace with that data, information and knowledge.

Of course, a firm might develop an amazing new product that contributes to environmental improvement and may want to make some money out of it, rather than immediately share it altruistically. But we are seeing industry cooperation in many sectors, from cocoa growing to plastic packaging, from human rights monitoring to reducing emissions in transportation. Humanity is facing huge challenges, and the power of collaboration is needed to make progress quickly.

Supplier (and Wider) Collaboration Recommendations

Here are some key points to note if you want to ensure success in terms of collaboration with your suppliers, and indeed potentially more widely.

1. Collaboration is time- and resource-consuming, so don't think you can do it with every supplier. Focus on where the benefits are potentially the greatest – that applies actually whether you are collaborating for a purpose-driven reason or to drive value and innovation.

2. Suppliers must see the benefits to them of collaboration. The benefits and value created must be shared.
3. Successful collaboration almost always involves internal stakeholders beyond the procurement and sustainability teams. Operational managers, technical staff and finance people may all have critical roles to play. The same applies in the supplier side – it must go beyond the sales people.
4. Benefits may take years to come through – look at some of the successes in terms of new recyclable materials which have taken years of development. Be ambitious and drive for action, but understand when it is appropriate to be patient.
5. Collaboration across multiple buying and/or supplying organisations can be particularly powerful to address major issues. That can be based on similar firms in a sector, or geographies, or a shared interest in a particular purpose-related issue.
6. Do consider where collaboration might lead to real competitive advantage for your organisation. But balance that with the benefits of sharing in terms of resources and cost, and the wider benefits of sharing positive purposeful outcomes and results.

The End-to-End Procurement Process – A Summary

The last five chapters have looked at the end-to-end procurement process from strategy, through supplier selection to contracting, contract and supplier management. The table below summarises what you might consider in terms of how you work with suppliers at each stage of the process.

Stage	Activities
Pre or outside the procurement process	• Education • Information
Supplier selection	• Qualification • Assessment and evaluation
Contracting and contract management	• Contractual Ts & Cs • Measurement, feedback, action
Supplier management and collaboration	• Collaboration with suppliers – short and long-term
Wider collaboration	• Collaboration at sector, industry, national or global level

Fig. 5 – Working with Suppliers

Chapter 10 - A Refreshing and Inspiring Conversation with Heineken

Many of the interviews Mark Perera and I carried out for this book were inspiring for us (and we hope for readers, too). Our discussion with Hervé Le Faou, Chief Procurement Officer of Heineken, certainly refreshed the parts that other procurement with purpose interviews couldn't reach!

OK, we couldn't resist that, although the famous advertising slogan has not been used by the brewer for 20 years or so, but it entered general usage long before the adverts stopped. While Heineken is still one of the world's leading advertisers in terms of marketing quality and spend, it has also developed a reputation for being at the forefront of sustainable procurement.

Le Faou himself is very much one of the new breed of CPOs. He has worked for a range of blue-chip consumer goods firms including Danone and Unilever, working in general management roles in India, Europe and the US, and has now been at Heineken for 5 years. So whilst his background is in operations and supply chain, his general management experience means he sees his current role as having "a business focus rather than a functional focus". Most of his roles have involved transformation, and he looks to leverage the skills of whichever area he is working in "to drive the organisation towards a successful future".

Through the company's ownership structure, the Heineken family involvement and vision are being retained, which helps keep the focus on "the long term and the top line," Le Faou explains. This perhaps makes supporting sustainability actions easier than in a company that is always focused on the next quarter's bottom line results. So what is the strategic positioning of procurement in the firm?

Procurement used to be about the flow of goods "into the box", Le Faou says, "but now, we see ourselves as the owners of the ROI that the supply base provides to the stakeholders within the business. We are powered by suppliers, we plug them into our business like electric plugs, not just in raw materials but even in marketing. Simply, if we choose the wrong agency, then that budget doesn't work." It is the quality and performance of suppliers that help you win, "and we must constantly reshape the supply base to meet our needs".

But the future focus includes what happens after the box, as it were. The billions of cans and bottles the firm buys annually could go around the planet over 30 times, and without responsible and clean recycling schemes in place, a significant proportion can end up going into landfill. "We have a responsibility to the planet. The circular economy and care for the environment is vital for us and the communities we operate in."

That procurement with purpose attitude extends into indirect spend, too, and a focus on developing an ecosystem of diverse suppliers. "We depend on a network of complex supply chains and we need to make sure there is wealth there." Indeed, in some countries such as South Africa, demonstrating supplier diversity is key to doing business.

Collaboration is key to the strategy, too. For instance, Heineken has also been helping some strategic suppliers with supplies of PPE during the COVID-19 pandemic. "We were able to share supplies through our contracts because these firms are critical for us" – and this approach is going to accelerate, he thinks. "We're being transparent with key suppliers, asking, 'how can we best get through this crisis?' Things will need to change, for instance, as we redesign bars and social gatherings."

So the focus now for Le Faou and procurement is on three main (and linked) areas – technology, sustainability, and the agility of the supply base.

"Agility is key. We work in an uncertain environment – I mean macroeconomic developments, political shifts, the environment, trade – but whatever happens, an agile and diverse supply base should help you manage." The firm is also sensitive to the growing focus on social issues, such as the need for responsible drinking behaviour. The focus of the firm's marketing now is on fun and creating "memorable experiences", whilst also focusing on global responsible drinking campaigns such as: 'When You Drive, Never Drink' or the recent Heineken® #SocialiseResponsibly campaign.

"Experiences could be at the centre of what we do in the future", Le Faou believes. Hence links to major sporting or music events, and maybe consumers buying something that is much broader than just a bottle of beer. That might bring some interesting challenges and opportunities in terms of procurement activities, we suspect, and "there might even be subscription models in future to 'create a dream', as we say."

But let's return to the technology angle. "Our role is to challenge our supply markets – not just in categories such as glass and cans but also in logistics, or media or marketing spend. Digitisation moves so fast, so maybe in the future media will be totally different. So creative thinking is important."

"This is the link between sustainability and innovation – it is about designing the future," Le Faou says. If you don't think about the future, you will lose it. "We need to paint a picture of a possible future, and create a sense of purpose for that vision".

He believes that negotiation will "disappear" as we design new ways of doing business. Artificial intelligence will give total transparency of the supply chain, so we will see ecosystems with a shared P&L. "It will not be about stealing margin from your suppliers. It is about speed, and using innovation to create competitive advantage and grow market share."

Moving from the vision back to current activities, Le Faou is one of the co-leads of Heineken's sustainability programme. The firm has cut carbon emissions from its breweries almost in half since 2008 and has committed to using 70% renewable energy within ten years. "Regenerative agriculture" is another priority, which in areas such as barley cultivation looks to improve the soil, and develop healthier water systems and increased biodiversity, as well as improve the lot of farmers. Heineken is working to make logistics and cooling greener, too, which matters as the firm has no less than 150,000 of its green fridges out in the marketplace!

Water is another focus. The "Every Drop" programme is reducing the amount of water used for every litre of beer brewed. 10 years ago the usage was 10 litres, now it is 3.2 and the target is 2.8. The programme extends even to "replacing" the water in the product that is eventually drunk by consumers; for example, through reforestation programmes. We have a number of breweries around the world using solar power to provide the energy needed for brewing – another demonstration of how sustainability thinking and innovative technology are closely linked.

To achieve this progress, procurement must engage with suppliers on sustainability and technology issues. A few years ago, the metals (cans) and glass markets were dominated by a few large, conservative suppliers. "Bringing these firms into a sustainability mindset was not easy," Le Faou acknowledges.

"We asked questions like how could we make the primary packaging 'smarter' and lose the secondary packaging?" This was radical, and changing the approach meant moving away from traditional commercial negotiation. But Le Faou is (rightly) cynical about the results of the old adversarial procurement approach in many firms. "Let's be honest, you beat up the supplier, you think you are making savings, but at the end of the year, somehow your supplier's P&L is better and yours is worse!"

But making real change in terms of sustainability and the circular economy needs the involvement of not only suppliers but also whole sectors, governments, retailers and more. So procurement must work with a wider range of external – and internal – stakeholders. "We are now closer to our people in corporate affairs and we go outside the business, too, talking to regulators and governments."

In terms of making circular economy ideas work, for instance, Le Faou explains that "whole industries have to move. No one will change how they do things for just part of the sector." So there is a major job to be done in terms of persuading many different people and organisations.

But while some suppliers weren't sure at first that Heineken was serious, now the messages associating sustainability, innovation and technology are getting through. The can and bottle industries are getting into renewable energy and circularity. "Some thought they would lose revenues, but we had to say, you will die if you don't adapt!" Eventually that message was heard and firms are acting.

Le Faou feels that for procurement functions and people, the discussion with very top management is easier if you talk about sustainability and innovation rather than purely commercial matters. And the pressure is continuous. "Being the best doesn't last long today. We want to be the best, to be the first – but then we will also share ideas and collaborate with others to innovate." People are vital, too, with the ongoing "competition for talent", and you must have the best people to sustain that advantage.

We then moved on to social matters. Le Faou has a fascinating perspective here: "Environmental issues used to be defensive and regulatory. Now they can be a competitive advantage. The same thing is now happening with 'social' issues, such as human rights. We can turn this into a positive, proactive issue, not just think of the regulations and the risks."

For instance, he believes that "multinational firms can make things better for people, and help bring them out of poverty. That is a real sense of purpose!"

Heineken believes it can create many jobs directly and indirectly – but of course measuring how many people move out of poverty is not easy. As you might expect, this enlightened attitude in Heineken has come from the top. But "not all CEOs are mature enough to listen to these ideas, they still focus on year-end. So we think we can help to move the needle on purpose, help to move whole industry sectors. And when you find a CEO who is passionate about this, who will allocate resources to the future, then they will win."

In our opinion, the same applies to CPOs. Those, like Hervé Le Faou, who can focus on sustainability, innovation, technology and agility in the supply base, taking both internal stakeholders and suppliers with them, will be the success stories of the procurement world. It is not always easy, and you need that supportive Board, but it is surely the way that procurement is moving, as Le Faou (and other successful leaders) show.

Chapter 11 – Greenwashing and Other Risks

Greenwash(v) – "the process of conveying a false impression or providing misleading information about how a company's products, process or practices are more environmentally sound than they really are. To make people believe that your company is doing more to protect the environment than it really is."
(Investopedia)

For anyone who cares about fundamental issues such as the future of our environment or basic human rights, the opportunity to use third-party spend to support such goals seems sensible and worthwhile. But that positivity should not stop analysis of the risks involved, or blind us to poor practices evident when organisations claim they are "doing the right things", without actually delivering on their claims.

The word *greenwash* (a play on "whitewash") first entered the *Oxford English Dictionary* back in 1999, but has become used more often in recent years as the focus on climate change has increased, and activist movements such as Greenpeace and Extinction Rebellion have become more vocal.

Greenwashing is usually an attempt to capitalise on the growing demand for firms to do the right things and jump on the sustainability bandwagon. The same principles apply to misleading information about human rights or other PwP topics, but "greenwashing" tends to relate to environmental issues in particular. It has the potential to confuse and mislead the consumer, or even make them sceptical about truly green products or actions. Firms that are genuinely concerned and active in this area might then suffer because of the greater cynicism and lack of trust caused by the guilty parties.

How Clean is Coal?

Greenwashing can take the form of outright false or irrelevant claims, or simply language or media that suggest something that is not actually correct or true. There have been many examples exposed over the years, a high proportion relating to the energy industries, perhaps unsurprisingly.

The term was coined by environmentalist Jay Westerveld in 1986, although there are older examples of the practice. For example, in 1962, Westinghouse advertised its nuclear power division, calling the plants "clean and safe". As meltdowns had already occurred in other nuclear plants, "safe" was debatable, and there was no mention of the issues around nuclear waste in the campaign either.

The 'Clean Coal' advertising campaign was brought to US consumers by a front group for the coal industry – the American Coalition for Clean Coal Electricity. It talked about clean coal and carbon capture, something that might happen one day but is a long way off, and in the meantime, coal remains far from "clean"! Similar pro-coal campaigns have been seen in different countries, including recently in Australia.[44]

Meanwhile, for years, Exxon Mobil funded the "climate change denial" movement, offering scientists money to undermine the findings of IPCC (the Intergovernmental Panel on Climate Change) reports, while

---

44 https://www.abc.net.au/news/2019-08-07/coal-lobby-hopes-to-make-australians-proud-about-coal/11388830

lagging behind other oil companies in their investment in renewables. That didn't stop the firm launching advertising campaigns boasting about their green credentials.[45]

Oil companies promote the money they are spending on renewables research, which sounds impressive, but is a tiny percentage of their overall spend on oil exploration and exploitation. In 2019, lawyers from campaign group ClientEarth said that oil firm bp was creating a "potentially misleading impression" that it is moving towards renewables rapidly, when in fact the vast majority of its planned investment is in oil and gas. bp also used the slogan "beyond petroleum" to indicate its direction of travel – but is it moving fast enough to justify this advertising? However, Bernard Looney, the new CEO appointed in 2020, has committed to making bp a purpose-driven business, and the firm is becoming more credible as it implements its strategy.

But It's Not Just the Energy Industry ...

Greenwashing also involves the use of complex technical terms or data that most people won't understand, with the purpose of presenting a false picture. Vague language and "buzzwords" that are misleading or don't come with factual explanation are another common tactic.

The food industry is another that has long been guilty of using this tactic. "Fat-free" or "low in fat" on a food product sounds good if you are watching your weight, but the product may be high in sugar and stuffed full of numerous additives, preservatives, and chemicals, making it far from healthy by any reasonable measure.

Other products make green claims that are meaningless. "CFC-free" on aerosol products looks impressive, but is actually required by law, rather than being a selfless decision by the manufacturer. (Although it can

---

45 https://www.desmogblog.com/exxons-greenwash/

be argued that pointing this out does at least reassure customers). There have also been claims that "bottled water is the most environmentally responsible consumer product in the world", which seems unlikely at best!

Some examples of dubious claims even ended up in court. In February 2017, Walmart paid $1 million to settle greenwashing claims that alleged the huge US retailer sold plastics in their stores that were misleadingly touted as environmentally responsible.[46] The automotive industry has been another culprit here. Car firms have advertised new models as being somehow environmentally friendly, when in fact they had worse fuel consumption than the average car.

At worst, behaviour can be criminal. The emissions scandal that engulfed Volkswagen in 2015 came about as the firm tried to bypass US legislation on diesel engine emissions and fool the customer by cheating on the tests for car engines. The engines were adjusted to meet the standards during testing, but in day-to-day use, emissions could be many times higher. In January 2017, Volkswagen pleaded guilty to criminal charges and signed an agreed Statement of Facts, paying a $2.8 billion criminal fine for "rigging diesel-powered vehicles to cheat on government emissions tests".[47]

In February 2020, leading airline Ryanair was told to stop making claims about how environmentally responsible it was. The firm claimed that it provided "Europe's lowest fares" and was also the continent's "lowest emissions airline". That was based on the "lowest carbon emissions of any major airline", measured as CO2 emissions per passenger per kilometre flown. That may be true, as the firm has a fleet of relatively new planes, with the latest most fuel-efficient engines, and the highest proportion of

46 https://www.sfgate.com/bayarea/article/Walmart-to-pay-1M-to-settle-suit-over-10901772.php

47 https://en.wikipedia.org/wiki/Volkswagen_emissions_scandal

seats filled on flights. But the claim was ambiguous.

When the firm was challenged, it presented evidence to the Advertising Standards Authority to back up its claims. But one of the charts presented was dated 2011, which the watchdog said was "of little value as substantiation for a comparison made in 2019". The ASA also commented that: "In addition, some well-known airlines did not appear on the chart, so it was not clear whether they had been measured." It also did not consider seating density, which has an impact on the data.[48]

It is also doubtful that packing more and more people into planes is really in the spirit of carbon emission reduction, although clearly there is no benefit in almost empty planes burning fuel (as unfortunately happened during the pandemic). But the explosion in low-cost flights, driven by firms such as Southwest in the US and Ryanair in Europe, has been a major driver of emissions, even if it has also brought benefits to many travellers. That growth has come to a crashing halt because of the COVID pandemic; but whether air travel will see a longer-term moderation, or more growth as everyone wants to make up for lost time (and holidays), remains to be seen.

TOP TEN TAKE-AWAY

Communicate your successes *and* remaining challenges honestly and openly to stakeholders. Avoid greenwashing, be proud of achievements but be prepared to explain and highlight where further work and effort are needed..

---

48 https://www.thedrum.com/news/2020/02/05/asa-bans-ryanair-ads-misleading-lowest-emissions-claims

Consumers Are More Cynical – and Better Informed

The public is becoming better informed about these issues, and it is likely that consumers will become savvier and more likely to spot attempts at greenwashing by corporates (or indeed governments). A touch of cynicism is healthy, too, given what is being claimed.

For instance, whilst pension funds, investment firms and fund managers are all expressing more interest in purpose and sustainability, their actions don't always live up to their words. Blackrock is one of the world's largest investment firms, and founder Larry Fink has been vocal about climate change. Yet his firm has voted against climate change-linked resolutions at company AGMs far more often than most investors.[49] Blackrock explain that they have put 191 companies "on watch" in 2020 and "those that do not make significant progress risk voting action against management in 2021". But these disparities between words and deeds are being noticed more often now.

In 2020, Jeff Bezos, the world's richest man (at the time of writing) and founder of Amazon, announced that he would dedicate no less than $10 billion to the Bezos Earth Fund, which would support "scientists, activists, NGOs – any effort that offers a real possibility to help preserve and protect the natural world".

He received both praise and perhaps more opprobrium than he expected for this move. Critics reminded us that this is less than 10% of his total wealth, and that the home delivery culture Amazon has driven leads to millions more shipments, journeys and emissions. Products from the firm also often appear to be overpackaged. Why does Amazon need a huge cardboard box, stuffed full of brown paper, polystyrene chips or plastic padding, to keep some tiny item safe? Then there are the direct emissions caused by Amazon Web Services, not to mention

49 https://citywireselector.com/news/blackrock-voted-against-climate-resolutions-over-80-of-the-time-in-2020/a1407553

accusations of poor treatment of Amazon workers, verging on abuse of human rights, according to some.[50]

And yet, customers use Amazon for a reason. Many people with disabilities or health conditions, who don't find it easy to trek around the shops, find the whole offering, the range and ease of finding information and ordering, absolutely invaluable. Through lockdowns in many countries Amazon has been a vital contributor to maintaining some sort of "normal" existence. So maybe Bezos should be applauded for making what is by any measure a huge commitment to fighting climate change.

As *Wired* magazine pointed out, Bezos "could fund 2,857 Duke University professors indefinitely, or almost three times the number of tenured professors at Yale"[51] with his investment. How he chooses to spend this money is key, of course, but his money could make a real difference. It's worth noting that Amazon has also now committed to meeting the goals of the Paris Climate Agreement 10 years early, by becoming carbon neutral by 2040.

It's also interesting that Bezos' ex-wife, MacKenzie Scott, has committed to giving away the vast majority of her fortune, and in 2020 she started the process in an extraordinary manner. She gave charities some $6 BILLION during that year, including $4bn (£3bn) to 380 organisations – chiefly food banks and emergency relief funds – in four months as a response to the COVID crisis. She does not seek publicity, but deserves praise and thanks.

How to Avoid or Counter Greenwashing

It is easy to be cynical about Davos-type pledges from CEOs. Pierre-

---

50 https://www.businessinsider.com/nyc-mayor-orders-investigation-amazon-warehouse-worker-firing-coronavirus-protest-2020-3?r=US&IR=T

51 https://www.wired.com/story/jeff-bezos-control-planet-future-10-billion-fund/

François Thaler of EcoVadis says that "quantifiable, time-bound pledges can create change, but some statements are made more for the publicity value". However, Thaler does believe that the world is really changing. He and his firm have close links with top French business school INSEAD, so he talks regularly to other senior executives and "there is an encouraging desire to pursue sustainability amongst leaders. Amongst the younger students that is even stronger."

So organisations that engage with PwP activities should be proud to tell stakeholders what they are doing – whether that means talking to staff, regulators or, perhaps above all, customers. After all, there are real business benefits to acting with purpose, as well as more altruistic goals. But there is also increased awareness of greenwashing, so you need to be careful, honest and reasonable when making claims about what you have achieved or intend to achieve in the future.

Here are some recommendations in terms of avoiding greenwashing, picked up from various sources, as well as from personal experience:

- Ensure that any green or other PwP-related claims you make are true and relevant to your stakeholders' expectations.
- Be humble – even if you are doing a great job, and want to communicate that (which is fine), do it sensitively. Even firms like Unilever constantly talk about where they need to improve, rather than simply boasting about their leadership position on PwP issues.
- On a related note, be honest if you are falling short; focus on 'the journey' and stress how you are moving in the right direction rather than claiming to have 'arrived' if you haven't.
- Use straightforward language when you're talking about the issues or your achievements. Don't try and confuse matters with 'the science'.
- Be transparent and use objective measures or independent,

external verification where possible. Make it easy for customers (or others) to check out your claims.

- Where appropriate, put the emphasis on collaboration (with suppliers, industry, the wider supply chain) and talk about how you are working with others for the wider good.

In October 2020, food giant Mars issued a press release relating to its **2020 Cocoa for Generations report:** *Reshaping the Future of Cocoa.* The quote below is a good example of how to communicate. It was well judged, highlighting key issues and emphasising progress, but being honest about work still to be done, and the need for more collaboration.[52]

"Today we recognize the progress we've made on our goals of increasing cocoa farmer income, protecting children, supporting women's social and economic empowerment, and tackling deforestation. While some in the industry are accelerating with us, collectively we must go further and faster to reshape the cocoa sector. We're calling for robust public-private collaborations so that human rights are respected, and the environment is protected, as we create a modern, inclusive and sustainable cocoa supply for the next generations to thrive."

(Andrew Clarke, Mars Wrigley Global President)

---

52 https://www.mars.com/news-and-stories/press-releases/mars-wrigley-releases-2020-cocoa-for-generations-report

Chapter 12 – Amplifying Procurement with Purpose

"We all contribute and have a critical role in ensuring responsible supply chains. We are concerned and care deeply about the future of our planet and its people. We believe in the necessity of leapfrogging the current efforts and in the power of the crowd to foster change. Because of the impact of Procurement decisions on a future sustainable planet, we pledge and commit ourselves to making sustainability the central mindset of our daily decision-making."
(The Sustainable Procurement Pledge)

Whatever stage your organisation is at on the procurement with purpose (PwP) journey, you are not alone. Others will undoubtedly be in a similar position. And as well as peers, the good news is that there are many organisations that can help you move forwards. Some have already cropped up, but the following can all prove useful when implementing your programme.

Leveraging Peers, Colleagues and Business Networks

In general, organisations appear to be very open about sharing standards, information, knowledge and ideas about purposeful business and PwP. There have been few examples of anyone saying, "we have done some great things, but we're not telling you what they are because we don't want our competitors to know".

That comes back to the debate about competitive advantage, already mentioned earlier. Can a firm steal a march on their competitors through their policy on recyclable packaging, or through buying commodities from more sustainable forests, or by paying workers in the supply chain better?

Hard evidence either way is lacking as yet, although some firms (such as Patagonia) have certainly built a successful business with sustainability at its heart. But that has arguably been about focus and determination rather than by doing anything absolutely unique or that couldn't be replicated. On the other hand, *not* following good practice in some of these areas can certainly lead to disadvantage and problems such as reputational damage.

No doubt competitive advantage built on purpose could emerge in specialist areas. If a food company comes up with a new healthy vegetable oil, created from old newspapers and sea water, they might well keep quiet about it – until they have a patent, at least! But in the vast majority of cases, organisations are being open about their work.

That is in part because they want their customers, staff and investors to know what they're doing, and in part (I would like to think) because they care about what they are doing. They want to see good work replicated. Indeed, many PwP initiatives are industry-wide, whether it is moves by chocolate firms to help indigenous cocoa growers, or industry projects around plastics recycling.

So talk to peers, contacts in other firms, use business networks such as Procurement Leaders, Procurious or similar professional associations (CIPS, IACCM, ISM, NIGP, etc) and other groups to gather information and ideas. There is now a wealth of conferences covering these topics, and more exchange of knowledge than ever before – there really is no excuse for saying "we just don't know how to get started".

At a personal level, the Sustainable Procurement Pledge movement, started by Thomas Udesen of Bayer and Bertrand Conquéret of Henkel, has proved very successful, with thousands of individual procurement and supply chain professionals signing up. That group provides another forum for exchange of ideas and best practice, and offers valuable support, particularly for those who personally care about purpose but work in organisations that have not fully embraced these ideas. Even if you are struggling to make progress, you are not alone.

In the UK public sector, David Shields has worked with Social Value UK to create the Contract for Change initiative,[53] and already over 200 people have expressed an interest, and 80 have volunteered to get involved with specific workstreams. A steering group has been formed, and various workstreams looking at good practice have been initiated, covering a range of issues across the whole procurement for social value life cycle.

There are also numerous sector and industry groups that encourage firms to work together to address issues. Oliver Hurrey is a veteran of sustainability initiatives of various types, and he works now with two collaborative industry groups. AIM-Progress is a forum of over 40 consumer goods manufacturers and suppliers "assembled to enable and promote responsible sourcing practices and sustainable production systems". Hurrey also founded and chairs the Scope 3 Peer Group, another collaborative group with a focus on reducing carbon emissions in the supply chain – "Scope 3" being the way that emissions in a firm's supply chain are defined in emission reporting schemes.

But perhaps surprisingly, given his own background, Hurrey is critical of the plethora of organisations (commercial firms, lobby or industry groups and third-sector players) who exist in the sustainability space, all trying to help firms make progress. Most of them mean well but *"there is so much nonsense and confusion out there"*, Hurrey explains.

53 https://www.socialvalueuk.org/contract-for-change/

> "There are at least 15 collaborative groups I know of just working in connection with human rights in the supply chain – 6 of them appear to have exactly the same words in their names, just in a different order!"
> *(Oliver Hurrey, Founder, Galvanised)*

He has counted no less than 187 sustainable procurement initiatives across different sectors, industries or issues. This makes it incredibly confusing for large firms in particular, who buy many different items from different geographies. How can they know which to support, and how best can they play a productive and collaborative role?

So organisations need to be careful and do their homework to identify which groups are effective and will be most appropriate. But the good news is that whichever industry you are in, or whichever purpose-related issues interest you, there will be an organisation to help or accept your input.

The Regulators – the Carrot and the Stick

We talked in Chapter 2 about the reporting requirements for companies, which are changing to reflect this agenda. For PwP evangelists within organisations, this can be useful leverage when looking to persuade colleagues to take a more active interest. Statutory reporting is particularly interested in risk issues, even more important post-pandemic. That will include risk around climate change and general business risk connected with a range of PwP topics.

There are also various "regulators" who have an interest in different elements of this agenda. In the UK, an Independent Anti-Slavery Commissioner has been established, whilst a Small Business Commissioner attempts to ensure larger firms treat small suppliers properly. Similarly, the Grocery Regulator takes an interest in unfair terms and conditions that bigger buyers might impose on suppliers. The situation is different in every country, but the number of such organisations is growing globally, with governance, advisory or regulatory roles supporting the drive for responsible and purposeful business. That can be helpful to organisations looking at such topics themselves. As well as providing that "threat" which can be used to leverage internal action, regulators often offer useful guidance and educational material to support improved performance.

I asked Russell Picot, who has worked extensively on issues around regulatory company reporting, how procurement and supply chain management should play into this new reporting paradigm. For example, if a company outsources manufacturing to a developing country, it might use less energy itself, but now causes more emissions via an inefficient supplier's factory elsewhere, one that might even be staffed by "slaves". How does that get reported in a transparent manner?

"These are sensitive issues. You might lose jobs locally, but create more in a location that really needs them. And as well as the factory's carbon emissions, the transportation involved in your example is another issue. Globalisation is problematic: we really need to de-carbonise global supply chains. But in their annual reports, I expect companies to be discussing their supply chains where these are significant to their business model."

So stronger reporting rules should help us highlight why this agenda is so crucial, both internally in your organisation and externally to citizens, investors and customers.

Technology to the Rescue?

Technology as a fundamental enabler for procurement with purpose was discussed in Chapter 6. It is essential to obtain and use the data and information needed for organisations to run successful PwP programmes. But as well as providing the infrastructure for successful programmes, technology is beginning to provide innovative solutions that will drive developments in this field.

Blockchain-based tools will enable consumers to understand the provenance of what we are buying – metals, materials or even food products. Frank Omare of SAP Ariba believes "we'll be able to scan what we are buying and immediately find out about its background, or the chances that modern slavery was involved". We might even get a clear view of where margin is being made in the supply chain and the make-up of final prices. Big data will also support decisions such as local versus global sourcing options.

Other developments underway include the use of drones to inspect regions at risk of deforestation, and the Mayflower autonomous ship, which is mapping the condition of the oceans.[54] This fascinating initiative is led by marine research organisation ProMare, supported by IBM and a global consortium of partners. The unmanned vessel will spend long periods at sea collecting critical data about the ocean, such as global warming, ocean plastic pollution and marine mammal conservation.

IBM is also working with Maersk on TradeLens,[55] an interconnected ecosystem of supply chain partners working together to digitise the shipping supply chain (using blockchain technology) and increase the efficiency around container shipping, customs clearance, and so on.

As Alison Smith from IBM puts it, "Data collection is often the hardest part of the process – you can't drive positive change if you don't have the right data". Technology can reduce the need for physical reporting, for instance, using the Internet of Things to obtain real-time data which can be interrogated, with AI looking for patterns, trends or concerns amongst the data. "That doesn't answer every challenge of course –

---

54 https://www.ibm.com/industries/federal/autonomous-ship

55 https://www.tradelens.com/

AI won't stop firms employing children in factories – but data can be powerful in many cases," Smith says.

She is a senior manager in the AI Applications business, helping firms use technology to manage supply chains more effectively, including the growing focus on the "triple bottom line" (profit, people and planet). She is an optimist, although there is a note of caution, too: "I do believe we can use technology for positive purposes; generally, the democratisation of information and data will have positive outcomes". But technology is neutral, she points out, and we have seen, for example, how social media can be used in positive or negative ways. "It is the intent that matters".

Another firm that has grown rapidly with the rise in importance of risk and sustainability issues is riskmethods,[56] a risk management platform and service to provide supplier alerts to clients. A buyer might gain awareness of natural risks such as earthquakes or floods, and also of cases where suppliers have broken environmental or human rights regulations, or industrial disputes that might affect a business and its reputation.

More advanced technology platforms that allow buyers and sellers to collaborate better, innovate more successfully, and share information quickly and easily across a cohort of organisations are also blossoming. Mark Perera's firm, Vizibl, is a leader in this field. The Vizibl platform helps buyers to manage relationships with key suppliers, covering innovation opportunities and new initiatives as well as the more risk- and sustainability-focused angles.[57] Vizibl "brings together your supply chain sustainability data in one place so you can identify new opportunities with suppliers, accelerate collaborative initiatives and advance your sustainability programmes".

Technology can also assist with project and programme management

---

56 https://www.riskmethods.net/

57 https://www.vizibl.co/

challenges, such as monitoring progress on specific PwP initiatives, capturing and reporting benefits. This can be particularly valuable for more complex collaborative programmes – for example, the development of new plastics or innovative packaging, where buyers and suppliers work together over long periods of time.

Then there are specialist solutions providers such as EcoVadis,[58] founded by the visionary Pierre-François Thaler with Frédéric Trinel back in 2007, when "sustainable procurement" was still something of a niche topic. The firm rates companies' supply chains on sustainability, corporate social responsibility (CSR) and other issues related to ESG (environmental, social and governance). Industry analyst firm Spend Matters says that EcoVadis "has built intelligence technology and networks to study and monitor supply chains. It is part intelligence network (for CSR data), part SaaS/cloud provider (in support of CSR data gathering and intelligence), and part enablement partner to companies for data collection".[59]

Technology is also supporting more industry or product-specific initiatives. The global software firm SAP announced in 2019 the creation of a new marketplace using its SAP Ariba solutions to expand the trade of recycled plastics and plastic alternatives. This was an extension of "Plastics Cloud", a pilot programme launched in 2018 to "help reduce and ultimately eliminate the waste of single-use plastics".

In this second phase, SAP worked with partners to extend Ariba Network, the world's largest business-to-business network, to create a new global marketplace for recycled plastics.[60] As Frank Omare from SAP Ariba put it, "firms are being held accountable for plastic waste

58 https://EcoVadis.com/

59 https://spendmatters.com/2020/01/09/EcoVadis-gets-200-million-boost-for-its-environmental-ratings-and-supply-chain-technology/

60 https://news.sap.com/2019/09/plastics-cloud-pilot-new-global-supplier-marketplace/

in the oceans and elsewhere. Retailers and manufacturers are looking to reduce waste and increase recycling". So the Ariba Network is a potential force for good, helping buyers to connect with recycled plastics suppliers and alternative supply sources.

Intermediaries, Consultants and Innovators

As well as the more traditional software firms, there are many people and businesses looking to assist organisations to implement PwP-type programmes. That includes strategy houses such as McKinsey and the huge professional and technology services firms such as PWC and Accenture. Then there are more specialist consulting firms, who have made aspects of sustainable business their core capability.

There is also an increasing number of interesting organisations which can't quite be defined as consultants or software providers, but provide support to their clients and users, often involving a range of professional services. Their offerings and business models all differ somewhat, but it is well worth looking at whether they can help on your PwP journey.

Paul Polizzotto is a social entrepreneur who launched Givewith[61] in 2016, with the aim of "being the first technology to link commerce directly to the UN SDGs". The "commerce" Polizzotto refers to involves all the money spent by and exchanged between businesses. Givewith enables purposeful donations or work to be included as part of the supplier bidding and selection process. In effect, it aims to channel a very small percentage of those tens of trillions of dollars that are transacted between organisations (an amount that would still represent a huge sum in total) towards "people in need".

Givewith maintains a database on not-for-profits, social enterprises, NGOs and social impact organisations and analyses where social impacts

61 https://www.givewith.com/

create the most business value. Their platform helps firms match their programmes with the issues their shareholders and customers care about most. Work with Boston Consulting Group has also looked to identify the benefits from programmes and has also verified and validated Givewith's methods and processes.

Polizzotto quotes cases where a social investment of $20,000 linked to a contract creates six-figure sums in benefits – for both buyers and suppliers. Givewith is also integrated now into the SAP Ariba platform, so buyers can "embed social impact directly into their sourcing process to generate unprecedented business value and new funding for the world's most effective non-profit, social enterprise, and NGO programmes".

Many other organisations are playing useful roles in terms of purposeful and sustainable business. FRDM (formally Made In A Free World) provides software that helps buyers understand the potential issues in their supply chain, such as modern slavery risks. Electronics Watch provides a collaborative monitoring and reporting service that keeps an eye on electronics factories in various countries on behalf of its member (buying) firms.

Jacqui Archer worked in both private and public sector commercial roles before founding the Positive Impact Commerce Foundation.[62] She has developed an "integrated holistic framework" with tools and processes designed to support a model which considers sustainable value from the perspective of the business, focusing on making better decisions that drive the right outcomes.

The model has five pillars, which combine to give an organisation a "Positive Impact Commerce" rating. Archer wants the PIC rating to become a standard measure that organisations can use to measure themselves and track progress.

---

62 https://www.positiveimpactcommerce.com/

The Positive Impact Commerce "Pillars"

- ✓ Integrated Governance – business-wide and focused on impactful decision-making
- ✓ People – the internal social value gained from engaging the workforce and clients
- ✓ Planet – natural value such as mitigating climate risk and improving biodiversity
- ✓ Society – providing real social value and economic opportunities

Under each of the five pillars, there are eight materiality indicators, with the most important weighted accordingly in the final scoring process. If you score above a threshold, you get a PIC rating, a single number calculated from the rolled-up scores.

The process starts with a self-assessment questionnaire. Organisations gather financial and non-financial information and assess themselves against statements, many of which are based on the "perceived wisdom", as suggested by various international standard-setting organisations. The PIC assessor can then highlight gaps and suggest more impactful activities.

The PIC system is at an early deployment stage, and in 2021, the UK's Ministry of Justice (MOJ), one of the largest and most sensitive government departments, is running a pathfinder project, with a handful of their most significant suppliers. It will be interesting to see data emerging from this, and perhaps the PIC rating will become an established and useful tool.

Academia – Universities and Business Schools

Academic institutions are increasingly interested in sustainability and implementation of the United Nations SDGs. More universities are creating professorial chairs or centres dedicated to the study of such areas. Often, they have one foot in academia and one in the business world, looking to work with businesses on projects or to develop innovative start-ups in these areas.

The University of Cambridge Institute for Sustainability Leadership, for instance, is "a globally influential Institute developing leadership and solutions for a sustainable economy". It provides executive and academic education, conducts research and carries out collaborative projects as well as commissioned research.[63] Over in Oxford, the Saïd Business School has carried out interesting research including a project working with the Mars Group[64] to examine the concept of "mutuality" in business, central to that firm's philosophy.

At Harvard, the Business & Environment Initiative was founded in 2010 to serve as a hub for environmentally focused research, teaching, and discourse.[65] BEI examines a wide range of topics and says, "we're working to accelerate energy innovation, foster sustainable food production, reimagine capitalism, address climate change, identify sustainable business practices, and promote effective governance".

A study that ranked the top sustainability programmes at global business schools carried out by the Study International organisation in 2019 came up with a ranking that puts some slightly lesser-known names at the top. The University of Warwick in the UK came out on top, followed by York University of Canada. Bath (UK), the University of Vermont (US) and Griffith Business School (Australia) completed the top 5.[66]

Universities have also been active in terms of reflecting sustainability

---

63 https://www.cisl.cam.ac.uk/work-with-us

64 https://www.sbs.ox.ac.uk/research/centres-and-initiatives/responsible-business-network/mutuality-business

65 https://www.hbs.edu/environment/about/Pages/default.aspx

66 https://www.studyinternational.com/news/most-sustainable-mba-2019/

and purpose in their own procurement. The London Universities Purchasing Consortium, for example, has been a key supporter and driver of the Electronics Watch organisation, which campaigns to improve human rights in the electronics supply chain.

Charities and Lobby Groups – Promoting Various Causes

There are numerous charities and lobby groups whose role in life is to promote the causes and drive improvements in those areas that sit within the procurement with purpose agenda. Whilst they understandably promote their own causes, such organisations often possess considerable information, expertise and insight that can help those who are putting programmes in place. They may also be able to link you up with others who are pursuing a similar track, or provide training or advisory services if you require that sort of assistance.

For instance, if you want to support the use of more minority-owned firms in your supply chain, then WEConnect[67] is internationally expert in the women-owned business sector, whilst MSDUK focuses on BME-owned businesses in the UK.[68] Charities such as Greenpeace and WWF can provide considerable resources that explain how and why organisations can and should work in harmony with the natural world.

Whether it is human rights issues, disability, apprenticeships, even noise pollution or littering, there will be a charitable organisation somewhere that can help you understand the issues and may well have useful resources to draw on for your PwP programme.

---

67 https://weconnectinternational.org/MS

68 https://www.msduk.org.uk/

Chapter 13 – Leadership and People

> "When you have a leader who is driven by purpose, understands their people's talents and passions, is clear on values, can tell the story of who they are and how that connects with the purpose of the business... that is when real magic happens!"
> *(Bernhard Raschke*

Ultimately, sustainable business and procurement with purpose are driven by people. That applies at all levels of our organisations, but leadership is particularly important. Senior management backing is important to make PwP programmes effective, ideally with both the CPO (Chief Procurement Officer) and other senior leaders supporting the efforts. In virtually all the case studies and examples through this book, strong and effective procurement leadership is driving the purpose agenda.

Are Procurement Leaders Leading?

However, the picture is not uniformly positive. Whilst there has been considerable progress, a degree of cynicism is appropriate. Oliver Hurrey, who works with several different collaborative groups, is also part of the team driving the Sustainable Procurement Pledge. As part of that work, he has interviewed many of those procurement practitioners who signed up. What's interesting, he says, is that all the CPOs say that sustainability is "embedded in everything we do", and is incredibly important to them and their organisation.

"But when I talk to junior and mid-level professionals, they say that their bosses won't let them pursue sustainability ideas and approaches," Hurrey says. The reality is not always matching the rhetoric.

"In many of the initiatives I've seen over the years, it has been the sustainability profession driving progress, with too little involvement from procurement". But again, he is positive about the ability of the Pledge and the procurement community to address these barriers eventually: *"Most of what is needed exists somewhere – if we can help to curate and communicate that knowledge, we can make life less complicated for procurement."*

Undoubtedly, many procurement leaders are grasping the nettle. Our case studies featuring Unilever, Heineken and Vodafone are examples of procurement leaders working right at the heart of purposeful business in their organisations. But to get an informed view on the topic, we spoke to someone who has spent years identifying and supporting procurement and supply chain leadership.

Bernhard Raschke – a Man of Purpose

Bernhard Raschke spent almost 25 years in the supply chain consulting world, with KPMG, A.T. Kearney and leading PWC's procurement advisory network. He moved in 2013 to be EMEA lead for Supply Chain at Korn Ferry International, known to many as "headhunters", but now consultants in a range of areas concerning talent and strategy. In early 2021, he moved to become Chief Transformation Officer at Electrocomponents plc, but when we spoke in the summer of 2020, he had recently run Korn Ferry roundtables with supply chain leaders, looking at new ways of working post-pandemic; "react / restart / reimagine" being the advice.

Raschke was brought up and educated in Germany, but has lived in London for many years. He has a sharp intellectual curiosity, and any conversation with him is littered with suggestions that "you should read this..." and "have you heard about that...!" It is always stimulating, and in recent years his conversation often turned to sustainability and questions of purpose. So why is "purpose" so high on his personal agenda?

"The Korn Ferry leadership model forms the basis of our one-year CEO succession programme, which simulates through coaching being a CEO. It is rooted in the philosophy of the 'purpose-driven leader,'" he explained. He is also a big fan of Kevin Cashman's book *Leadership from the Inside Out.*[69] Cashman also leads the Korn Ferry Chief Executive institute and the firm's leadership model[70] is very much based on this thinking, and informs work in purpose and supply chain more generally.

When a leader has true purpose and can demonstrate that, then they create effective "followership". That enables people, even if they aren't natural extroverts, to articulate why they want to do their jobs. If that all sounds a little new-age, Raschke is very much a supply chain man by background, rooted in logistics, operations, and efficiency, even as he embraces this thinking about purpose. And the post-COVID world will reinforce the purpose movement rather than derail it:

"There will always be a space for very low-cost, lean businesses. But we see too many victims of globalisation, too many disenfranchised people. The pandemic has highlighted these issues. Companies that have not created a culture rooted in purpose will struggle to grow, to attract the best talent, or to justify premium pricing for their products."

He also sees the way different generations perceive matters. Greta Thunberg has tapped into the emotion and anger that many young people feel – *"all parents want their children to have a better future, but we see that there is a real danger it will be worse for our kids"*. Along with a coming

69 http://cashmanleadership.com/leadership-from-the-inside-out/

70 http://cashmanleadership.com/site/wp-content/uploads/2019/05/Korn-Ferry_CEO-Exec-Development_2019.pdf

recession, that is a potent and dangerous mix.

What does all this mean in terms of the role of the Chief Procurement or Supply Chain Officer? *"The role has already evolved dramatically in recent years, from policing to strategic differentiation. It's not just looking at cost and cash – although those factors will always be important."* Leaders need to look to find a new route between resilience and agility, focusing on sustainability and innovation as well, all supported by digital enablement. But as always, getting the balance right is key.

The Self-Disruptive Leader and Remote Working Challenges

Raschke also speaks of a new breed of "self-disruptive leaders". Apparently only 15% of existing leaders fit the profile, but the market wants more, and that discussion leads back to the purpose-driven issue and life post-pandemic.

"Increasingly, you can't just tell people what to do. That is even more true with everyone working remotely – which seems likely to continue. If you are purpose-driven, staff have a guide in terms of what they should do or should not do, they don't have to constantly ask."

That is a really important point. If staff work from home more often, or the nearest coffee shop, then organisations and leaders that can articulate clear purpose will set a framework for behaviour and decisions that will surely make independent working more successful. Firms that have a credo, like Johnson & Johnson, or Mars with its "five principles", are providing an underpinning in terms of expectations around staff behaviour.

Raschke also pointed out that younger staff – who aren't working from big houses with pleasant gardens – miss the office more than most. However, that "trust", letting go of tight control, will be key as we move forwards.

Back to specific supply chain issues, and he sees supply chain management as being central to the post-pandemic world. *"We do need to revisit supplier relationships, there will be more local supply, but critically there will be more focus on protecting our key suppliers. Firms such as Heineken are placing emphasis on the quality of their supplier relationships, and the purpose that underpins that."* That means taking a long-term view, and "digitisation can accelerate and support that process".

Raschke also had an interesting take on the discussion around the CPO role and the CSO (Chief Sustainability Officer) role. Some leading firms, in the consumer goods sector particularly, are combining these roles.

"Sectors like retail and FMCG are making that link with purpose more directly," he says. But he also sees that as a pragmatic response to the war for talent. *"There is a shortage of top-class CPOs, so organisations are broadening the role by including sustainability, which makes it more attractive to the very best candidates"*. That's interesting, but he was also clear that sustainability must be embedded into the CEO role as well if organisations really want to drive for success. Alignment between procurement and supply chain is also vital.

Most candidates for CPO roles now do "get it" in terms of purpose and sustainability. But *"we still don't have enough inspirational procurement and supply chain leaders who are both hard-nosed businesspeople, but can also articulate that sense of purpose,"* he suggested. *"You have to deliver on cost and cash to earn the right to develop the purpose agenda. But the best people know that these aren't really different agendas, they align together perfectly."*

Leadership is Critical in Key Industries

Deciding the right things to do from a sustainability or procurement with purpose viewpoint isn't necessarily a hard task in itself. However, in the world of energy companies – particularly oil and gas – it is somewhat harder to excel when you're dealing with exploration, extraction, processing and distribution tasks.

Mark Smith of bp is a procurement veteran in the energy and utilities sector, joining bp in 2012 and now working as Procurement Vice-President, Digital & Talent Supply. Those two spend categories are highly significant in terms of both spend and their strategic importance to the firm.

"Both people and digital technology are central to how we transform the company," Smith says. And that transformation is also huge, as bp transitions from a "traditional" oil and gas firm to a global, integrated energy company. *"For instance, we are going to need people with different attitudes and skills, and so that requires different thinking on talent acquisition. There are also cultural issues to consider, and we need to actively encourage people to apply to us who might not have considered joining us until recently."*

Unsurprisingly, Smith works closely with human resources in that spend area, and he is obviously relishing that people dimension. *"Many of us are personally motivated by the environmental changes required to protect the finite resources on our planet,"* he adds. *"What's been great in recent years has been seeing bp shift its corporate position and embrace a new purpose."*

Shareholder returns are important, of course, but as others quoted in this book have pointed out, the sense of purpose can provide additional motivation for staff. Smith continues: *"Procurement can play such an important role, the choices we make about how we work with suppliers can have a huge sustainability impact, so we have a great opportunity to make a difference."*

He explains that there have been examples of procurement with purpose in bp for some time, but this has accelerated since the firm declared its new purpose – reimagining energy for people and our planet in February 2020. CEO Bernard Looney has been very clear in the company's ambition to become a net zero company by 2050 or sooner, and to help the world get to net zero. A corporate sustainability framework provides an anchor for procurement with purpose, and the firm has also published clear positions on climate policy.[71]

Smith feels that the changes are good news for the status of the procurement function, too. *"Procurement people tend to worry about our seat at the top table – the purpose agenda has seen bp really recognise the key role*

71 https://www.bp.com/content/dam/bp/business-sites/en/global/corporate/pdfs/sustainability/group-reports/bp-climate-policy-positions.pdf

our suppliers have in terms of this agenda, driving up our opportunity to really partner deeply to achieve this," he adds.

The procurement sustainability team is quite new, and the model is to design the jobs in that team to align with the United Nations SDGs (sustainability development goals). That is an interesting approach to structuring roles which we have not seen before in other businesses. Understanding the baseline and setting targets are current priorities for the team, and the aim is for the sustainability professionals to work with category teams, providing expertise in a similar way to how HR business partners work with stakeholders. They will also ensure the line of sight is maintained from the SDGs, through the corporate goals to the category managers.

Smith clearly has strong personal values. So how does he feel when he hears others criticise the oil industry over its contribution to climate change and environmental issues?

"Oil and gas play a fundamental role in society, providing basic human needs. We have to be pragmatic to some extent," he says. *"But I personally recognise the need for change, as I think most of us in bp do – and we feel energised by the growing focus on purpose. There's also the argument that we need to embrace those who have the furthest to travel. I also believe in being proactive, that's a core value for me. If I want to see change, then it's up to me to play a part. So if the steps I take in my work help the company and the planet move in the right direction, then I'm having an impact."*

That sounds like a pretty good definition of leadership.

TOP TEN TAKE-AWAY

An organisation's sense of purpose and sustainability actions are relevant in the "war for talent". People want to be proud of their work and employer, and this agenda is an opportunity for organisations to motivate current and potential staff. It also gives procurement and sustainability professionals a route to develop their own profile within and outside the organisation.

Chapter 14 – COVID & Procurement with Purpose

> "COVID has taught us that many organisations didn't understand their supply base. All it takes is one supplier to fail – perhaps a factory closes because of COVID – and an entire complex supply chain can fall apart in a domino effect. So we need to simplify and streamline our supply chains. We'll see a recalibration of operating models and supply strategies, more onshoring, a mix of global and local sourcing, with more thinking about diversity in the supply chain, supporting local communities and social enterprises."
>
> *(Frank Omare, SAP Ariba)*

Much of this book was written through the initial and then second waves of the COVID pandemic period, with the final draft completed during the successful UK vaccine roll-out. But the third wave is still in mid-2021 hitting some countries very hard, and the pandemic will have a lasting effect on individuals and business. Bernhard Raschke in the previous chapter talked about some of the likely implications, but it is far from clear what the implications for sustainable and purposeful procurement might be over coming years. Indeed, two very different pictures of how matters might develop can be painted.

Hypothesis 1 – Procurement with Purpose will be sidelined because...

- Businesses will simply be struggling to survive as the world crashes into a major recession or potentially even depression. That will put the focus on cutting costs – and that will mean a brutal procurement environment with tough negotiations, delayed payments and the usual actions we see when times are tough.
- Internal resources will be cut in organisations as they address their internal cost base, too. That will include procurement, so as teams shrink, there will be less time for the "nice-to-haves", which will include procurement with purpose programmes.
- Younger people, who have been leading the drive in areas such as climate change, will be worst affected by the economic effects of the pandemic. They will have to put their energies into simply getting and keeping a job, rather than campaigning for good causes.
- Ironically, the economic downturn will make it more likely that climate change targets will be hit, so that might reduce the imperative to take more proactive steps to drive down emissions!

Hypothesis 2 – Procurement with Purpose will thrive because...

- Everyone has realised how much we all depend on each other. That many people doing minimum wage jobs are arguably more important to society than bankers or soccer players. Being kind and considerate, including to future generations, will be seen as a higher priority for society, supporting many of the procurement with purpose ideas and initiatives.
- There will be a backlash against firms that are seen to have behaved badly during the crisis, or afterwards (in terms of increasing payment terms for suppliers, for instance) and they will be punished by customers.

The concept of "predatory capitalism" will be much discussed, and that scrutiny will grow, with firms being reputationally damaged if they don't behave in a sustainable and purposeful manner.

- Young people will only accept their inevitable economic difficulties if they can see that society is moving in the right direction more generally, so pressure in areas such as climate change and plastic use will increase rather than diminish.
- "Socialist" solutions to the crisis such as huge government investment (cf. the USA) or renationalisation (rail in the UK) will mean the state taking a wider role, and less of the economy will be in the hands of profit-maximising bodies. The public sector is more likely to want to address "social value" and procurement with purpose issues.

On balance, I believe that the positive view will prevail, and it has been encouraging to see leaders in sustainable business reinforcing their commitment through 2020/21. But COVID has driven change, often rapid, and has already pushed many organisations into reviewing or even radically changing their supply chains. PPE (personal protective equipment) was suddenly a highly "strategic" spend category, and a matter of life and death, not a simple category where volume leverage was the usual procurement strategy.

It seems likely therefore that governments and businesses will to some extent move away from globalisation towards supply chain approaches that place more emphasis on local or national supply. Every government in Europe will want to know that critical items such as vaccines or PPE (and many others) don't depend on China in the future – or indeed on the USA.

Nandini Basuthakur, CEO at Procurement Leaders, thinks that post-pandemic, there will be a move from global to regional supply chains:

"Does it really make sense to ship materials and products back and forwards across the oceans? Not only is it not a sustainable business practice,

but it opens the supply chain out to increased risk. And there will be major changes in terms of office space or travel – firms are going to cut budgets in areas like that, as they have seen remote working being effective."

The pandemic has also highlighted how interrelated different parts of society really are. It has brought home perhaps how procurement strategies that put cost above all else have significant risks of their own. Many businesses had to move online and find a whole new world of suppliers and partners to help them do that. Think of the restaurants that started offering home-delivered meals, which meant they needed the support of specialist packaging suppliers, delivery firms, and IT experts to redesign websites and payment processes. Some of what we have seen may prove to be short-term responses, but there will be a lasting impact.

Some firms have really stepped up to the plate and demonstrated a sense of wider purpose. BrewDog in Scotland turned production facilities that normally make fine craft beer into hand-sanitiser lines. Many hotels including Chelsea Football Club's Millennium at Stamford Bridge offered free accommodation for health workers. Apparel manufacturers in many countries turned over their production lines to making gowns and aprons for health professionals.

Unilever announced 500m of cash-flow relief to small suppliers and retail customers to help them manage through the crisis. Vodafone offered free unlimited data to vulnerable customers. Smaller firms provided meals and other benefits to health workers or local vulnerable people, and all over the world, communities worked together to try and protect themselves and others.

COVID is certainly going to change the balance of power and perhaps how nations look at themselves and others. Those in Asia, for instance, that have escaped the worst economic effects have become relatively richer than European and American countries which have seen the worst virus numbers. Nandini Basuthakur also makes the point that it isn't necessarily the (supposedly) most "developed" and larger nations that have responded best to COVID-19. Smaller or poorer countries have used different approaches to halt the spread effectively, showing the power of innovation and agility.

New technology will also support some of the changes that may emerge post-COVID. Pierre-François Thaler, CEO of EcoVadis, believes that *"in the next few years, there aren't going to be as many auditors and inspectors flying around the world to inspect suppliers' factories and facilities"*. So, concepts of checking and verifying will have to change. Onsite inspection will be replaced by "virtual auditing", with innovative mechanisms such as virtual reality, smartphone interviews or even drones used to check out suppliers.

Thaler also expects increased focus on finding new suppliers and more local supply. There will also be suppliers trying to find new buyers, of course, given the economic effects of the virus. So EcoVadis is developing new features to help this process; as Thaler explains: *"It is our responsibility to create connections in this community of like-minded businesses"*.

Frank Omare of SAP Ariba works with dozens of client firms, so sees the big picture: *"As we come through COVID, I think it will be more important than ever for brands to be associated with sustainability, if they want to appeal to the next generation of consumers – and motivate their own workforce"*. COVID has made us all aware of injustices, and that some groups within society have been affected more than others. We've even developed a heighted awareness that healthy eating comes back to social issues and gaps.

Thomas Udesen of Bayer believes that post-COVID, new businesses and even new industries will emerge, and *"sustainability will be embedded in these businesses"*. And he makes a great point – the companies that responded best to the crisis have been those that *"already invested in resilient supply chains, which equals sustainable supply chains"*. Indeed, Bayer is a good example of that: the firm has invested in risk management and every factory continued running through the crisis. *"Everything is continuing – all the changes we are going through and big initiatives are continuing. We are not being slowed down"*.

But Udesen acknowledges some wider post-pandemic risks. He hopes that the future global economy is not one based around nationalistic views. And he hopes that sustainability does not become a focus for competition – *"collaboration and building relationships is the solution,"* he says. And of course, business will carry on, whichever politicians we have in charge. Commerce can bridge short-term political sentiments. The UN SDGs are not political, they are principles of good business.

So, procurement with purpose should come out of this crisis stronger than ever, with a renewed sense of the value that it can create for everyone: individuals, businesses and governments.

Section 3 –
The Issues and Options

Chapter 15 – Social Value

"We believe that suppliers who pay the London Living Wage find that it makes recruitment easier, they get higher-quality staff, with lower turnover, better productivity, motivation, and improved customer satisfaction."

(Tim Rudin, Transport for London

Section 3 covers major subject areas that sit within the overall procurement with purpose picture. There are at least 25 different topics that we could feature (see pages 310–11) but the focus here is on the most prevalent and widely discussed, with some grouping of activities where that makes sense. "Social Value" kicks off, because it is an extremely broad topic and one that causes some confusion because of that breadth. The terminology is predominantly used in the public sector, but many of the issues are relevant to every organisation.

What is Social Value?

The term "social value" has been applied principally in the UK public (government) sector but similar principles are applied in various countries. The phrase "social value" itself has led to some confusion, as it is generally used to cover *all* "three pillars of sustainability" – social, environmental and economic issues. In other words, the UK public sector "social value" definition includes *anything and everything* within our entire procurement with purpose (PwP) scope.

It is therefore broader in scope than the definition of "social" used in the much-quoted acronym ESG (environmental, social, and governance) or in those three sustainability pillars. It is important to understand that when the public sector talks about social value, it includes activities related to climate change or recycling, and economic growth issues, as well as what we might consider genuinely "social", such as promoting minority-owned businesses or fighting modern slavery.

When a city in the UK issues a tender and looks for "social value" through the procurement process, the buyer may be looking for all or any of these disparate benefits from the supplier, as well as a great product or service delivered at a fair price. In practice, and not surprisingly, the city is probably more interested in the bidder making commitments that have a local impact, such as local employment of disadvantaged citizens, rather than promises to stop forest clearance in Indonesia.

The Social Value Act

In the UK, the Social Value Act of 2012 required public bodies to consider these broader issues when they bought services. It was initially implemented mainly in local government organisations, but has become more regular practice in public procurement generally.

In September 2020, the UK government announced new measures which were launched to *"promote new jobs and skills, encourage economic growth and prosperity, tackle climate change and level up the UK"*. So from January 1st, 2021, a new social value in procurement model, as described in a Procurement Policy Note (PPN),[72] is used to assess a supplier's social impact. This extends the requirement to consider social value to all central government departments, their agencies and NDPBs (non-

---

72 https://assets.publishing.service.gov.uk/government/uploads/system/uploads/attachment_data/file/921437/PPN-06_20-Taking-Account-of-Social-Value-in-the-Award-of-Central-Government-Contracts.pdf

departmental public bodies).

The first key action point says: *"Social value should be explicitly evaluated in all central government procurement, where the requirements are related and proportionate to the subject-matter of the contract, rather than just 'considered' as currently required under the Public Services (Social Value) Act 2012. Unnecessary burdens should not be placed on commercial teams or suppliers."*

The PPN says that more detailed guidance will follow, so at the time of writing, this isn't the final product. And the PPN itself is a little obscure in places – for example, it says, *"it is the quality of what is being offered that will count in the evaluation, not the quantity"*. But in some cases, it must be the quantity that matters. If bidders are offering apprenticeships, or to employ ex-offenders in relation to a large construction project, then surely the quantity does matter?

The PPN also requires significant weighting for social value in the bid evaluation: *"A minimum weighting of 10% of the total score for social value should be applied in the procurement to ensure that it carries a heavy enough score to be a differentiating factor in bid evaluation; a higher weighting can be applied if justified."*

A Positive Case Study – Transport for London

Many organisations have already used social value to obtain positive results and outcomes. Transport for London (TfL runs transport in the UK's capital city, including the tube network, buses and more, and has become a leader in terms of various aspects of social value and purposeful procurement.

One initiative has been to support the introduction of the London Living Wage for staff working for certain suppliers. The organisation has implemented it in areas including cleaning, catering, and security, insisting that suppliers pay their staff some 20% more than the statutory National Minimum Wage.

What is interesting is that TfL does *not* expect suppliers to pass on to TfL the cost of any wage increase caused by paying the London Living Wage. Tim Rudin, who led sustainability efforts at TfL, said in an interview in 2016 that he believed the benefits to the suppliers should offset the additional costs. Perhaps that leads to some interesting negotiation with suppliers, but he is right in principle.[73]

In terms of a different PwP issue, TfL aims to engage directly with diverse and minority-owned suppliers, diversify the supply chain, and monitor and report on progress. In the procurement process for relevant tenders, equality and supplier diversity policy, action plan and training plans are all assessed at an early stage of the competitive process; they are "gateway" factors, where a bidder must provide satisfactory submissions in this area before quality and price are considered (see Chapter 7 for more on evaluation processes and approaches).

TfL was also the first public sector organisation to join the Ethical Trading Initiative and Sedex, and is now affiliated to Electronics Watch (discussed further on page 262). The organisation has also made considerable progress working with suppliers to encourage more women into engineering and construction roles – another worthwhile aspect of the PwP agenda.

The Scottish Experience

The Scottish public sector has so far embraced social value in a more coordinated and structured manner than in England. That is in part because of the nation's more manageable size, but it also reflects considerable political and managerial willpower that has not been so obvious south of the border.

Public procurement in Scotland is seen as a driver of social benefit, aiming to address broad and somewhat intangible issues such as

73 https://spendmatters.com/uk/transport-for-london-responsible-supply-chains-examples/

inequality, as well as more specific issues around employment or health. Public procurement also aims to boost competitiveness and deliver economic benefit, and is seen as "a key enabler of strategy development".

The Procurement Reform Act of 2014 provided a legal basis for the approach to procurement, including a "sustainable procurement duty". Standard tools and processes have played an important part in this initiative, from a map of the "procurement journey" (with underpinning guidance)[74] to common e-procurement portals and sourcing systems. Now, consideration of social, environmental and community benefits is a fundamental part of the process, rather than something tacked onto the end.

Success on major procurement exercises has come from new jobs created for local people, apprenticeships, and subcontracts being advertised to promote the chances of local firms winning that work. For some years, an electricity contract for the entire public sector has come entirely from renewable sources, and an entirely new supply chain was created to support biomass energy development, creating 275 jobs.

Recycling has been driven by the creation of the Scottish Materials Brokerage Service.[75] The service is a "one-stop shop for growing Scotland's reprocessing sector, helping local authorities and the public sector get a better deal for the recycled materials collected in their communities". It is sponsored by the Scottish Government as a partnership between Scottish local authorities, Zero Waste Scotland and Scottish Procurement.

Julie Welsh is CEO of Scotland Excel, which acts as a collaborative procurement body for local authorities across the country, and has worked with her team to embed social value in their procurement activities. Whilst it is illegal under EU procurement regulations to make

74 https://www.procurementjourney.scot/

75 https://www.zerowastescotland.org.uk/brokerage

it mandatory for bidders to pay the Living Wage, she says *"we have had successes. Across our portfolio, more than 80% of our suppliers pay the living wage and when our customers have a choice of rates, as they do in our social care agency staff framework, more than 90% choose to pay the supplier more in order to support the living wage."*

The issue of focus comes into play again. *"In social care, we've concentrated on sustainable rates and staff welfare more than other wider social benefits – we judged that was the real priority"*. Welsh has looked to agree standard rates with care providers, but *"agreeing what is a reasonable profit margin is a stumbling block!"* Welsh sees social care as *"an important moral issue – it is unique and also highly political"*.

Welsh has explained to the governance body to which she reports that focus on social value needs to be determined at the strategy development stage of the procurement process: *"So, for example, when we look at security services, there has been a major focus on combatting organised crime, as well as pushing for suppliers to pay the Living Wage to staff"*.

When it comes to a new-build housing construction framework, the social value element switches to sustainable job creation. *"We think clearly now about what sort of social value we want from each framework – it can't be one size fits all"*.

There are particular issues where a central procurement unit puts in place contracts that are actually used by a range of organisations. David Gigg worked for several years as Head of Policy Delivery with the UK's Crown Commercial Service (CCS), the central procurement unit for government, looking at these challenges:

"CCS frameworks and deals are used by local government and other bodies outside Whitehall, and increasingly those customers were asking us to incorporate social value into the contracts and frameworks we were putting in place. So what we have tried to do is structure frameworks that give users options in terms of the social value that suppliers can provide," Gigg explains.

For instance, a vehicle hire framework describes broad themes, but local users can tailor the social value they receive from suppliers to meet their own needs and priorities.

Assessing Social Value in Bids

The term "social value" is now widely used in the UK public sector, but there is still some confusion about when and how to implement it. Now that it can be a significant factor in choosing suppliers, working out how to score bidders' proposals in terms of social value has been one tricky issue. Scoring generally was discussed in Chapter 7, as an issue for both public and private sector buyers, but the need for transparency in the public sector brings particular process challenges.

Many organisations are giving social value a weighting of 10% or more in the overall scoring system, making a real difference to a bidder's chance of winning the contract. So being able to assess proposals and bring a rational approach to scoring is vital.

One route to overcoming that challenge has been proposed by the Social Value Portal, a private firm offering tools and consulting support in this area.[76] It has developed a "set of 'Proxy Values' that will allow users to assess the financial impact that any measure will make". This allows different types of social value offered by suppliers to be compared against each other by using these financial proxy values.

However, some organisations are implementing this in a manner that appears suboptimal. David Shields is a public procurement leader who has driven the "contracting for change" initiative though Social Value UK. He suggests buyers must make sure social value has a strategic link to what their organisation wants to achieve. It should not rely, in his opinion, on choosing a "random benefit" that the bidder happens to put forward:

---

76 https://socialvalueportal.com/

"I'm seeing tenders for £50k contracts that are going out to suppliers with a spreadsheet listing 50 different social value areas. Each has a 'value' against it, and bidders are supposed to literally tick the box and say what they are going to deliver. That's not how social value should be managed."

Rather, buyers, commissioners and senior managers (and even elected representatives) need to be thinking strategically about what really matters to them, and what suppliers can best deliver to support that. *"Even when I see suppliers doing things that carry some value, it doesn't always seem to optimise what they could be doing,"* he explains.

As an example, he talks about a contract for banking services for a local authority, perhaps a county or city council. Now, given a free choice, the banks bidding might offer to reduce their carbon footprint or employ more disabled people in their workforce as their social value contribution.

"But what are the council's top priorities? For many, it is economic success for local businesses, which brings more employment and tax revenue. So, couldn't the social value come from the bidding banks offering a service to support local firms in their financial management? Or offering preferential loans to start-ups or minority-owned firms in the area?"

Corruption and Social Value

A further issue with social value is that it introduces another element of subjectivity into the public procurement process. Whilst assessing bids almost always involves some degree of subjectivity (scoring or ranking the "quality" of different supplier's proposals, for instance), social value factors can have a high degree of uncertainty in terms of how they could be marked. For instance, the risk of political interference increases once the relative objectivity of traditional procurement is potentially reduced and less tangible supplier selection factors come into play.

Even if we are not talking politics or corruption, the focus on social value can lead to poor decisions being taken, which a harder-edged approach to the commercial and economic issues might have avoided. Indeed, too much focus on social value might prejudice actual core delivery of the contracts. If 20 or 30% of the evaluation weighting is on social value, a firm might win the contract and prove to be inefficient in terms of real contract delivery, even if they are impressive on the social value elements.

In Scotland, the Ferguson Shipyards case is an example of a firm that was awarded contracts, in part with a view to supporting Scottish business and employment. Unfortunately, it appears that the shipyard may have been incapable of building the two ferries for which the government contracted, and costs to the taxpayer will run to over £100 million more than planned.

Reports suggested that the bid "was the highest quality bid received, in other words the highest specification, but also the highest price" of all the six yards competing for the job.[77] It seems likely that a high mark for social value contributed to the shipyard being the top score on "quality" and winning the bid – yet, in fact, it has failed to do the work effectively. So proper procurement processes and a commercially sensible approach must be maintained, and suppliers must not win work on social value alone.

That issue extends to the risk of corruption in the procurement process. Indeed, some countries with public sector corruption problems are hesitant to introduce social value approaches for that very reason. Introducing variable elements into the process of selecting suppliers might lead to manipulation of decisions, which would be hard to prove. Alastair Merrill, one of the procurement leaders behind much successful social value work in Scotland, acknowledges that *"social value is only likely*

77 https://news.stv.tv/politics/ferguson-yard-ferry-deal-could-be-down-to-incompetence?top

to take off once you have a good basis of professional government procurement" – where corruption is not much of an issue.

Avoiding Barriers to Entry

Another area of concern around using public procurement for social value is that it could have unintended consequences in terms of increasing barriers to entry for the very firms that it should be helping.

In the US, provisions to support minority-owned businesses through public procurement are much more established than in Europe. But the whole bidding process is often so complex for government tenders it has created such barriers. So many US firms either focus entirely on public sector work, or won't even attempt to win contracts. That can't be healthy.

Already, the large government suppliers in the UK are on top of this agenda. A quick LinkedIn search brings up a "CSR Manager" for giant services firm Serco and a whole bunch of people at Capita (including "Head of Responsible Business at Capita Customer Management" and "Head of Responsible Business (Government Services)").

Now of course major suppliers to the public sector should take purpose and sustainability seriously. But if you are a small firm bidding against Capita to win a contract, you probably don't have a dedicated manager in this area. You may not have an all-encompassing programme, including carbon reduction, diversity and inclusion, a lengthy modern slavery policy, a whole bunch of apprentices, data available about staff with disabilities, and community programmes.

Yes, large firms should be doing all this. But it must not lead to a situation where small firms are at an immediate disadvantage when they are competing with the giants. If social value is weighted at 20% of total marks, and your start-up scores 5/20 whilst Capita scores 20, you are most unlikely to win that contract, however strong the rest of your bid.

There is no simple answer to this conundrum. Smaller firms might need specific education and training – outside of specific bids of course – to help them. More creative thinking from smaller firms can be encouraged, so they can come up with novel approaches. They may be able to play the "local" card better than the corporate giants. But this will all require thought and effort from public procurement leaders.

Ensuring that suppliers actually deliver the social value they have promised during the procurement process in another challenge, as it is for any PwP promises and for any buyer, public or private sector. The need for robust contract management was addressed earlier, but in the initial days of procurement for social value, public sector buyers were often not equipped to ensure that suppliers followed through. To drive real benefits, organisations must verify and monitor delivery of any benefits arising from supplier behaviour and actions.

Assessing social value benefit is another challenge, again one that is common to many PwP topics. If proposals from suppliers are being assessed, it is important that the benefit of different offers can be quantified in some way, so that we can compare bids and make sensible supplier selection decisions. Measuring benefits should also play into future decisions about which types of social value offers the best payback, and how relevant strategies and approaches can generally be refined and improved.

Social Value in Context

Clearly, for many in the UK public sector, implementing social value approaches within procurement is no longer optional. The law requires at a minimum consideration of social value. But even beyond this imperative, the concepts are relevant to many public bodies, and are likely to become more so in coming years. Post-pandemic, in a challenging period for Western economies, issues around localism, resilience of the supply chain, employment, and supporting disadvantaged people are going to have an even higher profile.

For the private sector, "social value" looks much like the totality of all the initiatives under the PwP banner. Some areas, such as how you assess offers of social value in bids, and how you manage compliance with contracted actions, have a relevance that crosses over all sectors – and indeed, the private sector can probably learn from some of the best early adopters in the government sector. The focus on having structure, process and policy in place to support the delivery of proper and legal public procurement has driven good work by many public bodies.

Taking Action

So let's summarise the key suggested actions and recommendations from this chapter.

- Understand what the organisation's key stakeholders want to see from social value actions. In the public sector, those groups are principally elected representatives, service users, citizens and voters – a challenging range of interested parties in many cases!
- When including social value in the procurement process, encourage suppliers to make proposals that reflect the aims of the organisation's overall social value strategy, rather than simply allowing them to come up with whatever proposals they want to put forward, or relying on a "tick-box" shopping list approach.
- Where social value is relevant to the contract, make sure its weighting in your evaluation processes is reasonable. It should be significant enough to matter, but beware the danger that too much focus might lead to selecting firms who really don't offer good value, or simply can't do the work.

- Be aware of the increased risks of corruption where social value is a significant evaluation factor, and also of the risks of increasing barriers to entry accidentally through social value requirements.
- Contracts should lay out suppliers' social value commitments, and robust contract and supplier management is essential to make sure suppliers deliver the actions they promise in proposals and contracts.

Chapter 16 – Climate Change

> "I want you to act as if the house is on fire, because it is."
> *Greta Thunberg, World Economic Forum, Davos, 24 January 2019*

The following chapters look at key purpose issues related to the *environment*, which are amongst the most pressing and serious issues facing humanity. Given that, they are central to many organisations' thinking and actions relating to sustainable business and procurement with purpose (PwP) activities. Let's start with perhaps the biggest issue of all, carbon emissions and climate change.

Climate Change and Carbon Footprints

For many, climate change is the highest-profile and most familiar issue discussed in this book. We will assume here that climate change is real. The scientific evidence very strongly supports the hypothesis that our planet is experiencing real change, and citizens of many nations have experienced extreme climate conditions in recent years.

The link between man-made causes and climate change is less certain, but it seems very likely that carbon emissions at the very least contribute to the end result. Turning the logic around the other way, it doesn't seem very likely that burning fossil fuels is making the earth cooler.

One of the few positive side effects of the COVID-19 virus was the initial step-change reduction in global emissions, as factories all over the world shut down, planes stopped flying and cars sat on driveways. The economic effect was disastrous; but for a time, less oil, coal and gas were burned. If the global economy emerges from the virus into economic recession or even depression, that will continue to dampen down emissions levels for some years to come. However, the problem is not solved forever. At some stage, economic development and growth, as well as population growth, will recover, with emissions and climate change remaining key issues.

So, organisations, individuals and governments are increasingly aware of their own carbon footprint, and (in the case of organisations) that of their supply chain. Wright, Kemp, and Williams proposed the following definition of a carbon footprint:[78]

"A measure of the total amount of carbon dioxide (CO2) and methane (CH4) emissions of a defined population, system or activity, considering all relevant sources, sinks and storage within the spatial and temporal boundary of the population, system or activity of interest. Calculated as carbon dioxide equivalent using the relevant 100-year global warming potential (GWP100)."

The carbon footprint for a business comes from its emissions, which result from energy it uses directly, to heat its offices, power machinery or run its fleet of trucks and cars. It also derives indirectly from all the goods and services that it buys from other organisations, who themselves produce emissions in the course of their activities. So, from a procurement point of view, everything you buy in your organisation, from stationery to heavy machinery, or even professional services, comes with a related contribution to your carbon footprint.

However, studies have pointed out that it is inherently difficult to establish accurate emissions data and therefore carbon footprints for households or businesses. A 2013 study by Carnegie Mellon's

78 https://www.tandfonline.com/doi/abs/10.4155/cmt.10.39

Christopher Weber found that the calculation of carbon footprints for products is often filled with large uncertainties.[79] However, even if the detail is not always accurate, the understanding that everything you buy comes with a carbon footprint has been an important element of more informed PwP thinking and action.

There is also the footprint related to how consumers use the products that organisations sell. One major consumer goods firm calculated that the biggest environmental effect from their shampoo products came not from the manufacturing process or the plastic packaging, but from the hot water used when customers washed their hair!

Looking on the Bright Side – Maybe

The UK government has committed to reducing emissions in the country by two-thirds by 2030. But is there any chance of that target being hit? Even its own advisers have their doubts. In June 2021, the Climate Change Committee (CCC) claimed that only a fifth of its pledges on climate change were being delivered. Progress on climate promises was too slow.

The CCC is an independent group that advises the government, and released two reports, saying time is running out. It was "absolutely critical" that a new strategy was published before the COP26 climate summit in Glasgow in October– November 2021. The strategy must not be purely aspirational but should be accompanied by clear policy plans, backed by the government. It must go along with a commitment to "prepare the country for the serious climate risks facing the UK".

But for many, those risks still seem a long way away, whilst the actions needed will affect everybody very directly. Up to now, many of the steps to reduce emissions have not really hit us as individuals but

---

79 https://www.cmu.edu/news/archive/2010/December/dec13_carbonfootprints.shtml

to hit these targets, citizens may need to eat less meat, give up most air travel or pay for new heating systems.

Yet the UK only accounts for 1.1% of global emissions, a tiny amount compared to China, the US or India. Indeed, China is a real concern, accounting for some 28% of all global emissions. Although the country has promised that its emissions will peak in 2030 and then decline to carbon neutrality by 2060, 58% of its energy consumption comes from coal, and China commissioned 38.4 GW of new coal plants in 2020. That is over three times the 11.9 GW total commissioned across the entire rest of the world put together! Indeed, Asia's share of global coal power generation has increased from just over 20% in 1991 to about 75% in 2019.

38.4 GW of new coal plants in 2020. That is over three times the 11.9 GW total commissioned across the entire rest of the world put together! Indeed, Asia's share of global coal power generation has increased from just over 20% in 1991 to about 75% in 2019.

So why should the UK citizen (and those in other similarly placed countries) go through "hardship" over the next decade whilst China focuses on economic growth and continues to increase it emissions? Answering that question might prove tough for politicians, as issues around emissions require tough decisions on policies that may not be attractive to everyone.

However, amongst considerable quantities of doom and gloom, it is good to remember that progress is being made. Whilst much of the reduction in emissions during the pandemic was short-term, there are more promising longer-term developments.

For instance, in early 2020 renewables were "on the brink" of becoming Britain's main electricity source, according to research by EnAppSys.[80] In the energy analysis firm's market review, renewables just missed

80 https://www.current-news.co.uk/news/renewables-on-the-brink-of-becoming-britains-main-electricity-source

out overtaking gas as the largest source of electricity in 2019. In 2019, 104.8TWh of Britain's electricity came from renewables, only marginally lower than the 115.1TWh produced by gas-fired power stations. That also represents continuing growth, with renewables accounting for 34.9% of the 2019 total, a huge growth from the comparable 8.9% in 2011.

The cost of energy from renewable sources has also declined. The average cost of solar panel installation in the U.S. was $8.50 per watt in 2009. By early 2020, that was down to just under $3 per watt.[81] Yet huge questions remain as to whether reducing CO2 emissions is really likely in the medium term. Total global energy-related CO2 emissions stood at around 34 billion metric tonnes per year in 2019 and were on track to rise to about 45 billion by 2050 under current (pre-pandemic) trends, according to International Energy Agency (IEA) data.

However, under the IEA's Sustainable Development Scenario, three broad areas of policy and technology can help slash energy-related CO2 emissions to just 10 billion mt/year by 2050.[82] The proposed initiatives include greater energy efficiency, use of electric motors and vehicles, more use of renewable energy sources and (controversially) nuclear energy. Most of the ideas individually are realistic and achievable; it is whether humanity can embrace enough of these major changes quickly enough to stem the increase in global heating.

How to Make a Difference

After that brief diversion into more hopeful news, back to the shocking facts. A 2020 report in the journal Advances in Atmospheric Sciences stated that the world's oceans were warmer in 2019 than at any point in

81 https://oilprice.com/Energy/Energy-General/How-Far-Has-Renewable-Energy-Come-In-The-Last-20-Years.html

82 https://www.spglobal.com/platts/en/market-insights/latest-news/coal/011320-all-policies-technologies-needed-to-achieve-15-degrees-target-iea-chief

recorded human history. The report, titled *Record-Setting Ocean Warmth Continued in 2019*, says that the oceans' warmest 10 years on record were all measured in the past decade.[83] Evidence suggests that the oceans have taken in 228 sextillion joules of heat, or 228 followed by 21 zeroes, over the last 25 years – "equivalent to 3.6 billion Hiroshima atom-bomb explosions".

The research, conducted by a team of climate and ocean scientists from around the world, found that the heating was occurring throughout the world's oceans, but the Atlantic Ocean and Southern Ocean had absorbed the most heat. It also found that the rate of warming over the 1987 to 2019 period was four and a half times that recorded between 1955 and 1986 – the conclusion being that global climate change appears to be accelerating.

So, there is general agreement between international leaders, business and citizens that "something must be done". But numerous summits and meetings highlight that moving from a general desire to reduce emissions to actually making it happen is a huge step.

The politics of change can be very difficult. Smaller countries look at larger nations, and say, "It's hardly worth us bothering, if the US and China don't change". Larger countries claim they are doing more than most, whilst more developed nations start from a higher base of carbon use, so arguably should take most responsibility. But the wealthier citizens and countries are the most likely to resist changes that might affect their standard of living or convenience.

---

83 Cheng, L., Abraham, J., Zhu, J. et al. Record-Setting Ocean Warmth Continued in 2019. Adv. Atmos. Sci. 37, 137–142 (2020) doi:10.1007/s00376-020-9283-7

> "Ahead of COP26 this November (2021), many nations are updating their pledges to reduce greenhouse gas emissions under the Paris Agreement. Global sea levels will continue to rise, even if we halt all emissions now, but our research suggests we could limit the damage: if pledges were far more ambitious, central predictions for the sea-level rise from melting ice would be reduced from 25 cm to 13 cm in 2100, with a 95% chance of being less than 28 cm… This would mean a less severe increase in coastal flooding.""
>
> *Dr Tamsin Edwards, King's Climate Hub, King's College London*

These issues can be very emotional. The great tennis player Roger Federer has been criticised for his sponsorship from Credit Suisse, a bank with close links to the fossil fuel industry. Extinction Rebellion brought parts of Central London to a standstill in 2019, and dug up lawns at Trinity College in Cambridge in 2020 to draw attention to climate change. But many people who struggled to get to work, or saw plant life destroyed might feel both sympathy for the cause and frustration with the means of protest.

There are also pragmatic economic issues to consider. If the entire oil and coal industries simply shut down tomorrow, millions of people would lose their jobs and there would be a significant global recession, as well as revolution in some countries. So, while few would disagree with the notion that we will all have to make major changes, and do that pretty quickly, the move to carbon neutrality has to be considered and implemented carefully.

That's where individual companies and the procurement with purpose movement really can make a difference. If large firms and government organisations take the lead, both in their own internal actions and through their supply chain, then real progress is possible.

Taking a Lead Internally

Whilst much of the advice here relates to how procurement can work with suppliers to drive these agendas, there are some internal policy and operational issues within organisations that often involve procurement and certainly contribute to the emissions debate.

Corporate travel policy is perhaps the most obvious. Even before the pandemic, many organisations were looking to adapt travel policy to address the need to reduce emissions, as well as to save money. The welfare and safety of travellers should also come into the discussion, of course.

COVID has accelerated this with much business travel coming to a complete stop and Zoom, Teams and similar tools taking the strain as executives communicate in the virtual world rather than over a coffee or a beer. The relative success of this forced change has made many individuals and firms question whether many meetings, conferences or working visits to distant places were really necessary. As we move into the post-pandemic period, it seems unlikely we will revert to previous practice, and that will have a positive effect, as air travel in particular is a major driver of emission. But no doubt travel will increase again.

At theta point, business policies will come back into play. To manage cost and reduce emissions, organisations can take steps such as encouraging staff:

- to always consider not travelling first of all;
- to use trains rather than planes;
- to share cars where possible (and where the train is not an option);
- to rent cars with lower emissions.

Procurement can also encourage travellers to use hotel chains, airlines or other providers that take a positive approach themselves to "purpose" issues, including moving towards carbon net zero.

Another area of interest to many procurement teams is the management of the company vehicle fleet, whether that is company cars (as a perk or a necessary tool), commercial or industrial vehicles. Here, the obvious trend is towards electric vehicles or even hydrogen power in some case. But there can be other worthwhile actions, such as training staff to drive more economically and use less fuel. Some organisations have stopped subsidising cars or offering that perk, perhaps offering staff a contribution towards purchasing a bicycle, or taking other steps to encourage walking, cycling or public transport rather than private vehicles.

Procurement professionals involved with construction and asset management (buildings from office blocks to airports) can also play a key role in making sure energy efficiency is built into the process and considered in terms of both construction and ongoing maintenance and management.

In these and other areas, procurement often has a role to play in terms of the function's position as the interface between the organisation and the external world. As well as considering the commercial options, increasingly procurement is expected to understand and reflect these wider issues around emissions.

Microsoft Aims to be "Carbon Negative"

In January 2020,[84] software giant Microsoft pledged to become "carbon negative" by 2030, which means the firm will remove more carbon from the environment than it has ever emitted. That would mean, the company says, that it will remove "all of the carbon" from the environment that it has emitted since the company was founded in 1975.

That is an impressive commitment. Microsoft says it will do this using a range of carbon removal, capture and storage technologies, and has laid out some of the options that might help it to achieve this goal. It

84 https://www.bbc.co.uk/news/technology-51133811

is a useful list for any organisation looking to make similar moves:

- **Planting new forests** and expanding existing ones.
- **Soil carbon sequestration**, a process which puts carbon back into the ground. This could be achieved by adding microbes and nutrients to soil, which may have the added benefits of making the soil more fertile and less susceptible to erosion. It is worth saying however that there are some practical problems around what sounds like a very good idea, as researchers have pointed out.[85]
- **Direct air capture** – sucking carbon dioxide out of the atmosphere, possibly by using large fans to move air through a filter that can remove the gas. This idea has potential, but it still a long way from widescale implementation.[86]
- **Bioenergy with carbon capture** – growing crops and then capturing the CO2 they emit when, for example, they are burned to produce heat or fermented to make fuels such as bioethanol. Negative emissions become possible if the amount of CO2 stored as a result is greater than that emitted during production, transport and use of the crops.

Clearly, not all of these ideas are proven and reliable. But given Microsoft's size, power and resources, at least some should become practical contributors to the climate change fight. And it is not just Microsoft: more and more firms are making commitments to become carbon neutral or even carbon negative. But to do so, they need to address the three levels of emissions – Scope 1, 2 and 3, as defined by the Greenhouse Gas Protocol Corporate Standard.

85 https://www.pnas.org/content/115/46/11652

86 https://www.vox.com/energy-and-environment/2018/6/14/17445622/direct-air-capture-air-to-fuels-carbon-dioxide-engineering

The Greenhouse Gas Protocol and the "Scope" Methodology

Chapter 2 highlighted growing pressure from governments and regulators for businesses to report on their carbon emissions. The discussion increasingly is around Scope 1, 2 and 3 emissions, terminology defined in the Greenhouse Gas Protocol and widely used in analysis and reporting. But what does that mean, and is this really a useful way of looking at organisations' performance?

Scope 1 emissions are direct emissions from owned or controlled sources. That includes, for instance, fuel used by offices or factories such as in gas boilers, fleet vehicles and air-conditioning leaks.

Scope 2 emissions are indirect emissions from the generation of purchased energy, such as electricity purchased and used by the organisation.

Scope 3 emissions are all indirect emissions not included in Scope 2 that occur in the value chain of the reporting company, including both upstream and downstream emissions (so from both suppliers and customers using the organisation's products or services). They include those originating from a wide range of sources, and this category is very relevant to the procurement discussion. Scope 3 includes emissions related to all goods and services the organisation procures, as well as those related to waste, product transportation, end-of-life costs, business travel or water use.

For many organisations, Scope 3 is the largest contributor to emissions. Kraft Foods, one of the organisations that piloted the Greenhouse Gas Protocol, found that value chain emissions comprised more than 90 per cent of the company's total emissions.[87]

How does procurement with purpose fit here? All three scope categories have implications for procurement, even Scope 1 which is about direct use of power internally. If the organisation can buy more

87 https://ghgprotocol.org/sites/default/files/standards_supporting/FAQ.pdf

efficient boilers, or electric vehicles, then this type of emission will clearly reduce. Procurement professionals can play a role in such initiatives.

In terms of Scope 2, there is the opportunity for procurement to be involved or even drive the use of "greener" electricity, from sustainable sources, although this is not always as simple as it sounds.

Moving on to Scope 3 emissions, this is core PwP territory. Understanding the emissions generated by your suppliers and supply chain is key to calculating Scope 3 numbers, although it is not always straightforward. Working with key suppliers to reduce those emissions – across a huge range of products, industries and sectors – is a central element of the PwP movement.

Getting to Grips with Scope 3

It is easy to see issues with the measurement of Scope 3 emissions. How can you even estimate your organisation's figure, given that data (which almost certainly doesn't exist) would be needed from every supplier? That includes understanding the impact of every piece of stationery or laptop bought, every component or raw material used, let alone emissions generated by suppliers of services, from legal advice to catering. Clearly, getting precise information at that level of detail is impossible.

Recognising this, the World Resources Institute & World Business Council for Sustainable Development, in conjunction with the Carbon Trust, produced a 182-page (!) document titled *"Technical Guidance for Calculating Scope 3 Emissions"* in 2013.[88] The guidance suggests various methods of calculating emissions, and states that using a combination of methods is allowable (and indeed seems sensible). Companies should take "practical approaches to reduce costs and complexity without overly compromising quality".

---

88 https://ghgprotocol.org/sites/default/files/standards/Scope3_Calculation_Guidance_0.pdf

That means using techniques such as these to calculate the numbers:

- Applying more accurate data/calculations for large contributors (i.e. major suppliers in terms of our area of interest).
- Applying less accurate data/calculations for small contributors (including suppliers).
- Grouping or combining similar activity data (e.g. goods and services).
- Obtaining data from representative samples and extrapolating the results to the whole.
- Using proxy techniques.

When it comes specifically to collecting data from suppliers, the guidance suggests four methods:

1. *Supplier-specific method* which collects product-level data from goods or services suppliers.
2. *Hybrid method,* which uses a combination of supplier-specific activity data (where available) and secondary data to fill the gaps. This method involves:
   - collecting allocated Scope 1 and Scope 2 emission data directly from suppliers;
   - calculating upstream emissions of goods and services from suppliers' activity data on the quantity of materials, fuel, and power used, distance transported, and waste generated from the production of goods and services, and then applying appropriate emission factors; and
   - using secondary data to calculate upstream emissions wherever supplier-specific data is not available.
3. *Average-data method,* estimating emissions for goods and services by collecting data on the weight or other relevant units of goods or services purchased and multiplying by the relevant secondary (e.g.

industry average) emission factors (e.g. average emissions per unit of goods or service).

4. *Spend-based method,* which estimates emissions for goods and services by collecting data on the economic value of goods and services purchased and multiplying it by relevant secondary (e.g. industry average) emission factors.

The degree of subjectivity and estimation in the guidance does emphasise that data collection is still an imprecise science. And of course, every firm in your supply chain has to gather data from their suppliers as well to arrive at their own emissions number.

As well as the issues around accuracy, there is another concern. The more firms rely on industry averages, the more they might assume that they don't need to do much themselves. One firm can't affect an average much, so why go through all the hassle? But this thought-process could lead to stagnation. Rather, the goal must be to develop the network effect, where positive pressure and reinforcement goes down, across and through entire supply chains and networks.

So if emissions reporting is to drive the right behaviour, organisations must look for data that is as specific and accurate as possible and is related to individual suppliers, at least for their most important suppliers in terms of emissions. That should encourage everyone to take responsibility for their own actions and enable buyers to put appropriate pressure on suppliers.

However, there are still some questionable claims on emissions and energy use being made. An excellent article on the oneZero website looked at the claims from the giant IT firms that they use "100% renewable energy".[89] It points out that this is not as straightforward a statement as it sounds, given that energy comes into the grid from many different sources, renewable and traditional.

89 https://onezero.medium.com/what-it-really-means-when-google-and-apple-say-they-run-on-100-renewable-energy-f6d1719fd865

It also explains the use of Renewable Energy Certificates (RECs) that clean power plants can sell to firms enabling them to make the "clean energy" claim. It is all rather complex, but the article goes on to look at firms that are being more proactive in terms of supporting new and better energy sources. As it says:

"RECs have earned a bad reputation in the past,[90] *and as a consequence, real progress and the '100% green energy' claims made by many companies have all been perceived in perhaps an unfair negative light. But if we look deeper into the claims, we can see which companies have made only REC purchases and those that are really contributing to the creation of new renewable energy."*

Isn't the Internet Great? And Doesn't It Use a Lot of Energy!

Many assume that the biggest generators of carbon emissions are traditional heavy industries. Picture large factories and plants, belching smoke out of huge chimneys, perhaps making steel, processing chemicals or building machinery. While those sectors do still play a major role in overall emissions, there are industries and firms that are apparently cleaner, but actually are now responsible for a considerable quantity of emissions.

Equinix is one of those. It must be one of the largest firms globally that virtually no one has heard of, with revenues of over $5 billion and a market capitalisation of $63 billion (as of December 2020). The firm provides data centre services largely on a "retail colocation" basis, which means that customers lease space within a centre, usually a rack, space within a rack, or a caged-off area. That means a single huge data centre might be looking after equipment and data for multiple customers, including in all likelihood huge firms, such as Amazon and Google. It is the global leader in terms of colocation data centre market share, with 205 data centres in 24 countries on five continents.

90 https://thinkprogress.org/clean-energy-trainwreck-why-most-recs-are-bad-and-how-to-find-the-good-ones-63975573c073/

Data centres require huge amounts of power to operate. That energy has two main purposes. Firstly, power is, of course, needed to keep the computer equipment running. But the cooling needed to keep the computers at the right temperature for operating efficiently and effectively is even more important in terms of carbon footprint.

As Chris Ayscough, the EMA Director of Procurement for the firm, explained, *"in some of our locations, we might be one of the two or three biggest power users in the city or area"*. So, the firm sees it as essential that it is doing the right things in terms of carbon, and indeed other PwP initiatives. *"Our facilities throw out a lot of heat. So, for instance, we're using that to heat a local college in the Netherlands, and we look to energy efficiency in all our operations."*

The theme of collaboration also comes into play here. *"Our customers define the maximum operating temperature for their equipment. If we can persuade them to increase that by a couple of degrees, the energy needed for cooling is significantly less"*.

Equinix has joined forces with numerous partners and peers, "on a committed path to achieve 100% clean and renewable energy across our global operations", according to its website. The firm has made substantial progress towards this goal, covering "over 90% of our footprint worldwide with net-zero carbon emission renewable energy products".

Ayscough explains that the process for buying equipment is very focused on this goal, with energy efficiency a significant evaluation criterion – *"it is a true total cost of ownership assessment"*. In 2018, Equinix joined the industry-leading NGO, the Renewable Energy Buyers Alliance (REBA) to help lead this agenda, and also received the U.S. Environmental Protection Agency's Award for Excellence in Green Power Use, for the second consecutive year "recognizing our outstanding efforts to purchase green power in the U.S."

As well as power, water is another issue that is on Ayscough's agenda. *"In some of our data centres, the local authorities won't allow us to use water because of shortages and conservation. So, we have to look at innovative technology for cooling, such as novel heat-exchangers." But everything has to work, too. "We run at 99.9999% availability service levels!"*

But as the huge growth in the use of digital technology and the Internet continues, it is good to know that a leader in this industry appears to be fully committed to the sustainability – and procurement with purpose – agendas.

Carbon Emissions in Context

When developing a procurement with purpose strategy, organisations cannot give full focus to every possible area of interest or concern. So why might this be a set of topics that an organisation would choose to place high on its priority list?

Simply, climate change is probably the most serious long-term issue facing the human race (at least before COVID-19 came along), and probably still carries the biggest risk to our overall survival. So it surely makes sense that every organisation should pay attention to emissions, and customers, business owners and regulators are all increasingly interested in the relevant steps that organisations are taking.

That means both addressing the risks of climate change to the organisation itself, an element that is behind the work of the regulatory bodies discussed earlier. But there is also wide interest in what the organisation actively does in terms of its own carbon emissions and those in its value chain, upstream and downstream.

This is therefore one of the PwP issues that *every* organisation needs to consider to some extent. It may be at the top of the priority list if your organisation is directly or indirectly a very significant source of emissions, perhaps operating in traditional heavy industries or in the energy sector, or running data centres, as with Equinix. But even if you are not in that league, it seems likely that stakeholders will expect you to be taking some action.

However, the description of the three "Scope" levels shows that the task of responding to the climate crisis can appear daunting. Moving beyond the Scope 1 and 2 issues that are somewhat directly controllable looks challenging for many organisations. How can suppliers be motivated to take action, so that Scope 3 emissions are diminished?

This is where the beauty of the PwP network effect comes into play. As firms look to reduce their own impact, that will help their customers. If every firm is encouraging its key suppliers to take action, soon that pressure (as well as support or assistance) will be amplified through and across supply chains and networks.

Taking Action

To round up this chapter, here are key ideas and recommendations for organisations that want to address the emissions issue.

- If your organisation is starting on this journey, the first step is to understand your current situation (as it is for many PwP issues). For some elements of this task, the challenge is not too onerous. Working out how much electricity is being purchased or how much fuel for vehicle use is being used internally should not be too difficult.
- Internal actions can then naturally follow from this analysis. Improving the efficiency of factory equipment; turning down the air conditioning or lowering the office temperature a degree or two; and incentivising company car drivers to drive less or travellers to take the train or use video conferencing are all well-established ways of reducing emissions. Even post-pandemic, business travel may see a continued reduction, so that will help in that regard. Procurement can play a role in helping to

drive these initiatives and may well play an important role – for example, when it comes to managing business travel policies and standards.

- When it comes to the more challenging supply chain issues around Scope 3 emissions, we explained in Part 2 how you can influence suppliers by including your expectations within supplier selection or approval processes. Asking potential suppliers what they are doing about emissions is already a line of questioning in many tender documents.
- Such action may relate to suppliers qualifying to be considered for your contract. A minimum threshold, standards or certification can be required. Or you can assess performance or proposals relating to emissions as part of the scoring and evaluation system by which you select suppliers.
- Influencing suppliers once contracts are in place, through effective contract and supplier management, can also drive action in the supply chain. In many cases, that will require collaboration between buyers and suppliers, or more broadly across industries and supply chains.
- Longer-term, there is also likely to be considerable innovation in this field, from novel ways of generating clean energy such as tidal power, to use of hydrogen vehicles. Many solutions will be offered to help reduce the energy needed and emissions generated in day-to-day life. The emerging role of procurement in this field should include maintaining awareness of new developments and promoting initiatives where innovation and collaboration with suppliers can drive reduction in emissions.

Chapter 17 – Sustainable Consumption of Natural Resources

"Deforestation *(in Brazil)* in 2020 surged to a 12-year high. Although the number of fires recorded in the Amazon basin ebbed slightly, an area seven times the size of London was destroyed, felled or deliberately burnt last year to make way for cattle pastures, mines and soya bean production."

("Deforestation in the Amazon: The world's lungs still gasp for breath", The Times, April 23rd, 2021)

Climate change often dominates the headlines when it comes to environmental issues and potential procurement with purpose (PwP) issues and actions. However, there are many other concerns relating to consumption and management of natural resources. Some of these are linked to climate change, whilst others are quite separate. Those that relate to living creatures are discussed in the next chapter; here the focus is on issues concerning other natural resources.

It's Not Just the Climate ...

In terms of challenges for humanity, water consumption, management and resilience is becoming a more critical issue. Climate change is exacerbating the issue as rainfall patterns are changing, with droughts and higher temperatures reducing water supply for some. But the basic issue is ever-increasing water consumption by humans for agriculture, industry and leisure purposes.

For some years, experts have warned that the wars of this century may be fought over water rather than oil or land, and international tension is growing – for instance, a paper[91] published in 2017 highlighted that *"In Cambodia, the (Chinese) dams in the Greater Mekong Subregion are considered instruments of economic growth and development, whereas downstream in Vietnam the dams are seen as potentially undermining national growth, development and security".*

The response to this should be a greater focus on initiatives for reducing water use by individuals and organisations. These can range from the simple and easy, to the highly technical and complex. More efficient toilets that use less water in flushing is an example of the straightforward action, as is ensuring water pipes are well maintained to avoid leaks. At the more high-tech end of the complexity scale, there are initiatives such as Oxwash, a laundry service that disinfects materials using ozone gas rather than washing.[92]

"Our factory in Mexico now produces no excess wastewater. We have achieved this by cleaning the water we use so it can be consumed again in production. Other Audi plants are optimising their water consumption as well to meet this end goal and decrease the by-products of our plants."

(Peter Kössler, Member of the Board of Management for Production and Logistics, Audi, writing for the World Finance website, January 2020)

---

91 https://www.ncbi.nlm.nih.gov/pmc/articles/PMC6128393/

92 https://www.businessgreen.com/news/4014779/space-age-sustainable-laundry-service-oxwash-cleans-gbp-backing

But industries such as agriculture (both plant- and animal-based), textiles, food and drink manufacturing and automotive are the really huge users of water. It takes an amazing 147,631 litres to produce the average domestic vehicle,[93] for example. In response to this, manufacturers are taking action, as in the quote from Audi above.

In the agricultural sector, as part of Unilever's sustainability programme, the firm is working with suppliers and growers to implement *"over 4,000 water management plans through our sustainable sourcing programme. These plans can result in changes across the farm, from the use of drip irrigation to deliver water straight to plant roots preventing wastage to the introduction of best-in-class crop varieties, and better soil and nutrient management. Enhancing soil structure so it can hold more water, and collecting rainwater from rooftops and run-off, can also make a big difference."*

A combination of new technology, more awareness, and a concerted effort to spread knowledge and best practice globally can make a big difference in this area. It may be hard to avoid some of the potential geopolitical conflict over dams, but there is much that firms (and individuals) can do to reduce the pressure on future water supply.

Where Have All the Flowers (and Trees) Gone?

Deforestation is another issue that has wide-ranging and concerning effects. It happens when forest land is cleared to make space for industry, agriculture or grazing, or for use as timber for fuel, construction or manufacturing. Today, it is mostly occurring in the tropics, whilst in some non-tropical nations, including the UK and the US, the proportion of forested land has actually increased in the last 50 years.

However, there are still issues even in these countries. Opponents of the new HS2 high-speed railway in the UK have pointed out that 108

93 https://smarterbusiness.co.uk/blogs/the-top-5-industries-that-consume-the-most-water/

ancient woodlands are at risk of loss or damage because of construction work. The biodiversity and environment destroyed cannot be easily replaced, even if thousands of new saplings are planted in response. The 250-year-old Cubbington Pear Tree, one of the oldest and largest wild pears in Britain, was named Britain's "Tree of the Year" in 2015, but will be felled for the railway.[94]

> "Of the ancient woodlands affected by the railway in Warwickshire, HS2 said about 86.5% would remain intact and unaffected. For those areas of woodland that are removed, HS2 is planting 14.5 hectares of new broadleaved woodland, almost double the area affected."
> *(The Guardian, April 2020)*

HS2 executives claim that much is being done to mitigate the environmental destruction. But HS2 is still going ahead, despite major protests near London Euston station and the likelihood that the post-pandemic world will see less business travel, and more use of video meetings and remote working. It seems unlikely, however, that a third runway will be built at Heathrow anytime soon, which is some consolation for conservationists.

Back to the tropics, and the Union of Concerned Scientists (UCS) reported in 2016[95] that just four commodities are responsible for the vast majority of tropical deforestation: beef, soy, palm oil and wood products. UCS estimates that an area the size of Switzerland (14,800 square miles, or 38,300 square km) is lost to deforestation every year.

The effects of deforestation include the risk to biodiversity, as the

94 https://www.theguardian.com/environment/2015/nov/08/pear-tree-hs2-woodland-trust-cubbington

95 https://www.ucsusa.org/resources/whats-driving-deforestation

plants, insects and animals of the rainforest, for instance, are increasingly threatened. Forests also provide food, fuel and construction material for indigenous people. In some countries, children miss school as they have to travel further to find firewood if natural forest has been replaced by a palm plantation.

Loss of trees can affect water quality, and there is emerging evidence that converting forest to agricultural land reduces rainfall in the region. Deforestation not only removes vegetation that contributes to removing carbon dioxide from the air, but the act of clearing the forests also produces greenhouse gas emissions in itself. The Food and Agriculture Organization of the United Nations says[96] that deforestation represents almost 20% of greenhouse gas emissions and is the second-leading cause of climate change (after the burning of fossil fuels).

That is quite a list of negatives, yet the issue has not had quite the focus that "global warming" receives. Perhaps that is because it is less visible, although the Australian bushfires of 2019/20 did hit the headlines. Or perhaps it is because there are difficult issues here. Why shouldn't poor countries help their own citizens to make more money from agriculture? And are manufacturers and consumers globally prepared to make sacrifices to reduce the use of palm or soya oil, for instance? Palm oil also requires less land to produce (per tonne) than most other vegetable oils, so there are tricky issues when developing sensible responses to the deforestation crisis.

Is Palm Oil Killing the Orangutans?

Demand for palm oil has increased greatly in recent years. Having first been used principally in soaps, toothpaste and cosmetics, its major use now is in huge number of food products, where it has replaced animal

96 http://www.fao.org/state-of-forests/en/

fats and has a number of advantages. It is easier to use than other vegetable oils, is commercially attractive, and is also "trans fat-free", so plays well with the growing interest in health and diet.

Palm trees are indigenous to West Africa, but in recent years, to meet the growing demand, farmers and agribusiness firms across Southeast Asia (and elsewhere) have been clearing biodiversity-rich rainforest to make room for palm plantations. Palm oil production is now considered to be the largest cause of deforestation in Indonesia and other tropical countries. That has a broad negative impact and there are some very specific issues locally as well as the global impact on climate change. For example, Indonesia's endangered orangutan population, which depends upon the rainforest, is estimated to have reduced by some 50% in recent years.

In 2003, some 200 commercial entities in the global supply chain established the Roundtable on Sustainable Palm Oil (RSPO) to promote the growth of environmentally friendly palm oil. RSPO works to develop definitions and criteria for the sustainable production of palm oil, while facilitating the adoption of more green-friendly practices throughout the industry. The group celebrated its first shipment of "sustainable palm oil" to Europe in 2008.

Greenpeace International considers RSPO to be "little more than greenwash", pointing out that at least one RSPO-certified producer – United Plantations, a supplier to Nestlé and Unilever – is deforesting Indonesia's vulnerable peatland forests. And Sinar Mas, another major RSPO player, has cleared tropical rainforest all over the country for its palm oil plantations, and is still expanding rapidly. Greenpeace is calling for a moratorium on deforestation throughout Indonesia so that the RSPO and the government can take stock and then proceed accordingly.

Scores of the world's biggest consumer brands agreed in 2010 to phase out deforestation through the use of sustainable palm oil by 2020, but this goal proved out of reach, according to separate reports from the campaigning groups WWF and Rainforest Action Network.[97]

Many of the companies highlighted as performing poorly or missing targets in analysis from the lobbying groups are household names, including Kellogg's, Mondelez and General Mills, whose brands include Yoplait and Häagen-Dazs. In the UK, major brands such as Greggs, Warburtons, Reckitt Benckiser and Associated British Foods also ranked relatively low in the table.

Mars (nearer the "top" of the table) said: *"RAN's conclusion is that, despite industry initiatives, a number of environmental and social threats to the landscape remain. This is precisely why we are working to radically transform the way we source palm oil at Mars with our Palm Positive Plan that aims to deliver 100% deforestation-free palm oil by the end of 2020 and to advance respect for human rights across our suppliers' extended supply chains."*

Unilever, which scored 34th of the 173 brands in the WWF table and came out best of the eight companies in the RAN report, said: *"Only by all parties coming together, using cutting-edge technology to carefully monitor our forests and engaging with the communities and stakeholders around them, will we create a sustainable future. We remain committed to working in partnership with suppliers, governments, NGOs and the wider industry to end deforestation."*

Whole Foods Market, which scored only 8.25 out of a possible 22 in the WWF table, said: *"We made a public pledge over 10 years ago to use only 100% RSPO palm oil in [own] brand food products. We recognise that there is more work to be done and are actively exploring opportunities for improvement."*

It is clear that there are plenty of good intentions; but there is some way to go before the challenges here are overcome.

---

97 Https://www.theguardian.com/environment/2020/jan/17/biggest-food-brands-failing-goals-to-banish-palm-oil-deforestation

But Is Palm Oil Really That Bad?

Generally, the largest firms are looking to do the right things in terms of deforestation. But there are problems. Clearing the rainforest brings immediate economic benefits to people and governments, even if the long-term effects might be tragic. People who are living a subsistence existence quite rightly don't appreciate rich Westerners telling them what they can and can't grow. There is also a major issue around understanding. Palm oil is so ubiquitous, it is hard to make consumers realise just how often they are potentially contributing to these issues.

But the alternatives also have their problems. Some environmental experts want us to use *more* palm oil, not less. Jane Hill, Professor of Biology at the University of York, was quoted in The Times as saying:[98] *"Boycotting palm oil could have the opposite effect to that intended, resulting in forests still being lost and more decline for wildlife."*

That's because palm is in some ways an environmental wonder crop. It needs less fertiliser or pesticide than other oil crops such as soya beans, and most importantly it requires up to ten times less land. To switch to soya or coconut oil could put more forest and wildlife at risk.

"Sustainable" palm oil is one way forward, for instance using certificates from RSPO. Palm-boycotting, which critics call "palm-phobia", is the other approach. Some big British retailers, such as Selfridges and Iceland, are trying to remove all palm from their own-brand products. They subscribe to the hard line taken by Greenpeace, claiming sustainable palm is just not achievable. And because of the confusion and some cynicism about RSPO, firms are often hesitant to use their logo on their products even where they could. That may be because

---

98 https://www.thetimes.co.uk/article/my-palm-oil-problem-how-can-i-save-orangutans-vm0pj8gsl

they don't want to draw attention to the fact that palm oil is present in their products, even if it is "sustainable".

Perhaps the move to sustainable palm oil will gain traction and credibility, and lead to less destruction of rainforests. Perhaps governments of nations such as Indonesia will realise that their rainforests are a huge asset in a number of ways, from tourism to water management, and that destroying them is not a sensible approach.

For the individual, boycotting palm oil appears to be neither practical nor helpful. But if consumers continue to put pressure on the big industrial buyers, and those firms continue to follow a sincere PwP path in this area, the future of palm oil might be economically positive for the whole supply chain, whilst also being environmentally acceptable.

Natural Resources in Context

So why might an organisation choose to put this type of issue high on its priority list?

Firstly, these issues do really matter to a lot of people, including many customers, investors, and staff. Deforestation and loss of habitat are seen as important, and the emotional reaction to issues such as rainforest destruction and potential extinction of species has emotional power. That has been obvious through the reaction to David Attenborough's television programmes in recent years.

These are also high-risk issues in terms of the future of the human race. Species extinction may have unexpected impacts, and those are unlikely to be positive. Destruction of rainforests exacerbates climate problems and increases the risk of natural disasters. Ultimately, businesses will not gain if humankind is struggling economically or environmentally, or the world is thrown into wars based on the fight for resources such as water.

Firms may well find that there is a strong stakeholder drive to take action here, particularly for those businesses that can have an impact.

That is a key point here: not every organisation can do much about these issues. As described in Chapter 5, when developing a PwP strategy, it is important to consider if your organisation really can make a difference. Even Unilever realised that they couldn't address every issue they found in their various supply chains for raw materials; they had to focus most strongly on those where they could have real impact. That is a critical point for any organisation to consider here.

But those who *can* have an impact may well find that the contribution they can make is significant. Being able to say that you are protecting natural habitats and contributing towards addressing climate change is a powerful message. Certainly, these areas come with the potential for real achievement, success that can reflect well on the organisation.

Taking Action

For those who do choose to prioritise this sort of issue, there are a range of actions that can be taken:

- Often, as in the case of palm oil and deforestation, it will be a case of collaborative actions, working with both suppliers and others in the industry. Even the largest food firms in the world are looking for collaborative initiatives in these areas.
- As usual, the starting point is to make sure you understand your suppliers and supply chains. That isn't easy in all cases; getting back to the level of farmers and growers in the developing world takes considerable effort, and not every firm will have the resources to go that far. But you need to understand as far as possible what impact your organisation, your suppliers and supply chain are having in terms of these issues before you can develop a plan of action.
- Tracking progress is key, as with any significant PwP initiative. Ultimately, whilst getting accurate data and information is not

always easy, firms are looking to measure progress and success with metrics such as:

- % of spend from sustainable sources (by spend category or material)
- % of spend from known suppliers (traceability back to grower)
- reduction in water use – direct and indirect

- The different steps to achieve positive change then relate to the earlier discussion in Section 2. These issues can be incorporated into the supplier selection process, for instance, by insisting that potential suppliers sign up to certain standards or rules or agree to act in a certain manner. Supplier actions or proposals can also be evaluated and scored as part of a formal selection process.
- Activities can also be driven with existing suppliers and managed as part of an ongoing, continuous contract and supplier management programme. That is very much how some of the leaders in this field (such as Unilever, Mars or Nestlé) have viewed it, looking to persuade their supply chain partners to act in a particular way. Collaborative approaches and using the carrot as well as the stick work well.

Chapter 18 – Plastics, Pollution and Obsolescence

In March 2021, Mars Wrigley and Danimer Scientific announced a new two-year partnership to develop compostable packaging for Skittles in the US, estimated to be on shelves by early 2022. It involves a type of polyhydroxyalkanoate (PHA) that will look and feel the same as plastic, but can be thrown into the compost where it will break down, unlike regular plastic that takes anywhere from 20 to 450 years to fully decompose.
(BBC website, May 2021)

This topic could be split into several separate chapters, as it covers broad and diverse issues. The common theme, though, is "waste" – the tendency of modern economies and societies to produce a lot of unwanted "stuff" that has to be disposed of somehow, from chemical waste to plastic bottles, from unwanted T-shirts to obsolete laptops.
The volume of waste humans produce has multiplied in recent years, and now there are a range of serious problems that must be addressed before the negative consequences for life on earth escalate further. Those issues include plastics disposal, waste and landfill, pollution such as chemical emissions, discharges and toxic waste. On the more positive side, there are exciting opportunities and developments in terms of the "circular economy".

The Blue Planet Effect

Very occasionally, a TV programme can drive real change. One of the first examples was back in the 1960s, when *Cathy Come Home* highlighted the problem of homelessness in the UK and led to political action. More recently, the David Attenborough series *The Blue Planet* highlighted the problems of plastic pollution in the ocean, creating a huge amount of debate and prompting many firms to review their own use of plastic.

Sequences in the programme that showed a dead albatross, killed by a plastic bag, and a baby whale with part of a plastic bucket caught in its mouth brought home the reality of how plastic waste is affecting marine wildlife. The World Economic Forum has forecast that with current trends, plastic will outweigh fish in the ocean by 2050. One of the lasting negative outcomes from the pandemic (one of many, unfortunately) has been the explosion in the use of personal protective equipment such as disposable masks and aprons, often made from single-use plastics and eventually adding to the waste in the oceans.

In 2018, reports suggested that the Great Pacific Garbage Patch, a giant floating accumulation of plastic situated in the ocean between California and Hawaii, was now three times the size of France. It was estimated to contain at least 79,000 tonnes (72,000 tonnes) of discarded plastic, covering an area of about 617,800 square miles (1.6 million square kilometres), according to a study published in *Scientific Reports*.[99] That is not surprising: plastic use has grown at an incredible rate, such that over the last ten years, more has been produced than during the entire 20th century.

But it is not just the visible pollution of bags, buckets and bottles. *Microplastics* are very tiny pieces of plastic that pollute the environment. They are not a specific kind of plastic, but any type of fragment less than 5 millimetres in length. They enter natural ecosystems from a variety

99 https://abcnews.go.com/International/great-pacific-garbage-patch-massive-floating-island-plastic/story?id=53962147

of sources, including cosmetics, clothing, and industrial processes. The understanding of microplastics and the effect they have is at an early stage. However, as they are now being found in drinking water, the soil and the air, it is important that scientists do gain an understanding of what they might be doing to humans, other animals and the whole natural environment.

Some campaigning groups have called for a total move away from plastic. A Plastic Planet says: *"we are all plastic addicts. Our simple goal is to ignite and inspire the world to turn off the plastic tap"*.[100] Sian Sutherland, a co-founder of the organisation, believes that we should *"increase the use of materials that nature can handle and eliminate the use of those nature can't"*.

Even some plastics that are presented as "biodegradable" actually take hundreds of years to break down into microplastics and nanoplastics that still pollute the planet, the critics say. However, bio-plastics, made from plants rather than oil, and which do compost at the end of their lives, are a step forward and their use is growing.

It's Not Quite as Simple as That...

By taking an extreme position, that all plastic production should cease, groups such as A Plastic Planet have successfully gained a lot of attention to publicise problems. But yet again, the issues are not simple, and there are complexities and challenges to be faced. If all use of plastics were banned tomorrow, there would be an immediate range of crises – economic, practical, and in day-to-day life.

Plastic has many positive qualities, which explains the growth in use and its ubiquity. As food packaging, it is light, flexible, and protects food from degradation and contamination. It can also be incredibly strong and robust for its weight and cost. So in some cases, substituting other materials

100 https://aplasticplanet.com/

could have an overall negative impact on the planet. More fuel would be needed to transport heavier glass bottles, more food would be wasted without plastic packaging, and more metal would need to be mined to replace plastic in certain cases, such as in automotive manufacture.

A report from the Green Alliance in 2019,[101] titled *Plastic promises – What the grocery sector is really doing about packaging*, pointed out that since 2017, the proportion of plastic packaging on supermarket shelves has barely changed. But it also explained that *"decisions to switch away from plastic are often made without considering the environmental impact of the substitute materials chosen, or whether or not there is adequate collection and treatment infrastructure in place for them"*.

Despite the difficulties, there has been a rapid increase in firms announcing positive initiatives in recent years. In January 2020, consumer goods giant Nestlé announced[102] that it will spend up to $2.1 billion to develop recyclable packaging that is safe for food use. That will be made up of two main elements. Nestlé will be prepared to pay a premium for such plastic to encourage manufacturers to develop and produce the right products. With similar aims, the firm has created the Nestlé Institute of Packaging Sciences to develop sustainable packaging materials and collaborate with industry partners to scale up research and innovation.[103]

In addition, about $250m will be allocated to a venture capital fund to invest in sustainable packaging start-ups and advanced recycling technologies. *"Making recycled plastics safe for food is an enormous challenge for our industry,"* said chief executive Mark Schneider. *"That is why in*

101 https://www.green-alliance.org.uk/resources/Plastic_promises.pdf

102 https://www.nestle.com/csv/global-initiatives/zero-environmental-impact/packaging-plastic-pollution

103 https://www.nestle.com/media/pressreleases/allpressreleases/nestle-institute-of-packaging-sciences

addition to minimising plastics use and collecting waste, we want to close the loop and make more plastics infinitely recyclable."

Less, Better, None

Unilever is another firm leading the drive for business to address these issues. The firm aims to move away from single-use plastic and talks about "less plastic, better plastic, and no plastic". The most dramatic reduction in use could come from cases where the plastic use stops altogether – "no plastic". So, for instance, Unilever says that in France, *"we are piloting a laundry detergent dispensing machine in supermarkets for our Skip and Persil laundry brands to eliminate single-use plastic".*

Other examples are food stores that are selling products such as vegetables, nuts or cereals loose rather than in pre-packed plastic bags (although the COVID-19 pandemic may call into question the hygiene issues around such initiatives, unfortunately). Cardboard packaging for deodorant sticks is another Unilever idea.

Some dairies are moving away from plastic containers back to the old-fashioned milk bottles, although this highlights the tricky issues in considering these issues. A detailed analysis of environmental impact here has to take into account the transport emissions around the additional weight of the glass bottle, the water used to clean them, and so on. But there is no doubt that many other products (grocery and non-grocery) come with unnecessary plastic packaging that could be reduced or removed altogether.

> "Our plastic is our responsibility, so we are committed to collecting back more than we sell, as part of our drive towards a circular economy. This is a daunting but exciting task which will help drive global demand for recycled plastic."
>
> *(Alan Jope, CEO, Unilever)*

"Less plastic" could mean redesigning packaging structures to use less material, reducing unnecessary plastic or substituting lighter materials. Or it could be a change in what is being packaged. Again, Unilever has a good example. *"We launched a three-litre bottle for our OMO laundry detergent brand in Brazil, with a formula at six times the concentration of the original, so it can be diluted in people's homes. This has reduced the volume of plastic used by 75%."*

Many of the examples of this type require the sort of collaboration with suppliers that was discussed in Chapter 9. Again, Unilever provides an example. Innovation such as the foamed plastic layer in the middle of plastic bottle walls using MuCell™ technology, developed in collaboration with MuCell and Alpla in 2014, reduced plastic use by up to 15% per bottle.[104]

Finally, the "better plastic" option primarily means moving to recyclable plastic or using recycled material in the manufacturing process. The Unilever "Love Beauty and Planet" range *"has put packaging at the centre of its consumer proposition. Its packaging is made from 100% recycled PET (rPET) and is also 100% recyclable"*.

Closing that loop on plastics so that it items are reused rather than thrown away is a huge opportunity and challenge. The benefits of plastic mean it is unlikely in the foreseeable future that firms will just stop using the material. So, a combination of reducing use dramatically and recycling what is still used seems the best option.

In 2019, Unilever committed to help collect and process more plastic packaging than it sells by 2025. Coca-Cola has committed to use at least 50% recycled materials in its bottles by 2030, and also has a goal to recover 100 per cent of the cans and bottles used by 2030, *"so that none of our packaging ends up as waste and all of our bottles and cans are recycled and used again"*.

---

104 https://www.unilever.com/news/press-releases/2014/14-04-24-Unilever-launches-breakthrough-packaging-technology-that-uses-15pc-less-plastic.html

But this requires a considerable investment in waste collection as well as in processing capacity and capability. It will also require major changes in consumer behaviour. It is Coke drinkers and Snickers eaters who carelessly throw bottles and wrappers out of car windows or drop them on the street or beach, not Coca-Cola or Mars Confectionery who make the products. We all have a part to play.

Pollution Isn't Just Plastics

The problems around plastics have somewhat taken the focus away from other forms of waste and pollution in recent years, but there remain major issues that can be considered as part of a PwP programme. Indeed, for many organisations, these should be high-priority issues.

There are generally considered to be seven major types of environmental pollution: water, air, soil, thermal, radioactive, noise and light. However, Wikipedia includes several others such as littering, visual and electromagnetic pollution.[105] Each presents different issues and challenges.

Historically, most of the pressure on businesses that pollute has come from governments or direct action from citizens or the media. In cases such as chemical giant DuPont, which knowingly allowed a cancer-causing chemical (perfluorooctanoic acid or PFOA), used in manufacturing of Teflon, to pollute the air and drinking water in West Virginia, it was local residents and lawyers who finally got the practice exposed to wider attention and ultimately stopped.[106]

There are few public examples of buyers (business customers) exerting their procurement power to hold suppliers who are potential polluters to account. That is probably because such behaviour is often

105 https://en.wikipedia.org/wiki/Pollution

106 https://www.triplepundit.com/story/2016/case-duponts-pollution-and-importance-csr/29241

not obvious, and some polluters do their best to conceal their more dubious actions. Even inspections and quite direct contract management techniques are not guaranteed to identify problems.

But that should not stop the buyer understanding which industries, products or suppliers are high-risk when it comes to pollution. And the risks, reputational in particular, are similar to those from other sustainability issues. In 2017, firms including H&M, Zara and Marks & Spencer received a blow to their reputations when they were linked to polluting factories in Asia that produced viscose.[107] Investigators for the Changing Markets Foundation[108] visited 10 manufacturing sites in China, India, and Indonesia, and found environmental damage, including air pollution and water pollution from untreated contaminated waste.

Indeed, several different sustainability risks come together in viscose production. Viscose is made from cellulose or wood pulp, so there are issues around the sustainability of the wood sources in certain cases. Viscose production is then chemical-heavy, using carbon disulphide, a highly volatile and flammable liquid. The report suggested that carbon disulphide exposure was harming factory workers and people living near viscose plants. In China, viscose production has contributed to the pollution of China's largest freshwater lake, Poyang, killing aquatic life.

But of course it is not just viscose. Pollution can be generated by and through many different industries and sectors. From battery recycling to the dye industry, from gold-mining to tanneries, many different pollutants are generated as by-products of the main activities. As always, the starting point for procurement with purpose is to understand what

---

107 https://www.theguardian.com/sustainable-business/2017/jun/13/hm-zara-marks-spencer-linked-polluting-viscose-factories-asia-fashion

108 Changing Markets Foundation was formed to "accelerate and scale up solutions to sustainability challenges by leveraging the power of markets". https://changingmarkets.org/about/

goes in your supply chain – at all levels – and to be aware of the risks in this particular area.

That's Rubbish!

In 2016, the UK produced 222.9 million tonnes of "waste", not necessarily pollutants, but unwanted "stuff" of some sort. Incredibly, that is over 3 tonnes for every person in the country, although most of the waste isn't household; construction and demolition account for over 50%.

But the average individual still produces over 400 kilos a year of household material, and around a quarter of the overall total goes into landfill sites. The UK and many other countries also export waste; the BBC suggests that 611,000 tonnes of plastic packaging waste went to China in 2018, but after China introduced new regulations concerning this trade, other countries such as Malaysia, Indonesia and Turkey picked up some of that volume.[109]

Aside from the moral issues here, waste can cause health issues and devastate natural environments, and the effects may be felt for generations to come as the earth (and the oceans) are used as dumping grounds. So for any organisation, reducing the quantity of waste material produced should be seen as a good and worthwhile objective. It is also interesting from a PwP point of view, as good practice principles can be adopted usefully by *every* organisation. It should also be close to the top of the priority list for certain businesses and industries.

At the more day-to-day level, initiatives can include use of recyclable paper and other materials in the office, collecting food waste for recycling and composting, and ensuring that manufacturing, technology or other equipment has an end-of-life route which avoids it ending up in landfill sites. Taking those whole-life issues into account when carrying out

---

109 https://www.bbc.co.uk/news/science-environment-49827945

initial procurement is clearly the best practice approach here.

But some firms are adopting more dramatic approaches where this is a major issue for their business. In January 2020, Wates, the construction firm, committed to eliminating waste and carbon from its operations by 2025. The first of the three targets is "zero waste from Wates operations by 2025 – Wates aims to reduce and then eliminate the production of all waste created from onsite operations". That will be a challenge, but more sustainable building methods are becoming more common, such as extracting gypsum from waste plasterboard so it can be reused.

In a very different industry, brewing historically had a waste problem with "spent grain", the by-product from malting barley, obtained once the substances needed for the beer have been extracted. Historically, spent grain was fed to livestock, but that wasn't always possible, so it could end up in landfill. Now, firms are turning it into human food products, including malted flour which apparently makes beautiful barley flour and tasty bread![110]

The Circular Economy

> "Circularity is a move away from the traditional thinking about our economy. We've got good over the centuries at the linear economy. We take materials from mines or forests, we make something, we use it, we throw it away. The problem is what we throw away. The circular economy is about getting more value out of that "waste", or designing it out altogether where possible. Waste streams become value streams."
> *(Deborah Dull, supply chain professional and circular economy evangelist)*

When I first heard about the idea of the circular economy, some years

110 https://www.perishablenews.com/bakery/susgrainable-duo-in-vancouver-makes-breads-and-healthy-baked-goods-out-of-beer-waste/

ago, the phrase that brought it to life was this – *"we have to move from cradle to grave costing and analysis, to cradle to cradle"*.

In February 2020, National Geographic magazine dedicated its cover story to "the end of trash".[111] A major element of that vision is the concept of the "circular economy". Recycling plastics is one example of that; but some of the ideas under this heading are more complex and novel. The magazine reported, for instance, that "*in London, researchers are feeding beer waste to insects, which are made into animal feed*".

The Ellen MacArthur Foundation was launched in 2010 to support the "transition to a circular economy". The organisation has done great work as a leader in educating and promoting the cause since then, and this is how it defines the circular economy:

"Looking beyond the current take-make-waste extractive industrial model, a circular economy aims to redefine growth, focusing on positive society-wide benefits. It entails gradually decoupling economic activity from the consumption of finite resources, and designing waste out of the system. Underpinned by a transition to renewable energy sources, the circular model builds economic, natural, and social capital. It is based on three principles:

- *Design out waste and pollution*
- *Keep products and materials in use*
- *Regenerate natural systems"*

But it is only relatively recently that procurement people and others in business really started thinking about even true "cradle to grave" thinking, by including the costs of disposal into the picture when looking at the initial buying process. But the circular economy takes it one step further, and looks at how we can move from "disposal" to recycling and reuse.

Firms across many industries are now embracing this thinking,

111 https://www.nationalgeographic.co.uk/environment-and-conservation/2020/02/why-we-dedicated-our-cover-story-end-of-trash

including some we might not consider obvious candidates for the approach. For instance, Nike has been a global partner of the Ellen MacArthur Foundation since 2014, and has worked to create products made from waste materials. One example of this is 'Nike Grind', a material made from recycled sneakers collected through the company's Reuse-A-Shoe programme,[112] plastic bottles and manufacturing scraps from Nike's factories.

In a very different sector, UK-based company Circular Computing[113] claims to be the world's first computer re-manufacturer to support the circular economy concept, by refurbishing enterprise-grade discarded laptops into brand new products ready for a second life.

The fashion industry, which has not exactly been a watchword for sustainable behaviour in the past, is now embracing some circularity concepts. There was much media comment when the British Prime Minister, Boris Johnson, and his bride, Carrie Symonds, got married in May 2021 because she hired rather than purchased her wedding dress. But that is a very sustainable behaviour; the "waste" of a beautiful garment worn only once is obvious.

A number of entrepreneurs are now looking to exploit this opportunity. Jade McSorley, who worked as a successful fashion model herself, is a co-founder of LOANHOOD. The LOANHOOD App will enable those who own clothes, particularly higher-value / cost items, or indeed entire outfits, to hire them out for a fee. "Think of it as Airbnb for clothing," she says. Getting more use and value out of products of any sort is a fundamental principle of recycling and reuse.

The Future of Circularity

112 https://www.nike.com/help/a/recycle-shoes

113 https://circularcomputing.com/about/

Deborah Dull, a procurement professional and active advocate of circularity, expects to see shorter supply chains in future and more local and regional activity: *"Most regions have the raw materials they need, we don't need to ship materials around the world. If you want to repair and renew, that needs local support and skills, and a more flexible approach to manufacturing."* That all promotes a less global approach, as well as local innovation – she talks about a firm making packaging material from mushrooms to replace Styrofoam as an example.

"It also costs less to remanufacture than to start from scratch," she says, although she also believes that 3-D printing will get more common. *"It should be a local township option. And we should never have to drive 20 miles to a store to buy a screw again."* She wants to see more decentralisation, and local economies becoming as self-sufficient as possible.

Dull thinks that in ten years' time, firms won't be buying from primary commodity markets – it will all be secondary markets (for example, selling recycled/recovered plastics). She believes it won't be long until landfill sites will be (literally) mined, to extract valuable materials, helped by new technology. And as key materials such as some metals run out, *"AI will be a game-changer, helping us find alternative materials to those currently used, making connections from all the data that is available"*.

In some cases, thinking about how circularity might apply requires a degree of creative thinking and innovative approaches. But for most businesses that produce or sell products of some sort, the circular concept is well worth considering, and is likely to receive growing attention from the different stakeholder groups.

As Dull says, we should all "realise that decisions you make impact the world, and ultimately you can contribute to real shifts in global behaviour. Start to be aware of the inputs to the system and the outputs. For instance, as a simple way to get started, I suggest that people literally weigh what they buy and what they throw away – even reducing supplier packaging can be a big win."

"Waste" in Context

Organisations cannot give full focus to every possible area of interest or concern. So why might this be a set of topics that an organisation would place high on its priority list?

Fundamentally, these are important issues for humanity and the planet, and key stakeholders such as customers often really care about them. So, the reputational risk if a business gets it wrong can be considerable. We have seen examples of this arising from pollution of various types and particularly plastics, where *The Blue Planet* TV programme educated a new generation to the dangers of filling the oceans with empty drinks bottles!

There is also likely to be increased regulatory pressure in many countries to reduce pollution, drive recycling and make firms more responsible for the waste they produce directly or that comes via what they sell. Getting on the front foot in terms of recycling, reusability and simply producing less waste will help firms avoid potential issues and stay on the right side of the law.

But it isn't just about the risks and regulations. Firms that take action and are innovative in these areas can reap positive benefits. Consumers increasingly look to support firms that are seen as leaders in areas such as use of plastics and recycling. And successful supply chain collaborations have developed innovative new materials and approaches to packaging, processes and products.

For many businesses, this is a positive area of focus because they *can* make a real difference. Unlike, for instance, the incredibly challenging battle against deforestation, almost any organisation can reduce the waste it sends to landfill, or consider how it can replace some plastic use with other products. Progress and success are usually tangible and measurable, with meaningful metrics such as quantities of waste sent to landfill or percentage of materials used that are recyclable.

Taking Action

So what should organisations be doing to address these areas? There are obviously different steps depending on whether we are talking about plastic use, pollution or circularity.

- In all cases, the understanding of suppliers and supply chain is (yet again) a vital starting point. Understanding of the actual *materials* that are being bought is also critical here. As seen in case studies about new types of plastics, or circularity reuse options, a detailed understanding of the properties of materials or products used is often vital. A clear view of both suppliers and specifications is critical.
- In terms of *general waste*, steps can be as basic as good housekeeping actions for staff around what is used in the factory, office, or tearoom. Where your organisation produces more "industrial waste", look at what others in the same sector or who produce the same waste are doing. Suppliers can often provide insight, too. More general guidance is difficult, as the possibilities vary so much across different products. But in most industries, new ideas and approaches are allowing firms to reduce waste significantly or put it to better use rather than just sending it to landfill.
- Managing *plastic* use has many potential actions. Remember Unilever's mantra – "less, better, no" plastic. So, can you reduce use by making plastic packaging products lighter-weight, or by substituting more environmentally friendly products? Can you find better plastics, that are recyclable or reusable – or even compostable? Finally, can you remove the need for the plastic

altogether?

- Pollution must be managed in terms of what the organisation generates itself, and then buyers need to identify where risks may lie in the supply chain. The full range of PwP techniques may then be applied, including: requiring potential suppliers to pass thresholds or sign up to codes of conduct; incorporating the issue into supplier selection processes; inspections, audits and checks; and working with existing suppliers through collaborative processes to improve the situation.
- In terms of *circularity*, almost every business will face different issues and opportunities, so it is hard to generalise. Creative thinking about reducing or eliminating waste streams can draw on experience of others in similar industries or situations. And putting waste to better use may well mean partnering with others who see your waste as their "raw material", as in the case of the flour made from beer "waste".
- In all these cases, make use of industry and collaboration groups, technology firms, charities, academia and other bodies (see Chapter 12) that potentially can provide resource, information and assistance. There is a vast amount of work going on in these areas, and firms should draw on this emerging knowledge.

Chapter 19 – Animals and Food

> "The coronavirus (COVID-19) pandemic has put a spotlight on animal welfare. From the overwhelming support and comfort provided by pets, to the importance of a secure food supply chain founded upon high-welfare farming, high welfare standards have never been more important.... This is not the last word on animal welfare. The way we treat animals reflects our values and the kind of people we are. We will continue to raise the bar, and we intend to take the rest of the world with us."
>
> *(UK Government, Action Plan for Animal Welfare, May 2021)*

This procurement with purpose (PwP) topic contains a whole range of somewhat different issues, but the common thread is that they directly involve the animals that share our planet. Perhaps humans could live happily and healthily in a world where we were the only remaining life form – but that seems unlikely. Our fate is almost certainly tied up with that of our fellow creatures.

The Revenge of the Pangolins?

Whilst the source of the COVID-19 virus may never be known with total certainty, many believe it originated in the animal "wet markets" of Wuhan, in China's Hubei Province. These sell a wide variety of living and dead creatures for food and medicinal purposes.

COVID has led to greater awareness of animals in the food (and medical) supply chain, hygiene around selling animal products, and whether it is sensible for humans to eat certain animals. The virus may have originated in bats, and then entered humans via an intermediate species, perhaps pangolins, which are prized as a delicacy and for the unproven medicinal properties of their scales.

Whether or not this is true, there are subjective and cultural issues here as well as some that are less contentious. In the West, most people find the idea of eating dogs, monkeys and pangolins unpleasant or even disgusting. Yet we cook live lobsters, shoot and eat wild deer or rabbits, and eat pigs, creatures that are as intelligent as dogs (and can make good pets).

Some have suggested that the virus is in some sense the "Revenge of the Pangolins", as *The New York Times* headline put it.[114] That might be going too far; a pangolin is unlikely to be sitting in a James Bond-type villain's lair, stroking its white cat and plotting the downfall of the human race. But more reasonably, some of the world's most eminent biodiversity experts said this, reported in The Guardian.[115]

"Rampant deforestation, uncontrolled expansion of agriculture, intensive farming, mining and infrastructure development, as well as the exploitation of wild species have created a 'perfect storm' for the spillover of diseases."

Actor Idris Elba, who caught the virus and recovered, described the virus as the earth's revenge on the human race. Whilst positioning the earth as a sentient creature that is capable of plotting and executing "revenge" is perhaps even more far-fetched than the idea of a pangolin uprising, I share his feelings. There is an increasing sense that humans have over-exploited the earth and living creatures, leading to potentially disastrous consequences for all.

---

114 https://www.nytimes.com/2020/03/05/opinion/coronavirus-china-pangolins.html

115 https://www.theguardian.com/world/2020/apr/27/halt-destruction-nature-worse-pandemics-top-scientists

That explains why interactions with the natural world, across the range of issues from climate change to animal welfare, is core to many purposeful business approaches and actions. But understanding the various issues in detail is key to successful action and outcomes.

Extinction and Biodiversity

There have been previous mass extinctions of plants and animals in the past, caused by asteroid strikes, volcanic eruptions, or natural changes in the climate. But for the first time, the current extinction – the sixth, according to scientists – is totally created by humans. Yet like many of the issues discussed here, much of this is driven by business considerations. So equally, a more sustainable and informed approach by firms and consumers could reverse this terrible trend.

Extinction occurs naturally, with what is defined as a "background" rate of one to five species a year being affected. But that is now progressing maybe a thousand times faster, with dozens of species *a day* disappearing, because of loss of habitat, climate change or introduction (by humans) of exotic species to new habitats. There is a link here to the discussion about sustainable consumption of natural resources; the destruction of rainforest, largely to create farmland for cattle, soya or other food process, is one of the biggest threats to the natural world. But species diversity is just as important in grasslands, tundra or the oceans, and humans can have a major impact, positive or negative, everywhere and anywhere in the world.

The increased use of pesticides and weedkillers in agriculture, for instance, and the destruction of hedgerows and woodland to create mega prairie-type fields, has created huge areas where almost nothing living can be found. Conservation scientist from Princeton University, David

Wilcove,[116] estimates that there are 14,000 to 35,000 endangered species in the US alone.

Pressure on food supply and new methods of fishing have put the oceans and fish stocks under great pressure, too. Historically, communities fished in a "sustainable" manner, consciously or unconsciously understanding that if they wanted productive seas for their children, they should not catch every single fish that they could now. But huge industrial trawlers now dredge the sea, many miles from their home countries, with little regard for the long term. In the process, they also kill millions of creatures that aren't even suitable as human food. Fish farming brings its own problems, with evidence that farmed fish are less healthy than their wild counterparts, and problems such as salmon lice can spread into the broader community when fish escape their "farms".[117]

But whilst people tend to think about polar bears, tigers or whales when worrying about extinction, there are issues much closer to home. Many businesses and public sector bodies have run into criticism for actions which are potentially harmful to the less spectacular natural world and reduce local biodiversity.

Sheffield Council in England ran into problems when it started removing thousands of trees in the city, supposedly as part of a programme to improve and make safer roads and paths in the city. Mass protests and the involvement of riot police followed, and residents were arrested as they demonstrated against the destruction of much-loved and mature trees. There were accusations that this was really about the profit that contractor Amey could make as part of a long-term agreement

---

116 https://eu.azcentral.com/story/opinion/op-ed/2020/01/12/wildlife-corridors-conservation-act-nice-must-do-more-public-lands/2837568001/

117 https://www.ciwf.org.uk/media/3818689/in-too-deep-summary.pdf

with the council. As *The Independent* newspaper reported, *"over the length of the company's 25-year highway maintenance obligations, so ran the theory, a newly planted sapling is far cheaper to look after than older, larger arboreta"*.[118]

Netting trees to stop birds from nesting or roosting has also been criticised. It is often done prior to building works, but has an impact on local fauna. Even Cambridge University, generally an organisation that is sensitive to environmental issues, had to apologise for netting trees prior to building work.[119]

Indeed, every time a firm develops a greenfield (or even a brownfield) site, there is potential to affect biodiversity and the natural world negatively. So it is not just buyers of palm oil and other exotic crops, or retailers buying canned tuna, who need to be sensitive to biodiversity. Any organisation that is engaging firms to carry out construction work should consider how they can avoid harming the living environment.

Animal Welfare

Conservation of wild species is not the only way in which PwP connects to animals. Another whole set of issues concerns animal welfare, food provenance and safety. While welfare and food safety are in some sense very different issues, they are linked where animals in the food supply chain are kept in unsatisfactory conditions, or treated inhumanely. It seems likely that in such cases, there is also more chance of food safety problems emerging from those providers.

Production of meat and other animal-based food products such as eggs or milk has for some time now been a high-profile topic, with campaigners highlighting bad practice and at times exposing awful

118 https://www.independent.co.uk/news/long_reads/sheffield-tree-massacre-parks-green-city-spaces-felling-street-council-yorkshire-a8286581.html

119 https://www.bbc.co.uk/news/uk-england-cambridgeshire-51666004

stories about the treatment of animals. In 2019, a French investigation found very unpleasant conditions and processes around production of duck foie gras in a French factory.[120] This horrified even many famously carnivorous French consumers, as ducklings were starved or suffocated, and beaks were removed even before the force-feeding to create the delicacy started.

Consumer and charity campaigns against foie gras have led to many restaurants and retailers stopping sales of the item, and some cities, including New York, have even banned it from restaurants.[121] Its production is banned in the UK – but chef Alexis Gauthier from the eponymous London restaurant has created a vegan alternative which he claims is "better than the original".[122] It is indeed delicious, I can confirm, with no less than thirteen different ingredients.

There are many other worrying case studies and stories. "Free-range eggs" conjures up an image of happy hens, roaming through fields and woods. But investigations have found a very different picture in some cases, as the legal definition of "free-range" in some countries allows hens to be crammed into sheds with limited access to the open air. Other larger farm animals such as cows, pigs and sheep are sometimes (and in some places) treated in a manner that many of us would find cruel or unacceptable.

Any retail, wholesale or catering organisation that is buying animal products, for processing or to sell directly, needs to consider these issues. This is another area whether consumer views continue to develop rapidly, and the growth of veganism is potentially a disruptive change for the

---

120 https://www.onegreenplanet.org/environment/ducklings-starved-to-death-while-ducks-were-force-fed-and-suffocated-at-french-foie-gras-factory/

121 https://www.nytimes.com/2019/10/30/nyregion/foie-gras-ban-nyc.html

122 It is delicious, we can confirm…

relevant industries. Artificial meat products and new food technologies are opening up the possibilities and may well drive even faster change.

As in many other PwP issues, the starting point for buyers is to understand suppliers and supply chains. You might not be able to identify every farm (let alone every animal) if you buy bulk meat to create frozen ready meals or dog food, but increasingly consumers may expect that level of understanding. They also expect you as the buyer to try and ensure that animal welfare considerations are a high priority. The actions described in Section 2, around supplier verification and selection, contract provisions, and collaborative management of suppliers, all have a part to play here.

Provenance Is Paramount

For any firm producing or selling animal products, the risks are obvious if the consumer feels that the basics of animal welfare are not being respected. There are also risks around the regulatory framework, as well as that reputational damage that negative stories can bring.

But even if animals are being treated well, or we are talking about wild creatures rather than farmed, other issues around provenance come into play. Provenance means *"the place of origin or earliest known history of something"*. It can also apply to a *"record of ownership"*, as in the case of a work of art, for instance.

In this context, it means understanding the origins of whatever you are buying, and the route it takes through the different tiers of the supply chain. In theory, it could apply to buying automotive components, pharmaceuticals or packaging materials, but it tends to apply more often to understanding the source of natural products, including foodstuffs, but also minerals, precious metals or gemstones. This is an area where technology is providing interesting new possibilities, such as the use of blockchain-based platforms to record and manage provenance through the supply chain.

Issues around conflict minerals and similar are covered later, but here the discussion in terms of provenance is most often centred around more upmarket products. That includes controls to make sure products are linked to place of origin. "Champagne" can only be produced in a certain region of France, in a particular manner, and the premium Jersey Royal[123] new potato, the only potato that carries the EU Protected Designation of Origin mark of authenticity, must come from that island. [124]

"Agridex, the world's first digital market place for the 'farm to fork' $9 trillion agricultural and food sectors, today announces that it will go live before the fourth quarter of 2021. The Agridex market place, which already has garnered serious interest from [over 150] corporates across this global industry, automates the interactions between farmers, food producers, industrial, commercial, financial and governmental players around the globe and across the supply chains. By exploiting the efficiencies of smart contracts and the immutability and the quantum-safe security of the L3COS permissioned blockchain operating system, Agridex enhances transparency, food provenance and reduces transaction costs for every participant."

(Agridex press release, February 2021)

But provenance can be important even in less glamorous cases, such as the infamous scandal in 2013 which ended up with horsemeat finding its way into "beef burgers" and other processed food products. This had major repercussions for many firms from top to bottom of the relevant supply chain, and perhaps even contributed to the growth in veganism seen in recent years. It wasn't just the revulsion many consumers felt; other risks emerged. For instance, horses can be fed drugs that are not

123 https://www.jerseyroyal.co.uk/

124 Personally, I've always found you just stick seed potatoes in the ground and they grow, pretty much whatever you do or don't do to them!

safe to be introduced into the human food chain.

That case also highlighted the complexity of the supply chain – even for a non-manufactured product such as meat. Food manufacturer Findus announced that in a sample of eighteen beef lasagne products it tested, eleven contained between 60 and 100 per cent horsemeat. The source was a French firm called Comigel, which made the finished product in a factory in Luxembourg.

But Comigel blamed French meat supplier Spanghero. It looked like the meat had originated in Romanian slaughterhouses, and legally left there labelled as 'horse'. It then went, according to investigations, to a Cyprus-based firm, Draap Trading Ltd (Draap backwards spells Paard, which is Dutch for horse). Draap was owned by Jan Fasen, who had previously been convicted for horsemeat fraud in 2007. It was then sold to Spanghero in France, labelled as beef when it arrived at their plant, they claimed. Some processing took place, then Spanghero sold it on to Comigel. A tangled web indeed …

Fish as well as meat can be vulnerable to trickery. In 2019, Oceana, a not-for-profit organisation which campaigns to protect the world's oceans, conducted an analysis around US shops, restaurants and catering outlets. No less than 21 per cent of the 449 fish tested were mislabelled, and one out of every three establishments visited sold wrongly labelled seafood. Restaurants and smaller markets were the worst offenders, and sea bass and snapper were the species most often mislabelled – an incredible 55 per cent of the supposed 'sea bass' weren't in fact that fish at all.[125]

What is the motivation behind this? Imported seafood may be disguised as regional favourites, which can command a higher price, and tricks buyers who think they are sourcing local products. Vulnerable

125 https://usa.oceana.org/press-releases/oceana-finds-seafood-fraud-persists

species, such as Atlantic halibut, may be sold as more sustainable catches to get around the rules and quotas. And seafood is sold with generic names like 'sea bass', disguising lower-value species or masking health or conservation risks.

Animal Welfare, Biodiversity and Provenance in Context

Unlike issues such as waste or climate change, where almost every organisation can play its role, this is one of the PwP topics that is relatively binary. In other words, it is likely to be either a particularly important issue for a business, or one that does not matter much at all.

For a professional services firm, or a manufacturer of laptops, issues around biodiversity or provenance in the food supply chain don't come across the radar often – although when it comes to building a new factory or office on a greenfield site, bats, toads and rare plants might suddenly matter! But for a food manufacturing firm that buys meat and commodity raw materials, or a restaurant group or an industrial user of palm oil, these issues increasingly matter to consumers and other stakeholders.

This is also one of the more emotionally sensitive issues that we cover here. Many people feel passionately about issues such as animal welfare, and at the extreme, the actions of some groups have tipped over into what has been considered "terrorism". That can't be condoned, but it does provide more reasons for firms to be seen to act responsibly and sustainably when it comes to issues such as biodiversity and animal welfare.

The positive news is that it is often possible for organisations to have a real impact in these areas quickly. A more rigorous approach may well generate worthwhile benefits that appeal to stakeholders relatively easily. Switching to buying organic produce from certified farms might well be a "quick win" for a food manufacturer or restaurant chain. But don't underestimate the complexity in some areas. No single firm or even government seems to be having much success persuading President Bolsonaro of Brazil to try and stop deforestation in the Amazon, for instance, currently accelerating for commercial reasons.

Targets and metrics to assess progress can be useful in some of these areas. Moving to organic produce, or being able to show that your firm is not causing deforestation, or only buys sustainably caught fish are typical initiatives that are tangible and measurable.

Taking Action

- What should organisations be doing to address these areas? Different issues under the overall heading for this chapter do require somewhat different actions, but here are some ideas.
- In all cases, the understanding of suppliers and supply chain is a vital starting point. And in some of these examples, gaining that understanding right through the supply chain from top to bottom is vital. That can be seen in the horsemeat case, with its complex web of firms involved in meat processing.
- Many of the actions under this heading also require deep product (as well as supplier) understanding. To understand the provenance of your sea bass or "meat" needs more than a cursory understanding of specification and involves quite technical issues.
- For many procurement professionals, the help of internal colleagues in research, operations, or quality functions will be essential here to understand the complexities and drive change. These are often also areas where collaboration at industry, product or country level can be vital. One firm may find it hard to really make a difference; but all the major players working together in a certain market can make a big difference.
- Defining standards, codes of conduct or insisting on accreditations that suppliers must sign up to can provide a

useful starting point as part of the supplier qualification process. Adherence to standards can be used as a "yes/no" selection criterion. Evaluation of supplier process, product quality or sustainability actions taken by suppliers can also be assessed for rigour and quality as part of the supplier selection process.

- As usual, robust contract and supplier management processes need to be applied to make agreed supplier behaviour or actions "stick". Key provisions should be incorporated into contracts with appropriate incentives and penalties.

Chapter 20 – Sustainable Living with Unilever

Of all the businesses mentioned in this book, Unilever's name crops up more than any other. That is in part because of the breadth of their product range; but also because of their leadership position in the world of sustainable business and procurement.

But when Unilever's Sustainable Living Plan was launched in 2010, many weren't sure it was a very good idea. That included both outside analysts and insiders at the global consumer goods firm, who looked in shock at new CEO Paul Polman's pledges, made on behalf of the business. The three overarching commitments, to achieve by 2020, were:

- cut by 50% the environmental impact of its products in terms of water, waste and greenhouse gases;
- source 100% of its agricultural supplies from sustainable sources; and
- improve the health and well-being of one billion people across the world.

Those top-level targets were backed up by commitments including an increase in renewable energy to 40% of the total; reducing water consumption by 65% on 1995 levels; reducing waste sent for disposal by 70% on 1995 levels; and reducing levels of salt, fat and sugar in Unilever's food products.

Many thought there was no chance of hitting the targets, and some staff weren't sure how they were going to go about even trying! But since then, the firm has become a global leader in sustainable business. Whilst not every target has been achieved in full, Unilever was awarded the top corporate leadership ranking in the 2020 Sustainability Leaders Survey, for the tenth year running (2011–20).[126]

So, there were plenty of topics for discussion in the spring of 2020 when we spoke to Dave Ingram, the Chief Procurement Officer of the firm. He has been in the CPO role since March 2019, but is a Unilever veteran, having filled operational and supply chain roles all over the world for more than 20 years, although his Scottish accent is still evident. "That initial set of targets seemed impossible, and were way ahead of what we could have set. But really, you will never move past your current thinking if you don't start with something off the charts. In reality, we have probably hit 80–90% of the goals, which was way beyond expectations, given where we were starting from."

Stephanie Schmid was also part of our discussions; she has a very interesting role. "I lead on strategy and communications for the sustainability programme in procurement. That includes ensuring it is implemented with rigour, as well as talking about it, explaining why we are doing it and getting people excited, internally and externally."

Given he is still fairly new to procurement, how does Ingram see the function? "We are well regarded internally, but like the rest of the business, we can always improve. It was a shock when Heinz and Warren Buffett tried to buy the firm in 2017, but that maybe helped to increase focus. In procurement, we want to contribute to bringing purpose to the centre of the brand, be the number one partner of choice for innovation from our supply chain, and also deliver great value to the business."

In 2019, Unilever reviewed its sustainability commitments, "looking at

---

126 https://globescan.com/unilever-patagonia-ikea-interface-top-sustainability-leaders-2020/

how each brand lives the purpose, in terms of the product, the packaging, the advertising". Now, there are 15 long-term commitments, with the overarching aim that "brands grow, companies last and people thrive".

So, procurement has to work with purpose if it is to support those wider goals. "It has to be real if we're talking about what we're doing in our advertising, for instance," Ingram says. "It has to be impactful and meaningful, it can't just be about getting the right certifications." But it is not just about the customer drivers for sustainability; staff are important stakeholders, too.

"Of course, we still have to deliver value, and savings. But when people retire and review their contribution, they rarely say, 'I'm glad I saved a lot of money.' Staff want to feel they're here for more than that, they want to go beyond savings, to buy better and more responsibly."

Ingram, Schmid and their colleagues are helping procurement to "extend its wings", and work with a clearly communicated sense of purpose. But they recognise that this takes them into some difficult areas where nuanced discussions are necessary. "Sometimes it would be cheaper to move away from a sustainability position – we may be spending more than the competition. It might be tempting to look for the saving in that given year." But that temptation is resisted if it goes against the principles.

"Tea is a good example. We have stayed with our smallholders, the growers, even though we've been challenged by NGOs and charities, because those small growers are not always part of a certificated scheme". It would save money if Unilever just pulled out of buying tea from certain small countries altogether, Ingram explains. "But we commit, we stay, and try to drive change and improvements with them as partners."

He has mixed feelings about certification generally. "We look at sustainability and purpose through the lens of impact, not certification. We want to take action where that drives greater impact, independent of certification issues."

There are also challenges around innovation and partners who might help Unilever move into "white space" (new market and product areas). "Relationship management is a real challenge when half your business with a supplier is in these innovation and partnership areas, while the other half is in commodities – we need to use a range of procurement approaches".

For example, in the homecare sector, Unilever is working with the major petrochemical firms to develop innovative and more environmentally friendly products, but at the same time, those suppliers will be engaged in tough negotiations around bulk, commodity-type material supply.

Going back to the strategy and approach, Ingram is a believer in being stretched "beyond your existing knowledge base". The challenging targets drove that, but sustainability isn't always under your control. Governments, NGOs, financial markets can all impact on even well-made plans – "if you're looking at agronomy in developing markets, it is a complex picture".

One way procurement handles such complexity is by ensuring that the business owns various aspects of those key supplier partnerships that drive innovation and procurement with purpose. "We own the overall programme, the common platform and technology, but the business leaders own the relationships". It is key that this isn't seen as a land grab by procurement, Ingram emphasises.

What are the key factors that have enabled Unilever to become such an admired business in terms of these issues? We would suggest that the way sustainability is embedded in goals, deliverables and success measures must be part of that. "For senior managers, 30% of the long-term bonus is linked to sustainability metrics. And everyone in procurement will have some aspects of sustainability – relevant to their work – in their personal objectives." How many organisations can say that? we wonder.

Another impressive aspect is the three-way working between procurement, the business and suppliers. Procurement resources sit in each of the business pillars – whether that is a customer-facing division such as Homecare or internal services such as IT. And while cost is of course still important, "the focus has moved increasingly into working to drive innovation, growth and sustainable business".

For example, working with the American Cleaning Institute, the firm got 150 Homecare suppliers together to talk about the "clean future" strategy. As Ingram explains, "we were open with suppliers, we talked about how we want to move away from using virgin petrochemicals, and the long-term journey we've started. We were overt about the expectations we have of our suppliers, and our need to work with innovative firms who can directly impact our brands."

In Chile, a fully biodegradable handwashing product has been launched – "working with a partner, it took 10 years to design and launch this". So, there is great potential for suppliers but "we will want suppliers to make commitments to match ours – for instance, when it comes to providing a fair wage for staff".

Ingram and Schmid believe that technology is coming into play that will make supply chains much more transparent – in areas as diverse as land use (e.g. to check for deforestation), fair pay, or operational flows in commodities. "Some of the eye in the sky and 'sensing' technology has amazing potential – in some cases, this tech will be developed with suppliers, some will be third-party and industry-wide."

Such transparency might also bring a more positive view of some materials or products that are currently demonised, Ingram believes: "Also, it will help us know that the product we're buying is what we think it is – rather than risking a refinery blending good and less good products, perhaps". He calls it "unearthing the unknown".

But don't think this has all been easy for Unilever. There have been cost pressures along the way, but having purpose at the core of the business, and with a clear connection to the brand, have generally helped to resist the temptation to take the easy way out. There is also external pressure, even for Unilever with their exalted reputation, when "the media or NGOs expect you to achieve 100%, when that is practically impossible, and actually getting to 95% is a real achievement"!

Clarity from the top has also helped the firm handle these pressures – otherwise, "as soon as there is a hard call, it will be a commercial call". That's when we see greenwashing taking place. Too often firms talk a good talk, until taking the "right" action might actually cost them money. But Ingram believes that "we've made some big calls with suppliers, and we've tried to make them the right calls, not the easy calls".

Of course, Unilever aren't doing this purely to feel better about themselves. "The consumer will drive this, and we need to be ahead of the curve". Also, if businesses don't take action, ultimately there will be less business out there anyway. "You can't grow the business sustainably in a region that is water-starved or becomes uninhabitable through climate change"! That sounds like an obvious comment, but it is actually quite profound. A lack of action in these key procurement with purpose areas will affect everyone, including our businesses, in the long run.

We asked Ingram and Schmid if they had seen changes in the people working in procurement. "There still are different roles within the function – for many people it is still important that they understand how to run a tender, how to manage cost pressures. But even those people also need to be able to consider and address the innovation and sustainability goals. For a large proportion of the group, that's been fine, and indeed for some there is a real connection with the purpose agenda. But we do segment – we still have people for whom analytics, cost and negotiation are a major part of their role, so it does mean fitting personal capability and aptitude to the job requirements."

But almost everyone coming on-board now mentions the purpose agenda as one of the key reasons they want to join Unilever. Schmid reveals that they have surveyed this across countries to see where "purpose" seems to matter most to applicants. And the answer? Perhaps surprisingly, it is China! Young people in China are very concerned about these issues apparently, which seems very good news given that country's size and likely future impact on environmental matters.

The Unilever sustainability story in procurement and more widely is undoubtedly impressive, so it is well worth drawing some key learning points from it. Here are six important insights we took from our session.

- Having a clear and challenging goal or set of goals, even if they look scary to begin with, encourages innovation, focus and attention.
- Top-level support is vital, because there will be times when things don't go so well, and having both clarity of purpose and senior management backing is important.
- You will never keep everyone happy – you may feel good about helping small suppliers in the developing world to improve on certain issues, but someone somewhere will feel you should just get rid of them if they don't have the right "certification".
- Many key procurement with purpose initiatives require long-term and close collaborative working with key suppliers, and indeed with stakeholder colleagues. That needs considerable effort, and can be even more challenging if the same suppliers are also in the more "tactical supply" box in other supply areas.
- If you are serious about these issues, then they need to be embedded in functional and individuals' goals, objectives, and personal bonus plans. What gets incentivised, gets done.
- For the vast majority of procurement staff, the purpose agenda is a real positive – but be prepared to segment staff and jobs to reflect skills and aptitudes.

Chapter 21 – Modern Slavery and Human Rights

In 2019, a Sunday Times investigation uncovered the largest modern slavery ring found so far in the UK. Investigators found some of its 400 victims worked for as little as 50p a day, working on farms, rubbish recycling centres and poultry factories. Gang members, led by the Polish Brzezinski family, were convicted of modern slavery offences and money laundering. Farms which supplied top retailers such as Waitrose and Marks & Spencer were found to be using the slave labour.

This chapter was first drafted in early 2020, and was revised that summer when slavery had, perhaps surprisingly, knocked COVID-19 off the top of the national news headlines. The Black Lives Matter movement, the tragic death of George Floyd in Minneapolis and protests about statues which commemorated those involved in the slave trade centuries ago all brought oppression, inequality, discrimination and sheer human evil into sharp focus.

Yet there is a risk that some might think slavery is something that happened a long time ago. Knock down a few statues, and we can wipe our hands of it and move on. But such assumptions are false. The Modern Slavery Act in the UK in 2015 highlighted continuing problems, and issues remain all over the world.

Slavery – Yesterday and Today

A headline in *The Guardian* in 2019 was truly shocking: *"One in 200 people is a slave. Why?"* The lengthy article, from Kate Hodal, actually had an even more disturbing secondary headline, which was this – *"Slavery affects more than 40 million people worldwide – more than at any other time in history"*.[127]

That current-day figure compares to best estimates that about 12 million slaves entered the Atlantic trade between the 16th and 19th centuries, but about 1.5 million died on-board ship, so 10.5 million slaves arrived in the Americas. Just think about those numbers for a moment. The terrible days of the slave trade, with millions of individuals traded and transported across the seas with huge numbers dying in transit. The vast majority of those who did make it lived lives of brutality and oppression.

Yet in 2019, there were an estimated 40.3 million people living in some form of modern slavery, according to figures published by the UN's International Labour Organization (ILO) and the Walk Free Foundation. That represents more than three times the figure transported during the transatlantic slave trade.

There are some differences to acknowledge when we make those comparisons. A "modern slave" might have a tolerable life working in a factory in Southeast Asia, or in a cosmetic nail bar in Surrey or Sacramento. They are unlikely to be brutalised, or murdered, as plantation slaves often were. But if today's victims have had their passport confiscated until they have earned enough to pay back the trafficker who put them into the job, then they are not free. Neither are some young women working in nail salons or picking fruit in the fields for a few pounds a day, living in fear of their "gangmaster" deciding that they are a suitable

127 https://www.theguardian.com/news/2019/feb/25/modern-slavery-trafficking-persons-one-in-200

target for rape or other abuse.

According to abolitionist group Anti-Slavery International,[128] a person today is considered a "modern slave" if they are forced to work against their will; are owned or controlled by an exploiter or "employer"; have limited freedom of movement; or are dehumanised, treated as a commodity or bought and sold as property.

Slavery can often go hand in hand with other human rights abuses. Working conditions in terms of health and safety may be poor or outright dangerous. Those suffering may be involved in wider problems; "conflict minerals" may be mined using enslaved workers, for instance. So slavery can cover a number of different problem areas, including:

- people as property – traded between "owners";
- limited freedom of movement – through passport confiscation or physical restraint; and
- forced labour – through compulsory overtime, or long working hours.

In May 2019, The Sun newspaper in the UK reported that an "army of migrant workers are being paid just 82p an hour to build stadiums in Qatar ahead of the 2022 World Cup".[129] There were 28,000 people working in hot and often dangerous circumstances, and being paid £158 a month for a 48-hour working week. Amnesty International has claimed that some can't change jobs, aren't allowed to leave the country and, at times, have waited months to get paid.

Footballers and other sportsmen around the globe may be "taking the knee" to express solidarity with the Black Lives Matter movement, but there has been little apparent concern in the football world about the Qatar situation, or indeed about the stories of forced labour in the

---

128 https://www.antislavery.org/slavery-today/modern-slavery/

129 https://www.thesun.co.uk/sport/9110001/qatar-world-cup-stadium-builders-paid-82p/

factories of China. Here, the Uighurs Muslims of Xinjiang are being encouraged to renounce their religion and heritage, and according to reports are being conscripted into factory working around China.[130]

Some stories are even more shocking. Human trafficking often is linked to prostitution, so young women or even underage children are taken from their homelands with the promise of good jobs, then find themselves a long way from home and forced into the sex industry by their traffickers.

Understanding Forced Labour

There is also behaviour by employers that doesn't quite go to those extremes, but is still unacceptable. Forced labour is any work or service which people are forced to do against their will, or under threat of punishment. It may be linked to slavery, but it often happens to employees who are technically free, but are under pressure to work certain hours, or in a certain manner.

The classic example of forced labour might be people from one country who are working abroad, often a long way from home. They are forced by employers or agents to earn a certain amount or work for a period of time before their passport is returned to them. Or it might be factory workers told that they must work overtime or they will lose their job. At the worst extreme, even in supposedly advanced countries such as the UK, forced labour has involved women working in nail bars or even as prostitutes, or gangs exploiting vulnerable people in the fruit and vegetable picking sector. The boundary here between slavery and forced labour can be very thin.

Electronics Watch[131] is an independent monitoring organisation with the mission to protect the rights of workers in the electronics

130 https://www.bbc.co.uk/news/world-asia-china-51697800

131 https://electronicswatch.org/en/

industry. It encourages public sector bodies (in the main) to collaborate in order to monitor factories, mainly in Asia, that produce laptops, smartphones, servers and other equipment. It has found many cases of forced labour, sometimes in factories that produce equipment for the biggest names in technology.

Typically, those cases might involve young students from schools or colleges who are required to work in factories as part of "work experience" for their courses. In reality, they have no choice, and may not even be paid, or certainly not at the going rate for the job. Forced overtime for workers when orders are strong is another example. In recent years, Electronics Watch has been particularly successful in getting UK universities and colleges to support their work; a student in London (possibly of Asian origin themselves) really doesn't want to think that their laptop or smartphone has been made by someone their own age in a forced labour situation.

Bringing Transparency to Modern Slavery

The first UK government modern slavery statement was published in March 2020,[132] and it is more detailed than the word "statement" might suggest, being an impressive 29-page document. A "procurement policy notice" (PPN), guidance on the topic[133] and an assessment tool (MSAT)[134] were also launched.

The assessment tool is also very extensive and impressive. It is aimed at suppliers, and the top 34 "strategic suppliers" to government have all completed this. David Gigg was one of the senior civil servants heavily

---

132 https://www.gov.uk/government/publications/uk-government-modern-slavery-statement

133 https://www.gov.uk/government/publications/procurement-policy-note-0519-tackling-modern-slavery-in-government-supply-chains

134 https://supplierregistration.cabinetoffice.gov.uk/msat

involved in developing the policy and the tools, working within the Cabinet Office. *"The tool goes way beyond the Act, and gets into a lot more detail,"* he says. Crown Commercial Service, the central procurement unit for UK government, has also asked over 300 suppliers in high-risk spend categories like construction and IT to complete the assessment.

"It is relevant to firms large and small, and in many sectors," Gigg says, and he points out that cases such as the KozeeSleep prosecution[135] showed modern slavery could happen in the UK and even in a business which was supplying respected firms, including John Lewis. *"But in general, we haven't been using the big stick. It's been a case of getting suppliers on-board. We need businesses to want to do this, to look seriously at their supply chains, ask the right questions and take action where necessary."*

More positive work has been carried out by the University of Greenwich in London, a leading UK university in terms of research and education around modern slavery and related issues. Dr Olga Martin-Ortega and Anna Gorna from the University, along with the Business, Human Rights and the Environment (BHRE) Research Group, carried out a piece of research into how UK local councils were addressing these issues. This has been supported by the UK Local Government Association, and a very useful aide-mémoire has been published focusing on the "transparency in supply chains statements" that councils are required to produce under the Modern Slavery Act.[136]

It is presented as a series of "dos and don'ts" and makes a lot of sense. For instance, "if creating a stand-alone modern slavery policy, clearly set out the obligations on staff, suppliers, business partners and agents, as well as procedures to be followed". But equally, don't "make empty statements not

135 https://www.bbc.co.uk/news/uk-england-leeds-35363259

136 https://www.local.gov.uk/sites/default/files/documents/LGA_Modern%20Slavery%20Transparency%20in%20supply%20chains%20statements%20-%20Aide%20Memoire_May%202018.pdf

backed by policies or evidence – for example, a zero-tolerance approach".

That is a point made elsewhere in this book under a number of different headings. It is fine as a buyer to have a policy, saying "we won't tolerate this". But it is important to think carefully before (for instance) dropping a supplier instantly because of breaches of the policy. That often doesn't help anyone, even the victims of slavery themselves, who might just find themselves in a worse position if the better customers of their employer pull out.

"Should we exclude suppliers who don't have a robust modern slavery statement? It is an option in the procurement regulations currently, and it might be mandated one day. But it could have a negative impact on the actual workers involved, and the UK government guidance has up to now focused on working with current suppliers to improve the situation.""

(David Gigg, UK Cabinet Office senior official)

The best firms from a purpose point of view try and work with suppliers to put things right as a first step, rather than acting in haste. Electronics Watch has had considerable success in improving conditions for workers, by collaborating with factories and technology companies. It is a similar approach to that taken by the best food manufacturers, who have improved the lives of subsistence farmers through education and a collaborative, empathetic approach, rather than simply dropping suppliers who don't meet a target or standard.

Child Labour

A particularly emotive aspect of human rights abuse centres on child labour. In the world's poorest countries, around 25% of children are victims. Shockingly, in 2017, four African nations (Mali, Benin, Chad and

Guinea-Bissau) had over 50 per cent of children aged 5–14 working.[137]

There is good news; the number of children working around the world has fallen dramatically (from 25% to 10% between 1960 and 2003, according to the World Bank) as many developing countries have seen significant increases in wealth, meaning that families can survive without children needing to earn money. It is also worth remembering that not too long ago, young children worked in Western countries. Children as young as five worked in terrible conditions in Britain during the Industrial Revolution, and it is estimated that there were over 750,000 children under the age of 15 working in the United States in 1870.

Today, every responsible organisation wants to ensure that children are not working in their own supply chain. But stories still emerge with depressing frequency. For example, a report from France 24 looked at the mining of mica, a mineral much prized in cosmetic manufacturing.[138] Some 60% comes from two of India's poorest states, Bihar and Jharkhand, and there is evidence that it is often children doing the work (and missing out on their schooling) in illegal small-scale mining operations.

In Cambodia, children are working in brick kilns across the country, according to a Thomson Reuters Foundation exposé in 2020. Despite a government declaration that all furnaces were free of child labour following a crackdown, the practice continues, and often it is also combined with a form of forced labour, as families accept loans that then tie them into working for the owners.[139]

Agricultural work through history has relied on whole families contributing at busy times of the year – planting and harvesting, in

137 https://data.unicef.org/topic/child-protection/child-labour/

138 https://www.france24.com/en/asia-pacific/20200128-focus-dark-side-of-cosmetics-industry-child-labour-used-to-mine-mica-in-india-children-bihar-jharkhand-state

139 https://www.sightmagazine.com.au/news/14798-special-report-expose-reveals-child-labour-in-cambodian-brick-kilns-despite-crackdown

particular (the late-October school holiday was still called "potato picking week" in the north-east of England when I was growing up there.) While mechanisation has changed that in some countries and for some crops, child labour is still prevalent in many parts of the agricultural world. Whether it is cocoa beans in West Africa, roses in Southeast Asia, or vegetable seed production in India, there are still millions of children involved in work that at best affects their education and at worst puts their lives at risk.

In 2020, actor George Clooney, who comes from a farming background himself and is married to Amal Clooney, the leading human rights lawyer, was embarrassed, "surprised and saddened" after reports that coffee for use by Nespresso was being produced at six of its suppliers in Guatemala with the help of child labour. Clooney is very much the face of Nespresso, so the results of the investigation did not sit well with his (genuine) support for good causes and appropriate behaviour by business.

> "All of the farms in the cooperatives in this region of Guatemala are Rainforest Alliance and Fairtrade International certified. We rely on these organisations to certify compliance with all laws relating to child labour. On top of this, our 400 agronomists worldwide made 170,000 farm visits, many of which are unannounced. We will continue to engage with our partners to improve and strengthen the certification process."
>
> *(Nespresso website)*

Journalist Anthony Barnett was given access to farms in Guatemala, the world's 10th largest coffee producer, and film appeared to show children working for up to six days a week picking beans on plantations as well as moving heavy loads. Nespresso, which is a division of Nestlé, told CNN in a statement that it has "zero tolerance of child labour" and has launched a "thorough investigation" to identify the farms.[140] The company said it has stopped purchases of coffee from all farms in the region until they are able to guarantee child labour is not being used. But can any firm absolutely guarantee that their supply chain is perfect and free from issues?

Even with all of this effort from the buyers and well-intentioned organisations, there are still problems. So there should be sympathy for firms that are trying to do the right things, while recognising that procurement with purpose in areas such as this requires constant effort, vigilance and thought.

The Danger of Unexpected Consequences

As is often the case, sometimes the situation is more complex than it first appears. For instance, if a customer discovers that a supplier is abusing human rights – perhaps through forced overtime in their factories – and cancels the contract, the workers may find themselves out of a job and forced into penury or even prostitution in the worst case. In that Nespresso case, what happens to the families who depend on Nestlé's business, if that is suddenly withdrawn? It seems unlikely that would be good news, including for the children involved.

Even the seemingly obvious goal of eliminating child labour can have unforeseen complexities and consequences, as Bahar Ali Kazmi and Magnus Macfarlane of Warwick Business School highlighted in a 2003 book.[141] Their fascinating case study looked at the largely home-working industry of stitching leather footballs in the Sialkot District of Pakistan. In the 1990s, many households were engaged in this activity, and often everyone in the family contributed, including children.

140 https://edition.cnn.com/2020/02/26/business/george-clooney-nespresso-dispatches-intl-scli/index.html

141 https://www.amazon.co.uk/Business-Human-Rights-Dilemmas-Solutions/dp/1874719810

But in 1996, the international media, trade unions and others highlighted this use of child labour, and a strategy to eliminate it was agreed between the key business buyers, not-for-profit bodies and local organisations. Over the next few years, stitching was moved primarily into factories, child labour was virtually eliminated, and stitching became a more skilled and generally better paid occupation.

So that's a good news story, right? Well, yes and no. Alongside the undoubted positives, Kazmi and Macfarlane pointed out some negatives, too. For many families, the total family income declined because several of the youngsters who did contribute through a few hours' work a week no longer could. And if both parents had to take full-time jobs to recover that income, who would look after the children? In some cases, an older child had to give up their education to look after the younger, whilst mother and father went off to work in the nearest town. There was less flexibility, too – workers couldn't choose when and where to perform the work, but were locked into formal factory schedules and working hours. Again, that can be bad news for family coherence and happiness.

Now no one is suggesting that we want to see 8-year-olds spending 40 hours a week stitching footballs in a windowless, dingy shack somewhere. But this case does illustrate that there can be unintended consequences related to these tricky PwP issues, including negative outcomes for the "victims" themselves.

This is one of the reasons why the more enlightened charities suggest that firms should not instantly fire suppliers who are found to be "breaking the rules". Andy Davies was Head of the London Universities Purchasing Consortium and one of the driving forces behind campaigning group Electronics Watch. He is now procurement head at London's Natural History Museum, and puts it like this:

"It is easy to say we'll just drop a supplier if we find a breach of human rights, but that does nothing for the workforce involved if the firm just continues

as before minus your business, and perhaps even has to sack workers as a result".

Even if the employer has not been acting in a proper manner, the advice is for buyers to work with suppliers to improve matters, bearing in mind that the ultimate aim here is to improve the lives of the workers. Cutting ties should be a last resort if collaborative improvements don't work.

"Death Metal"

Most of the issues under this chapter's headings – child labour, modern slavery, forced labour – are evident when we look at conflict minerals or metals.

'Conflict minerals', metals and other materials are natural resources extracted or obtained in war zones and sold to help fund and perpetuate the conflict. Corruption and illegality often go hand in hand with these activities, and this process can even extend the conflict. A recent example was seen in the eastern provinces of the Democratic Republic of the Congo (DRC), where various armies, rebel groups, and others from outside the country have profited from mining, while contributing to violence and exploitation. Many mining operations are run by armed groups and militias, using slave labour to do the often unsafe or unhealthy work of extracting and processing the end products.

The provenance issues discussed in the context of food products can also be seen here, as the origins of what is bought and sold are often disguised from buyers. Diamond-mining and trading ('blood diamonds') is a major example of this problem, and even petroleum can be a conflict resource; ISIS used oil revenues from territories it controlled to fund terrorist and military activities.

There have been international efforts to reduce this trade, such as the Dodd-Frank Wall Street Reform and Consumer Protection Act in the US, which required manufacturers to audit their supply chains and report on the use of conflict minerals. However, problems remain.

Many large firms are taking action, though, as they see the potential reputational risk to their brand and also just want to "do the right thing". Apple has a good record in this area, being named the world's top company for responsible sourcing of conflict minerals for three years running up to 2017 by the Enough Project, a non-profit that works to put a stop to conflict and human rights violations in Africa's conflict zones.[142]

But other large firms fare less well. A study by the Responsible Sourcing Network in 2019 actually suggested that companies' attempts to conduct due diligence and report their practices had got worse overall compared to the previous year.[143] In terms of sectors, technology was the best, and the three bottom-performing industries were, for a second year in a row, integrated oil and gas, steel, and business services.

However, this is an area where new technology might prove useful, with blockchain technologies now being used to track and monitor provenance. De Beers Group, the world's largest diamond business, is working on Tracr, a blockchain-enabled solution that will provide a single tamper-proof and permanent digital record for every diamond registered on the platform. If the project is successful, it will be possible to ensure that all the diamonds registered on the blockchain platform are conflict-free and natural. Presumably, buyers will also be able to monitor the progress of the gems through the supply chain and from owner to owner.

Modern Slavery in Context

Why might this be a set of topics that an organisation would place high on its priority list? Firstly, in many countries, there is now legislation relating to modern slavery and related issues that organisations *must*

---

142 https://enoughproject.org/demandthesupply

143 https://www.mining.com/number-of-companies-ensuring-they-use-conflict-free-minerals-drops/

comply with or face penalties. For instance, the UK has the Modern Slavery Act, and conflict minerals issues are covered in the US by the Dodd-Frank Act.

It is also clear that many stakeholders – customers, staff, investors and more – do care deeply about these issues. Most employees would hate to think their organisation was enabling forced labour or worse; and there are cases where firms have been damaged by a lack of focus here. Reputational risk is very much an issue here, as in that Nespresso example, which was damaging not just for Nestlé but also for George Clooney, the brand ambassador.

Whilst eliminating modern slavery or child labour is a Herculean task, individual organisations can genuinely have an impact. Even making sure all your suppliers sign up to the right behaviour and legal commitments is a good start. Food companies (including Nestlé, Mars, Unilever and more) have had a real and measurable effect through the actions they have taken; it is very possible to create good news stories.

However, this is often a difficult topic to explore. The issues around human rights, forced labour or conflict minerals often lie at the beginning of the supply chain, with farming, mining or basic processing activities, and are often deliberately concealed or denied by the guilty.

That means it may be necessary to understand the supply chain all the way to basic commodities, metals, small-scale farmers or "artisan miners", a new expression which sounds rather lovely but can disguise extreme poverty and terrible working conditions. Indeed, some organisations may not even be aware of the metals or minerals used in the semi-manufactured products they buy, but these products might well be linked to these issues.

Determining the right steps to take is also challenging because there is limited data available. Firms or gangs who exploit workers don't tend to produce monthly statistics on "number of slaves employed". That means goals such as "eliminate modern slavery from our supply chain" are arguably meaningless, because it will always be hard to know for sure whether it has been achieved. Having a clear set of actions, well thought out and delivered, is more powerful than simply making bold statements.

So, whilst these challenges should not deter you from pursuing appropriate actions in this area, do be aware that persistence and effort may well be needed in order to make real progress.

Taking Action

What should organisations be doing to seek out and address human rights issues in their supply chains?

- The starting point again is to understand your suppliers and supply chains, in particular those that relate to your more significant spend items and highest-risk categories. That in itself may require some analysis to understand where the risks could lie.
- Organisations can implement codes of conduct or similar to which suppliers sign up, preferably with a verification process. Implementing auditing and inspection regimes within the supply chain to check on practices and behaviours can back up those actions.
- Building human rights-related issues into the supplier selection process is another option. That might be based on "yes / no" analysis (rejecting firms who don't meet the standards) or by favouring better suppliers in the scoring and evaluation process (see Chapter 7).
- Organisations can also pursue collaborative one-on-one activities with key suppliers through the contract and supplier management phase in order to help suppliers improve their

specific performance. That is often preferable to simply "sacking" suppliers, which may have serious unintended consequences for their staff, the very people who most need protecting.

- Wider collaboration is often a good option here. Organisations can work as part of industry, sector or geographically based groups that can conduct audits and inspections more efficiently, and can lobby effectively for improvements at government and senior levels.

Chapter 22 – Supporting Purposeful Causes and Associated Suppliers

> "Once the crisis has passed, we will need social enterprises working in our economy to ensure that the people who have been worst affected are supported and that we rebuild our economy in a way that helps people and planet. The climate emergency and growing social inequality are not going away due to COVID-19. If anything, they may get worse as governments focus on propping up the status quo."
> *(Andrew O'Brien, Social Enterprise UK)*

Most businesses exist with the principal objective of making profit for their shareholders. They may have other objectives, but profit and shareholder value are at the core of the capitalist system. But some organisations have different goals, and this chapter features those that exist also to support social goals and purpose. It also covers the ways in which buyers can support and promote a particular cause to their own supply base.

Charities, Social Enterprises and More

Charities are driven by a sense of purpose, so they exist primarily to help cure cancer, or to support ex-offenders, or to improve procurement skills in the economy. However, whilst many charities simply raise money from donations, some both support their causes and also act in a commercial manner. They can therefore be suppliers as well as simply fundraisers.

Other organisations may be categorised as social enterprises, *not-for-profits, or community-interest companies.* Other terms are used by various organisations in different countries, but all have at least some focus on underlying purpose beyond simple profit maximisation. There are also "standard" businesses, set up in a conventional manner, who nonetheless pursue purposeful social causes as an integral part of their operations.

From a procurement with purpose (PwP) standpoint, there are two options here. Firstly, you may wish to consider buying from organisations that already have a particular purposeful focus. In that case, you need to consider how best to support the supplier and the cause.

Secondly, buyers may promote a particular cause to their wider supply base, including those that do not currently support the purpose. For example, in the UK, the government department that supports disabled people within the wider benefits system (the Department for Work and Pensions) introduced an initiative some years back to encourage its major suppliers to consider employing more disabled people themselves. It did not mandate such action; but it did exert its persuasive powers quite strongly. The Department now supports the "disability confident" scheme, which 17,000 organisations have signed up to and encourages employers to make the most of the talents of disabled people.[144]

A Complicated Landscape

A charitable organisation or charity is a non-profit organisation whose primary objectives are philanthropy and social well-being (e.g.

144 https://disabilityconfident.campaign.gov.uk/

educational, religious, or other activities serving the public interest or common good). The precise legal definition of a charity varies from country to country, but most make their money from various forms of fundraising – donations, legacies and the like – and in some cases, also through commercial trading activities.

That might be charging for admission to a castle (the UK's National Trust), selling Christmas cards (every charity in the UK, apparently) or charging an annual membership fee (the Chartered Institute of Procurement and Supply), or providing services. Today, many larger charities earn money from governments: for example, through providing support in the health and welfare area on a contracted basis.

Kavita Cooper is the founder of consulting firm Novo-K, whose core business is working with charity organisations to help them improve their own procurement performance.[145] She therefore sees how those organisations are also implementing PwP initiatives themselves. Not surprisingly, many of them look to support suppliers who share similar values or focus on issues that are aligned with their own core charitable purpose. So, a charity focusing on refugees or modern slavery might take a particular interest in how human rights issues are being managed by their suppliers and in the wider supply chain.

But there are problems sometimes for organisations to find the sort of suppliers they seek, as smaller firms and charities in particular are often not good at promoting their own values. *"It's important they do that, for their own sake, as more organisations – including their own customers, of course – get behind the procurement with purpose movement,"* Cooper says.

She has also taken steps in her own business that are related to wider purpose. So, every time the firm wins a contract, it makes a donation to the MicroLoan Foundation, which supports women-owned businesses

145 https://www.novo-k.com/

in Africa with small loans. Micro-finance schemes seem to show very positive returns, both financially and in terms of social value. (Cooper herself was born in Hertfordshire but has both Indian and East African family background.) She also uses the Work for Good[146] fundraising platform, which makes it easier for small firms to donate to charity.

"Given our size, our actions may not mean much in the global scheme of things, but we've always tried to think about purpose in everything we do. We implemented a no single-use plastics in the office policy some time back, and we look at sustainability in everything we buy."

Social enterprises, unlike charities, are *primarily* commercial organisations, but they exist to drive improvements in purposeful areas (social, environment, or economic) alongside their business goals. There are several types of social enterprise and in different countries there may be different terminology used to describe them. Some may be "co-operatives", with staff or customers having ownership of some type, some are fully not-for-profit, and some make profit for their owners alongside their social purpose.

Whilst there is nothing intrinsically wrong with any of these approaches, the variety of organisations under this heading does provide a note of caution for buyers in terms of understanding just how much positive activity and social benefit is being generated by any specific enterprise.

There have even been questions about apparent fraud committed by the trustees of charities, and the logic of certain "social enterprises" appears dubious. For instance, a legal services venture, LGSS Law, set up by several UK local councils, lost money and was closed down in early 2021. Observers asked why it was ever set up as a social enterprise,[147]

146 https://workforgood.co.uk/how-it-works/for-businesses/

147 https://www.cambstimes.co.uk/news/law-firm-part-owned-by-ccc-loses-1-2m-1-6452237

and any buyer who gave work to that venture, thinking they were supporting a good cause, would appear to have been sadly mistaken.

Social Enterprises in Focus

However, on the positive side, there is no doubt that social enterprises can generate major benefits and achieve real positive outcomes. Social Enterprise UK (SEUK), an umbrella body for such organisations, has many positive stories concerning its members' achievements across a wide range of good causes. SEUK also published a report in 2019[148] based on a survey of over a thousand enterprises, which suggested they were outperforming UK business generally. 52% of the enterprises grew their turnover in the previous year.

Social enterprises tend to address a particular cause, which they do through the staff they employ, by raising money for that purpose, or through both those routes. For instance, *auticon* is an IT consulting firm that provides employment opportunities for people on the autism spectrum, who often have extraordinary technical or cognitive abilities. It employs more than 150 IT consultants on the spectrum in the UK, US, Germany, Italy and France. In the UK, consultants work on IT projects for clients including Linklaters, KPMG, RBS, Experian and GlaxoSmithKline. As the firm says:[149]

"By creating autism-positive work environments and offering highly individualised, sustained support mechanisms to autistic employees, auticon provides its corporate clients with a means to tap into the amazing talents of autistic people while creating well paid long term careers for its team."

There are many examples of such organisations, of different sizes and

148 https://www.socialenterprise.org.uk/wp-content/uploads/2019/10/Capitalism-in-Crisis-State-of-Social-Enterprise-Report-2019.pdf

149 https://auticon.co.uk/company/

structure. H.M.Pasties is a limited company, founded by a former young offender, that produces pasties and other baked goods and employs people with criminal convictions.[150] The Forward Trust is a charity with a turnover of over £20 million, and its work includes delivering services as a supplier to public sector bodies in the field of drug and crime rehabilitation.[151] It also employs ex-addicts and offenders itself. Other organisations focus on employing disabled people or youngsters who have had disadvantaged backgrounds.

In other cases, the social enterprise acts commercially to raise money for its cause. Frank Water was founded in Bristol, UK in 2005 with the aim of funding safe drinking water, sanitation and hygiene to marginalised communities in India and Nepal. To do this, they take their bespoke refill service to music festivals and events where they serve chilled, filtered water to customers and sell refillable water bottles, cups and other merchandise. They also sell artesian spring water in glass bottles to restaurants, bars and cafes around the UK. Profits fund their work in India and Nepal – "Water for Water".[152]

But social enterprises are not just a UK phenomenon by any means. One of the best known globally is Grameen Bank – "the bank for the poor",[153] launched in 1976 by Muhammad Yunus. He essentially started the microcredit revolution, and for over 40 years, he provided small loans and banking opportunities to small business operators around the globe without requiring collateral. That has shown the power of business solutions to tackle the underlying causes of poverty, as many of the recipients have thrived and created employment and wealth in impoverished areas.

---

150 https://hmpasties.com/about-us/

151 https://www.forwardtrust.org.uk/about-us/

152 https://www.frankwater.com/

153 https://grameenbank.org/

The Buy Social Corporate Challenge

So there is a wide range of potential purpose-related options for a buyer to consider. Your organisation might want to focus on a particular area, having carried out the strategic prioritisation process described earlier in the book. Or supporting social enterprises and charities as suppliers generally might be a worthwhile objective.

In 2016, Social Enterprise UK launched its "Buy Social Corporate Challenge", in which a group of high-profile firms set a target to spend £1 billion with social enterprises. Whilst the initiative has been very positive and has focused attention, spend to date (in 2020) is £65.2 million according to SEUK, which shows that there is still a long way to go to establish social enterprises as a significant force in the supply market.

The major firms who pioneered this initiative on the buy-side included Wates, Interserve, PWC and Johnson & Johnson (J&J). At an SAP Ariba event in 2018,[154] Timo Worrall, the Director of Supplier Social Responsibility from J&J, and Colin Downie, from WildHearts, a social enterprise, were interviewed by Martine Booth from SAP. WildHearts Group is "a portfolio of companies that, through their activities and profits, create global social change".[155] Booth asked whether this was all really a marketing ploy from J&J.

No, said Worrall: *"We don't market this activity, we don't talk about it much. But it is built into our culture – the J&J credo goes back 75 years, and our priority is to serve customers and communities. We are aiming to use our procurement power to support this. This is just the right thing to do, it makes us feel good, our employees want to contribute, and it is part of our culture. But in terms of process, we have a long way to go … the passion is great, but execution is key."*

---

154 https://spendmatters.com/uk/procurement-with-purpose-jj-and-wildhearts-take-centre-stage-at-sap-ariba-summit/

155 https://www.wildheartsgroup.com/about/

Colin Downie, speaking as a supplier, said this. *"Many social enterprises evolved from the not-for-profit sector. We started with a view to make profit for our foundation – if you can buy from us at same price as from other suppliers, why not buy from us, and help do some good at the same time? We report to every customer in terms of what they have spent and how many lives that has saved and how many people we have helped! We act commercially, we don't raise funds from other routes and we want your business."*

Talking to several firms who signed up to the Corporate Challenge, they are generally enthusiastic and willing to put more work the way of social enterprises. The difficulty is sometimes in finding suitable organisations who are producing the goods and services corporate buyers need. *"Many social enterprises are aiming at the retail market, which is fine, but that's not what we buy,"* the procurement head from a major construction firm explained.

Supporting Employees with Health / Disability Issues

Another aspect within this broad topic relates to the employment of disabled people.[156] In the Western world it is estimated that some 10% of the population have physical disabilities or health conditions that can affect their employment opportunities and capabilities. That can range from the very obvious – people who are blind, or paraplegic, perhaps – to those with less visible issues, such as those with diabetes or chronic fatigue syndrome. This area also aligns with the UN Sustainable Development Goals. Goal number 3 is "good health and well-being" and goal 10 talks about reducing inequality, including that based on disability.

Looking at mental health issues, the numbers are even more striking. An estimated 25% of UK citizens will experience issues at some time

156 We will use the shorthand of "disability" in this section to include all types of disability and health conditions.

in their lives. That percentage has grown, rather than shrunk in recent years, which may represent more diligent measurement of those affected, or the increased pressure of modern life. Blame social media, consumerisation, the Kardashians, the breakdown of religious and community values, or the Daily Mail sidebar of shame, but whatever the cause, more seem to suffer.

The history of disabled people in employment, particularly physically disabled, is interesting. In the UK, Remploy was set up after the First World War to provide employment for veterans who had returned from the front line with injuries, often terrible in nature.[157] Factories were set up, to this day termed "sheltered workshops" in European procurement regulations, where people could carry out meaningful work in a supportive environment. That ranged in the case of Remploy from packing car accessory kits for major automotive firms, to manufacturing furniture, or (in more recent years) monitoring CCTV film remotely as security operatives. Corporate buyers could support the cause by using Remploy as a supplier.

However, as time went by, charities supporting the sector, the disabled community and progressive employers started questioning whether this was the best approach. A consensus gradually emerged that for the vast majority of disabled people, working in a less segregated environment was better for the individual. As employing organisations became more progressive and legislation supported this (through pushing organisations into having better access for disabled people, for instance), the movement away from sheltered workshops continued.

There is absolutely no reason why an amputee can't do pretty much any office or management role. Individuals with Down's Syndrome are highly valued by many employers – there are great stories of those

157 Peter Smith served as a non-executive director for Remploy for several years.

staff being the only ones to make it to work when a blizzard hits the supermarket. auticon, as mentioned earlier in this chapter, provides employment opportunities for people on the autistic spectrum, many of whom have proved to be brilliant in certain IT roles. So helping those with disabilities or health conditions find meaningful employment in the mainstream has become a very worthwhile goal.

Putting Diverse Suppliers Into Context

Working with suppliers who themselves are achieving social good (by employing certain types of people, or supporting other social benefit actions) can obviously contribute to the buying organisation's procurement with purpose programme. But it also relates to a wider issue of *supplier* diversity that is relevant to general procurement approaches and strategies.

Underlying the PwP messages in this chapter and the next is the idea that organisations should seek to develop a diverse supply chain, including suppliers that support wider social purpose, or represent a different sort of business to the "usual suspects". Whereas some topics such as deforestation are only really relevant to certain organisations, this principle of diversity in the supply chain is relevant to every organisation.

Over the years, various strategies have led to a situation where too many organisations see a relatively small number of very large firms dominating their supply chain. The procurement profession has driven this itself to a large extent. Strategies around aggregation, leverage, and supplier reduction have led to organisations boasting that "we have reduced our supplier numbers from 10,000 to 1,000".

But is that really a good thing? Whilst there are some advantages in those approaches, it has often made it harder for small, minority-owned or new firms, or unconventional businesses such as social enterprises, to become suppliers to large organisations. And that can have disadvantages for the buyer, too.

Having too few suppliers can be just as problematic as too many, as seen in terms of PPE (personal protective equipment) supply to the UK National Health Service and other health organisations globally during the pandemic. Risk was not managed well, as "leverage" had driven the NHS to a strategy of aggregating, relying on a few very large suppliers and driving down the price.

Greater diversity of suppliers could bring benefits for many organisations. In general, smaller firms can be more flexible than giant businesses. Start-ups bring innovation. Social enterprises can provide different approaches or ways of looking at the world that can benefit their customers. This also creates more competitive markets; where a few giant firms dominate a market, that can lead to unhealthy behaviour or poor performance from a buyer's perspective.

So whatever PwP causes you and your organisation choose to support, bear in mind that being open to new and diverse suppliers and encouraging a dynamic supply chain is not purely about wider purpose. It can also have very direct benefits for organisations looking to improve performance through having a broad range of effective suppliers in place.

Taking Action

So how can buyers take action in this particular PwP area?

- Organisations can look to buy more from suppliers that demonstrate a particular purpose, or from a range of such suppliers, e.g. all social enterprises. That can be done by setting aside a certain amount or element of spend for such organisations, or by making sure they are represented as options when it comes to supplier selection. In that case, they may still be required to compete on a level playing field, or the buyer may want to "tilt" the field somewhat (see Chapter 7).

- Elements of "social value" (as defined in the public sector) or wider benefit can be included in the selection process, giving purposeful supplier organisations the chance to put that forward as part of their proposal. Or "conventional" suppliers might be encouraged to support the causes in their own supply chains.
- Where the approach is to encourage all suppliers to support purposeful causes, some buyers allow bidders to propose which aspects they want to focus on. However, it is usually better to direct propositions towards the areas of greatest strategic interest to the buying organisation. So, a buyer might stipulate that suppliers will be expected to take action to employ more disadvantaged people as part of contract delivery, if that is the sort of social value / wider purpose value that is most desired.
- Even if it is not part of the supplier selection process, suppliers (existing and/or potential) could be encouraged to adopt a more "purposeful" approach, perhaps using social enterprises in their own supply chain, or by adopting a particular social cause themselves.
- As usual, whatever is agreed with and by suppliers needs to be followed up through the contract and supplier management phase of the relationship.

Chapter 23 – Supporting Diversity in the Supply Base

"One company can create champions of change by choosing the right supplier. With inclusive supply and value chains, entire communities become more empowered, more sustainable, and more innovative. Accenture is committed to promoting inclusive, ethical and sustainable procurement practices that create long-term value for our clients, our suppliers and our communities."
(Accenture website)

This procurement with purpose (PwP) topic shares some similarities with the ideas outlined in the previous chapter, as both support the idea of encouraging *supplier diversity*, which can generate benefits for any organisation. But in this case, rather than buying from a supplier because that organisation is supporting a particular *cause*, under this heading the buyer is promoting diversity by:

i. encouraging suppliers to focus on diversity (as well as inclusion and equality in most cases) within their own organisation; and/or
ii. supporting suppliers that have a particular characteristic themselves, generally in terms of size, location or ownership.

Back to "Social Value" and Government Preferences

Whilst this type of purposeful activity is not restricted to the public sector, many governments have introduced policies to support certain businesses because of their ownership, size or business location. In some countries, that is primarily aimed towards support for SMEs (small and medium enterprises). Another common initiative is for public bodies (or indeed private firms) to support buying from minority-owned firms, through setting targets or even quotas.

The reasons for such government policies are varied. Some argue it is to support worthwhile causes, such as helping military veterans get back into civilian life. Smaller firms might be seen as a group that can provide economic stimulus to the country. But the cynics might say that such moves are primarily about winning votes; from small business owners, veterans, women, or whichever group is being favoured.

The definition of what is included under the "minorities" heading varies. It might cover firms owned by people from ethnic groups, woman, disabled people or military veterans. Or organisations may wish to support local businesses, based on where the supplier operates from or head office location. That is a significant aspect of "social value" as used now in the public sector sense, as it is often a key driver for local government at city, state or regional level. In the post-pandemic world, with economies struggling for some time to come, there is likely to be more focus on that sort of approach.

However, there are questions and issues to be addressed here, at both strategic and operational level. In some cases, the strategy is clear, but execution has not lived up to expectations. Various governments in developing countries, for instance, have tried to give preference to suppliers owned by their own citizens, or to certain ethnic groups. But the results have not always been as hoped.

Perhaps the best-known global example is the key role public procurement plays in South Africa's broad-based black economic empowerment (BBBEE) framework, aimed at reversing historic racial injustice and inequality. The US government also has policies in place to support a number of different types of businesses through "set-asides", when contracts are reserved for certain firms. According to the US General Services Administration website, these are:[158]

- Women-Owned Small Businesses (WOSBs)
- Small Disadvantaged Businesses, also called 8(a) Small Businesses
- Historically Underutilized Business Zones (HUBZone) Small Businesses
- Service-Disabled Veteran-Owned Small Businesses (SDVOSB)

But there is limited evidence that these policies really deliver against the stated goals. In terms of South Africa, for instance, a 2019 paper[159] from Shai, Molefinyana and Quinot found that there is a significant "knowledge gap" that makes analysis of the outcomes difficult, and that *"the intervention's effectiveness has largely been undermined by various challenges and demonstrates that it remains unclear whether BBBEE's observed achievements have translated into targeted impact of meaningful participation of all black people in the economy"*.

Many consider that the policies have led to more corruption in that country, by muddying the waters when it comes to choosing suppliers to win government contracts. Certainly, South Africa's economy has declined dramatically in recent years, with corruption a key element of that failure. If these policies around preference are not managed carefully, being seen as the right sort of business (and having the right contacts, of course) can become more important than your actual capability to do the work competently and at a fair price.

158 https://www.gsa.gov/small-business/-become-a-gsa-vendor/explore-business-models/-setasides-and-special-interest-groups

159 https://www.mdpi.com/2071-1050/11/24/7164/htm

The UK Government's SME Programme – Is There Any Evidence of Success?

In the UK, there has been no analysis of the government's SME (small and medium enterprises) policy, which has consistently failed to meet its targets for awarding a certain percentage of government spend to smaller firms, mainly because those targets were and still are fundamentally unachievable.

From the beginning, the UK government was never on top of this policy initiative. The initial talk of "target" then became an "aspiration", and spend by large suppliers with smaller firms down the supply chain was allowed to count against the target, despite the fact that few of the large firms actually measured that spend.[160]

The initial target of 25% of spend going to SMEs was not achieved, but then it was increased to 33%, presumably just to have something to say about SMEs in the 2105 election manifesto. (Experts and civil servants were allegedly not consulted about the increase.) But the Ministry of Defence, which buys aircraft carriers, fighter jets and tanks, is never going to spend more than a limited percentage of its money with small suppliers, and tiny construction firms aren't going to build motorways or power stations. A high proportion of the total spend was never suitable for SMEs, so the targets were and still are fundamentally unachievable.

Needless to say the government is still way short of 33%, and it seems that such approaches are really about politics. There is no evidence that any benefits have accrued from this policy over the years; no analysis has been published. There is also an argument that the efforts would be better directed at supporting innovative start-ups, or social enterprises

160 That all prompted a "Yes Minister" spoof on the Spend Matters website: https://spendmatters.com/uk/minister-another-change-sme-aspiration/

and other firms that have a real purpose, rather than firms that happen to be "small".

It is also important to note that there are ways of helping particular firms without introducing overt bias into the procurement process. Buyers can offer training in bidding techniques for smaller firms, or invite potential local suppliers to "meet the buyer" events. Engagement before formal competition starts can help bidders understand what is required of them. As Julie Welsh of Scotland Excel says, *"there is much that public bodies can do without bending the rules to help local companies.... We encourage leaders to be creative, to engage with suppliers and to think about a solutions perspective rather than simply process."*

Let's Be Positive!

Cynicism about the UK government's SME programme does not mean we should reject this whole category of procurement with purpose activity. There is no doubt, for instance, that small firms, start-ups in particular, can often provide the most innovative and appropriate goods or services to the benefit of their customers.

Every organisation should be open to innovation in its supply chain, and that means being open to new suppliers and pursuing a diverse supply base. Using the same huge, well-established firms as suppliers, just as all your competitors do, will rarely bring the competitive advantage that all private sector firms seek.

Smaller firms can also at times be highly competitive, as they may not be burdened by large firm overheads. They may be able to move faster, or offer a more tailored or personal service. And supporting minority-owned businesses can contribute towards more fairness and less discrimination in society. So this sort of PwP action has its merits, but it must be well thought out and executed.

Firms may want to demonstrate their support for a diverse supply chain in order to improve their own reputation with customers. They may also want to be seen to be a good citizen in a country, region or city; these are all worthwhile objectives that can be supported by a supplier diversity approach. One of the most impressive and successful examples of this comes from technology, solutions and consulting giant Accenture. In 2018, Accenture's Supplier Inclusion & Diversity Program was ranked as the best such programme by DiversityInc.[161]

One aspect of this[162] is the "Diverse Supplier Development Program" (DSDP), in which senior Accenture executive mentors are matched for 12–18 months with diverse supplier "protégé" companies to help them grow their businesses. In turn, the hope is that Accenture, its clients and communities benefit from innovative contributions from the firms involved. Developing diverse suppliers also strengthens communities by creating more businesses, jobs, and economic growth. The DSDP currently runs in four countries: Canada, South Africa, United Kingdom and United States.

Whilst the firm has implemented the wider supplier programme in 17 countries, it probably has the most benefit in less-developed parts of the world. It is also interesting that Accenture has spread its focus quite widely. So, it works with organisations that represent different issues – promoting women, ethnic minorities, LGBT and disability groups. The organisations include:

- WEConnect International (collaboration in 14 countries)
- Women's Business Enterprise National Council (WBENC)
- National Minority Supplier Development Council (NMSDC)
- National LGBT Chamber of Commerce (NGLCC)

---

161 https://suppliertynews.com/2018/05/13/diversityinc-releases-list-of-top-15-companies-in-supplier-diversity/

162 https://www.accenture.com/gb-en/company-supplier-inclusion-diversity

- MSDUK
- Disability:IN

Supporting Minority-Owned Businesses – the MSDUK Story

Back in 2014, I started writing on the Spend Matters website about MSDUK, an organisation that supports minority-owned businesses in the UK and helps them to become more successful.[163] Mayank Shah, the founder and CEO, is Indian by birth, and came to the UK in 2000 to do an MBA, then academic research into supplier diversity. Part way through his PhD, the idea for MSDUK was born and the academic life was put on hold. With backing from the East Midlands Development Agency, the not-for-profit organisation was founded in 2006, based in Leicester.

MSDUK works in a couple of ways. It actively looks to match minority-owned suppliers in their database with corporate buyers who make contact, saying, "we want to work with more or better diverse suppliers". Secondly, the organisation looks to proactively help their supplier base, by organising "meet the buyer" and other events, or providing training and education to help firms perform and bid better in order to win more work.

In 2016, I interviewed Ross Mandiwall for the Spend Matters website. At that time, he was IBM's Head of Procurement for UK / Ireland.[164] He spoke about his relationship with the organisation.

"Our work with MSDUK is an increasingly important route for us to identify diverse suppliers – around a quarter of our diversity spend in the UK is through MSDUK members now. And every one of our category managers has a personal KPI related to their use of diverse suppliers, so they will use different routes to find those firms but they are all incentivised to do that."

He explained one particular success story: *"We have a minority-owned*

---

163 https://spendmatters.com/uk/supplier-diversity-msduk-event-looks-to-make-it-happen/

164 https://spendmatters.com/uk/ross-mandiwall-ibm-thoughts-supplier-diversity-msduk/

provider in the staffing sector. We initially recommended that they might work through a much larger prime contractor. They didn't want to do that, and eventually they won a small part of our business. More recently, they have been appointed as one of our four prime contractors in that spend category, a large contract, and even our most 'challenging' internal stakeholders love them!"

But he acknowledged that sometimes using diverse suppliers bumps up against the supply base consolidation goal that is often another priority: reducing supplier numbers, more aggregation, and so on.

"We have to target which categories are most appropriate and be honest with the market, and firms have to be realistic about what is possible – that will give them a greater chance of success."

The IBM approach was not to create a bias in the procurement process either. *"We are trying to be open to these suppliers, but they have to compete on a level playing field, add value, and show innovation to become suppliers. But if you see where many of the MSDUK suppliers are based, in more underprivileged areas, you realise just what social impact they can have as they grow and succeed. I'm aiming to open doors for them that might not otherwise have been open, giving firms the opportunity to pitch their wares. Then it is up to them to bring their value and innovation to IBM."*

Helping "Disadvantaged" Firms – Without Introducing Bias

Overtly favouring firms with a particular characteristic, while sometimes politically attractive, is relatively unproven in terms of real results and outcomes at government level. Certainly, introducing a bias in selecting suppliers can lead to perverse outcomes if it is not done carefully.

However, there is much that can be done to support supplier diversity, including smaller or minority firms, without taking that step. The IBM comments and the Accenture scheme mentioned earlier are both excellent examples of that, and there are many ways of helping diverse suppliers without tilting the level playing field too much. That includes supplier open days, or mentoring and advising firms so they understand how they can compete better for work.

Making sure that procurement strategy and operations are not intrinsically biased against smaller or minority-owned firms is simply good practice, independent of outcomes. Over the years, a number of business and procurement strategies have (perhaps accidentally) made life harder for smaller firms.

Here are five key barriers; if you want to support diverse suppliers without introducing overt bias into your selection processes, then you should at least ensure these issues are not accidentally making life difficult for such firms.

- *Buyers aggressively aggregate their own spend*, believing they'll get better deals if they offer bigger contracts – until in some industries, only the largest can meet the needs.
- *Buyers value consistency above innovation and experimentation*, and prove unwilling to take the "risk" of new suppliers.
- *Buyers set tighter and tighter specifications* either directly or through demanding accreditations and so on, again locking many potential suppliers out of the picture.
- *Buyers group together disparate bundles of goods or service*s into larger packages of work, such as "total facilities management" contracts or using "IT integrators", meaning fewer suppliers can handle that large span of work, particularly smaller firms.
- *Buyers make tendering and bidding for work expensive and difficult*, so small firms find it hard to compete against bigger bidders.

Good procurement should always mean seeking the best suppliers, whatever their nature, and that means being open to new suppliers, and having approaches that help ensure dynamic, competitive markets in all key supply areas. Being mindful of those warning factors, and how they can restrict competition, is a key part of achieving good results.

Dinosaurs!

Andy Davies was mentioned earlier as a contributor to making Electronics Watch, a successful collaborative organisation, focused on improving human rights in the electronics supply chain. But he also provides a case study of how a buyer can maximise market interest and achieve a strong field of potential suppliers, including diverse businesses, for an interesting and specialist procurement.

Actually, for "specialist", read "unique". Davies now leads procurement for London's Natural History Museum, a global leader in its field. The role is always fascinating, but occasionally something very unusual hits his desk. In 2020, the Museum decided that it should commission metal models of a handful of its most iconic dinosaur exhibits, such as the famous *Diplodocus carnegii*. These would be displayed outside the museum as part of the Urban Nature Project to develop the green spaces around the building.

This procurement was potentially of interest to specialist metal foundries and other quite small, specialist businesses. However, the museum also had to follow government procurement regulations, and run a formal competitive process. Davies realised that this might create barriers for certain potential bidders. *"I talked to a number of small foundries. They wanted to bid for it, but I was concerned that when they download the document and start reading about award criteria, insurances, terms and conditions, and so on, they might not feel like even trying!"*

So Davies organised a webinar that all bidders could participate in, during which an independent expert talked through the public procurement process, highlighting key issues and generally demystifying the process. Bidders were encouraged to ask questions, but Davies himself did not participate. *"I wanted to create a safe space, where they could ask anything and not worry that they might seem to be asking daft questions!"*

Around a dozen firms participated in the session, and while at the time of writing the winning bid has not been selected, it looks like a good field of bidders was achieved, with several small but impressive firms in the running.

There are other notable examples of buyers in local government providing training and education for suppliers, particularly smaller, minority-owned or local firms. This appears to be a useful and positive initiative that supports diverse suppliers, without risking some of the potential downsides of using overt favouritism.

Encouraging Actions within Supplier Organisations

Up to now, this chapter has focused mainly on supplier "diversity" in the sense of the organisation's ownership or size primarily. But there is also the question of how diverse a supplier is in terms of its own staff, which is relevant to the wider drive for greater diversity, equality, and inclusion (DEI). For instance, a supplier owned by a female from a minority background might look good in terms of ownership, but if it turned out to employ exclusively white middle-aged men other than the owner herself, that would hardly help to achieve the desired wider societal goals.

The logic here is about both fairness and performance. Most people agree that firms should not discriminate purely on gender, age, race, appearance or sexuality when recruiting or making decisions on jobs, pay or similar. There is also emerging evidence that diverse organisations tend to succeed compared to those with a more mono-culture. The dangers of "groupthink" have been highlighted in cases ranging from the Space Shuttle disaster to various financial crashes, and organisations that embrace a diverse workforce are perceived to have a better change of avoiding such problems. Both of those imperatives suggest that buyers should encourage diversity within each of their suppliers, as well as looking at the *overall* diversity of their supply base.

So buyers are increasingly asking to know more about the make-up of suppliers' workforces, and about the policies and practices that support DEI. That can be done using the tools and techniques discussed at greater length in Section 3. Buyers can start by asking potential suppliers to confirm whether they have DEI policies in place. That might be a "tick-box" exercise, but it would at least start to focus attention.

The next step might be to ask for diversity data – what is the male/female ratio at different management levels of the firm? How many women or non-white people sit on the Board? What about pay differentials? In the UK, since 2018 the Government Equalities Office has required all organisations with more than 250 employees to publish their gender pay gap figures annually. And similar questions could apply to racial data, disability, or sexual preferences, although few firms collect extensive data yet across all those areas.

The next step for buyers is to actually assess potential suppliers' performance and incorporate that into the supplier selection process (see Chapter 7). In a recent major tender for the UK Government, the Crown Commercial Service (which puts contracts in place on behalf of many public sector bodies) asked bidders to describe their existing and planned activities to tackle inequality and to improve diversity in their workforce, covering women and what was described as "Under-Represented Groups", across issues including recruitment, employment, skills and pay.

The tender also asked how bidders would collect data, report on progress and drive improvement, which was good to see – effective contract management is vital in so many of these areas, as discussed throughout this book. That question was worth 5% of the total marks for the tender, supporting the social value procurement legislation and guidance now relevant in the UK, with similar approaches increasingly seen elsewhere.

Once contracts are in place, organisations can continue to work with their suppliers both in that formal contract management sense and also with collaborative actions to encourage better performance in the DEI areas. Such collaboration could be one-to-one or apply across a wider group of interested parties. Again, this principle applies in everything from human rights in the developing world to employment of more people with disabilities; it is clear that organisations working together can often achieve much more than if everyone works individually.

Putting Supplier Diversity in Context

Looking to achieve a diverse supply chain and supplier base is simply good procurement practice, and making sure you don't accidentally make it difficult for certain firms to win business with your organisation must be sensible.

If you want to go further and make supplier diversity central to your PwP efforts, that could mean focusing on local firms, or minority- / female-owned businesses, as well as encouraging all your suppliers to develop a more diverse and inclusive workforce and approach generally. But why might you choose this as a preferred strategy within the wider PwP arena?

As discussed earlier, some organisations can make a real difference in dramatic sustainability areas such as climate change or reducing plastic pollution. But many firms can't have much impact in such areas, including many service businesses, for example. Accenture can achieve little in the greater scheme of things around deforestation or plastic usage; but literally any organisation can have a positive impact by looking to develop more diversity in their supply base.

If you can help just one small firm with minority ownership by awarding them a contract, or support local start-ups with mentoring and advice, you will have achieved something. Positive results can also be achieved relatively quickly, and the initiative is not inherently too difficult or expensive to implement. You don't even need to introduce bias into the evaluation process when it comes to supplier selection, as described in several examples here, including IBM, Accenture and the Natural History Museum.

There can also be benefits in terms of customers, staff and investors. If your customer base is largely female, it could be a positive step to show you are supporting female-owned businesses as suppliers, or encouraging large suppliers to address unfair pay differentials. If your operations are based in a region with a high ethnic minority population, looking to support local ethnically owned suppliers may improve the firm's reputation as an employer and in the eyes of customers. And looking at the opposite view, there were even successful moves a few years back to boycott Russian vodka brands in strongly LGBT-friendly venues because of the alleged anti-gay stance of that country's authorities![165]

Other positive examples have come from various public sector organisations that offer training and support to small or minority-owned firms to help them get better at understanding how to compete for work.[166] There are arguments that this is a better way of supporting such firms rather than overtly favouring them in bidding situations, as it avoids the market distortions and potential for corruption that direct favouritism can create.

Large corporates have also helped smaller suppliers by providing better payment terms, paying very promptly or up-front for goods and services not yet provided. Buyers have even set up joint ventures or invested in start-ups that they see as having potential. (That can play into the whole issue of capturing innovation from the market, too.) And there

165 'https://www.businessinsider.com/russian-vodka-boycott-theres-a-better-way-2013-7?r=US&IR=T

166 I developed a training course in the UK government way back in 2009 aimed at helping smaller firms understand better how to bid under formal public procurement rules.

have been very positive examples during the pandemic of larger firms explicitly supporting their smaller suppliers by improving payments or even launching support funding for those firms. Take a bow, Unilever, Vodafone and others.

Taking Action

So how can buyers take action in this particular PwP area? There are some similarities with the last chapter, but the emphasis here is more on the nature of the suppliers, rather than the causes that they support. So here are some ideas for promoting this agenda.

- Clearly, organisations need to understand the current make-up of their supplier base if they want to start promoting or favouring certain types of firm. If you don't know how many SMEs or minority-owned firms you currently use as suppliers, it is hard to implement a focused programme and impossible to monitor progress. If you don't have that information, you need to get at least an estimate, perhaps from sampling if you cannot easily achieve a full 100% analysis.
- Buyers can set "quotas" of some sort, looking to give a certain number of contracts or percentage of spend to businesses of a certain type. That can be done by formally setting aside some contracts for the type of firm in question, or by taking steps that are likely to achieve the targets by more across-the-board success for those firms. Some buyers, for example, set a policy that at least one (or more) SME or minority-owned firm must be on the shortlist for every procurement competition.
- The playing field may be tilted, so that firms with the particular characteristic are given a head start in the supplier selection process. However, do consider the dangers of this, as per the South African experience.

- Elements of "social value" or social benefit, or a positive approach to DEI, can be included in the selection process, giving organisations with purpose the chance to put that forward as part of their proposal. So, a minority-owned business might include its efforts to employ more disadvantaged people as a social value benefit when bidding for work. Public sector organisations are now formally including "social value" as an evaluation criterion in many procurement processes.
- As described in several examples here, there are other ways in which buyers can help firms (or social enterprises) without touching the evaluation process: for example, by mentoring and training, or by providing better payment terms for certain suppliers.
- As usual, whatever is agreed by suppliers needs to be followed up through the contract and supplier management phase of the relationship. There is also the issue of firms "cheating", as in US cases where firms lied that they were run by military veterans, so they could bid for reserved contracts.

Chapter 24 – Standing Tall with Vodafone's Three Pillars

Ninian Wilson is a well-known leader in the procurement world, a regular in the CIPS "Procurement Power List". He held senior roles from an early age at British Gas, Cable & Wireless, and the Royal Mail. He joined Vodafone back in 2009 and is now the Group Procurement Director and also the CEO of the firm's procurement company, so "I'm in the fortunate position that everyone in supply chain management in Vodafone reports into us in Luxembourg".

We asked him how he has seen procurement change in that time. "The biggest change is perhaps what technology has done in terms of our ability to use data and analytics, to talk to the top table with real information and facts at our fingertips. So the eProcurement and eCommerce revolution has elevated the function more than anything else. I remember making a pitch – at very short notice – to get a £20 million investment at Cable & Wireless signed off, which we used for both new technology and also to transform the whole function."

In Vodafone, procurement has been transformed from individual firms doing their own thing, to a more centralised function that is highly digitised. "When people ask us a question, we're not rummaging around or asking the supplier for information, we have detailed analysis of spend, suppliers, preference, metrics, compliance…" It's taken a decade or more to build this, and Wilson explains that "Detlef Schultz started this and I've inherited the great foundations he built".

The agenda has moved on from the traditional view of procurement's role, too, with the function playing a broader role now – for example, in the "innovation ecosystem", as Wilson calls it. And now, Nick Read, the CEO since late 2018, is leading a drive for Vodafone to become a purpose-led company. He was the CFO previously, so it is interesting that a bottom-line-focused executive sees these issues as key to the firm's future.

Wilson explains that the supply chain strategy must reflect the corporate strategy – "so we are making sure we get that alignment to purpose – and it is the right thing to do, we have a moral duty, to society and the planet. And we do believe that if we put purpose at the heart of the business, our customers will respond to that, too."

At a Group level, there are three pillars to the strategy. "The first is about how we help society to digitise – partly our own internal technology but also working with other organisations and customers to help them become more effective and purposeful. And it's not the same in every country in which we operate – in some places, your mobile phone is about your education, your business, your life."

The second pillar is around diversity and inclusion. Events in the US have brought the race element of that even more to the fore recently, but Wilson has also been the Group executive sponsor for the LGBT+ community in Vodafone for two years now. Vodafone's push on diversity has been mainly around gender until recently, but now there is also consideration of sexual orientation and more in terms of inclusivity both within and through the supply chain. There is also some evidence that a diverse supply base can help to develop more innovation, so that fits well with his core priorities.

"Taking on that role has made me realise how easy it is to exclude people. When the world seems to be polarising into people being very for or very against things, companies can perhaps be a sort of sensible voice. We take human rights for granted in many Western countries but in some countries, people still hide their private lives because of prejudice. We think you get more out of people when they feel comfortable, and accepted. And as well as the work within Vodafone, procurement can reflect these values and culture more widely when we work with our supply chain."

The third pillar for Vodafone is around the planet. Supply chain management sits on the sustainability committee and works closely with Andrew Dunnett, the Group lead on SDGs and sustainable business.

"Even when I was at university, doing Geography in the late-1980s, my professor was starting to talk about global warming, but many didn't take it seriously. There was a peak of environmental activism in the 1960s, but it kind of disappeared in the 70s with the economic shocks, and now it is building back again. I think there is no question that humanity is having an impact on climate, and large firms like Vodafone have to take some proactive steps around energy use and greening of the supply chain. And customers are demanding it, so I think it will only get stronger – even post-COVID, I think we will see firms building back better and greener."

Wilson also sees that staff respond to this sustainability agenda. "People engage with the diversity and inclusion agenda, and the planet issues. I'm proud that we've been able to help people through COVID, keeping people engaged – even if Zoom isn't as good as a coffee or a beer!"

We asked how Vodafone procurement is actually implementing some of the purpose-related ideas. "We're changing our tendering processes to reflect diversity, inclusion and planet issues, as well as safety and risk issues where relevant. That means hard scoring that goes into every tender. On some recent bids that's been 10% on safety and risk, 5% on diversity and 5% on planet issues – so sustainability-related issues can be 20% of scoring. That will change buying decisions."

As Wilson says, it is easy to say the right things but "embedding change is the key. So we started talking to suppliers about safety years ago, but we didn't really see a difference until we embedded that in tenders. Since then we've improved our safety record by 90%. When it affects marking and scoring, that's when the rubber hits the road."

But Wilson acknowledges there is more to do on enriching data. "We've joined a couple of groups including the blockchain-based IBM Trust Your Supplier initiative. Many of our large suppliers have really good programmes, too, that we can learn from. Then we're producing educational materials to help our smaller suppliers. They want to know how to do this, and we need to make sure SMEs aren't disadvantaged through this. We noticed recently on some of our proof of concepts, the smaller firms were struggling with our mandatory questions in tenders, so we need to help them."

Vodafone have also looked at paying smaller suppliers faster – paying 15 days from invoice, which is excellent practice. Wilson is looking at how to handle that issue longer-term, too: "90-day payment terms for small suppliers may not be the right approach".

He has also looked to reach out to other top companies on this issue: "the power of scale", as he puts it. "If we can get to £100 billion rather than the £20 billion of Vodafone spend, that can really create momentum, and I want to learn from companies who are ahead of us, learn from their mistakes." There is also work with other external interested organisations, such as Stonewall in the equality area. "We're looking at how to embed diversity in tenders, and we will share learning with others."

And of course Vodafone will talk about their programmes when the firm bids for work with their customers, including government. "I think when we start coming back out of COVID, people are going to be way more selective who they work with, and who they pay money to".

The firm is also looking at SIM cards and how to reduce plastic use.

"There are billions of cards in use, and that's increasing because of their use in Internet of Things devices. So we've saved 500 tonnes of plastic by putting more than one SIM on a card, and we've moved away from plastic bags in Vodafone shops. We're making equipment vendors think about more energy efficiency, too – this benefits everybody so it's also just great business sense."

We asked whether the circular economy was being considered in terms of spend areas such as equipment. "We're thinking about it, but we're not there yet". But, despite Wilson playing down this area, the firm is doing more than most. There is a huge logistics programme, looking at coordinating and consolidating physical operations to reduce cost and emissions, with forward, reverse and repair supply chains all being considered. There is also an internal marketplace for equipment, so if the UK is going to scrap a piece of kit, it can be offered to other business units first.

"In procurement we see all the equipment coming in and going out – that's a useful control lever, too. Our target is to recycle 100% of network equipment, but that is very challenging, the last 1% is really tough! But if you set challenging targets, you get the right ambition, the right mindset in the company."

Collaboration is another key theme for Wilson. "We talk to suppliers about their approach to the UN SDGs, to see how they compare with us, and we are learning from them on any issues. For instance, US firms are often ahead of us on diversity issues. You realise how little many of us know – if you are like us, white, affluent, middle-aged straight guys, it is very hard to understand how it feels to be in other shoes. Your people and company need to be open and make an effort to understand these issues".

Another great example of that was the #CodeLikeAGirl programme, launched in partnership with Code First Girls in 2017 to provide a free, 4-day coding workshop to girls aged 14–18 from 26 countries across the world. "We want to see more women in engineering and science – but we need to support that through the employment life cycle, so that means having good policies in areas such as maternity and paternity leave." Wilson says that he is "not a religious man". But he clearly does believe sincerely, at an ethical and philosophical level, in these approaches and actions. "If you do them really well, you enable societal change, but as an individual you also feel really good about what you're doing." And of course, the firm will be viewed as a better employer, a better place to work, a better investment and a better supplier in its own right.

Section 4 –
A Directory of Procurement with Purpose Topics

Introducing the Directory

In this final section, no less than 26 different procurement with purpose topics are summarised. Some have been covered quite thoroughly in Section 3, so this will act as a recap and a summary of key points for issues such as plastics, climate change and modern slavery.

In other cases, there was not the space in previous sections to discuss the issue at any length, or it may be a relatively less prominent topic that generally receives less attention in the PwP debate. That's not to say issues such as GDPR or corruption and sanctions aren't incredibly important in their own right, and all of these topics have some linkage with the "purpose" agenda.

However, they are often not considered by organisations to be quite so central to sustainability or purpose programmes compared, for example, to carbon emissions or human rights issues. Hence the summary here, rather than the more detailed discussion and analysis provided in the previous section.

This section is intended to be a useful reference guide, rather than material designed to be read from start to finish in one sitting. The topics covered under the three key headings are:

Social

Modern Slavery and Human Rights
Rehabilitation of Offenders
Workplace Diversity and Inclusion

Diversity in the Supply Base
Supporting Charities and Social Enterprises
Supporting Local Business (and Communities)
Health and Safety
Apprenticeships
Wage Discrimination
GDPR

Environmental

Carbon Emissions
Deforestation
Plastics
Species Loss
Pollution
Waste
Recycling and Circularity
Food Provenance and Animal Welfare
Water Conservation and Management
Local Environmental Issues

Economic

Treatment of Suppliers
Fraud, Corruption and Sanctions
Fair Wages
Paying Taxes
Promoting Supplier Innovation
Promoting Employment

SOCIAL – MODERN SLAVERY AND HUMAN RIGHTS

Overview

This is one of the widest topics in the list and could be split into several component areas – for instance, human trafficking, forced labour, persecution of union members, or bad treatment of minority groups in the workplace. But they all represent basic violations of fundamental human rights, such as the right to have your own opinion, and not to be mistreated by the state, your employer or anyone else.

Awareness of this set of issues has grown immensely in the last couple of decades. Most buyers until recently did not worry too much about how staff were treated in the factories of suppliers on the other side of the world, or building contractors working in the heat of the desert to earn enough money to return to their home countries, or the working conditions of subsistence farmers growing the crops that went into our processed foodstuffs.

But as communication has improved, we have all become more aware of these issues, and organisations have become aware of the potential for reputational risk if they are linked with such human rights violations. It is not just in distant countries either, as seen in 2020 with the case of garment workers in factories around Leicester, England, who were being paid far less than the minimum wage. Questions of trafficking and forced labour were raised here, too.

So, taking action to address such risks has become a common element of procurement with purpose programmes. However, there are some difficult issues here: from the unintended consequences of sacking a supplier (what happens to their staff?) to the difficulty of knowing exactly what is going on in factories or on farms in remote areas. But most leading procurement and supply chain functions are now working to improve matters. Often the most effective programmes involve collaboration across sectors or industries, or between buyers and key suppliers.

Which organisations should consider this issue?

- Any organisation claiming a sense of "purpose" needs to consider action in this area given the importance and high profile of these issues.
- Organisations with supply chains involving people working in unskilled or low-pay jobs in factories (or on farms, or in mines), should consider action. That is particularly relevant for supply from less affluent countries and those that are perceived to have human rights challenges.

What can organisations do?	What are the barriers and risks?
• Require suppliers to obey the relevant laws and sign up to charters, codes of conduct or similar relating to human rights. • Include issue as part of supplier selection process, qualification process, or in proposal section of tenders and similar. • Manage suppliers and contracts to verify that behaviour is as it should be, and take appropriate action where it is not.	• Gaining insight into relevant issues in the supply chain can be difficult, particularly from remote areas or in multitier supply chains. • Getting behind the supplier "façade" is sometimes essential in order to see what really goes on at working level. • Dropping firms who transgress can lead to even greater problems for their staff if good customers simply abandon the supplier.

How do you measure success?

- Number or percentage of suppliers who sign up to code of conduct or similar.
- Percentage of tenders or contracted spend that incorporates human rights issues into supplier selection process.
- Lack of reported cases of human rights abuse in the supply chain ("no news is good news").

SOCIAL – REHABILITATION OF OFFENDERS

Overview

This is one of the least "fashionable" causes featured here. Some people see helping people who have committed crimes, particularly those who have been in detention, as something that is not a good use of anyone's time or money.

Yet this is a significant issue for the individuals concerned and also for society more widely. The prison population in most countries includes a higher than representative proportion of people from minority groups; who are illiterate; who have drug problems; or who were abused as youngsters or brought up without parental support. Many are arguably "sad" rather than "bad". They also create huge costs for the rest of society. As well as the direct damage they do – though violence, theft or similar – they cost the taxpayer vast sums of money. That is not only in the direct costs of incarceration but also in benefits, healthcare, and in the opportunity cost of unproductive lives.

Encouraging suppliers to support this population, by offering training, jobs and support to that community, can therefore have real benefits. This has been an area where public sector buyers have probably been more active than private, although some social enterprises and charities that support offenders have been well supported by private sector buyers, too.

Buyers can simply suggest to suppliers that this is worth doing; or it can be included in "social value"-type proposals that form part of suppliers' bids and feed into supplier evaluation processes. As usual, any supplier commitments in this area need to be monitored as part of the contract management process.

Which organisations should consider this issue?

As explained above, this is perhaps not a fashionable cause. But this is a purpose that any organisation could embrace and gives a good payback for society generally. It might particularly resonate with:

- Any public sector organisation, but especially those involved with policing and criminal justice systems.
- Private sector firms that want to show they are concerned about social issues and are not afraid to address a challenging area like this.

What can organisations do?

- Look to offer direct opportunities to such individuals.
- Ask potential suppliers as part of the supplier qualification process to commit to support recruitment of offenders.
- Take organisations' approaches in this area into account when selecting suppliers.
- Follow up with appropriate contract management when suppliers make commitments.

What are the barriers and risks?

- Lack of sympathy generally in society for offenders.
- Reluctance of organisations to recruit individuals who might be seen as a risk or "high maintenance".
- Verifying what suppliers / potential suppliers offer in the bidding process and checking that with their actual actions and behaviour.

How do you measure success?

- Number of offenders helped / offered jobs via programme.
- Number or % suppliers committing to appropriate programmes or policies in this area.

SOCIAL – WORKPLACE DIVERSITY AND INCLUSION

Overview

This is an atypical issue as far as this book is concerned. That is because it is generally seen as more relevant in terms of how the organisation conducts itself internally, rather than how it acts through the supply chain and influences suppliers. But in fact, it can have relevance in both spheres. In many countries, organisations have legal requirements to treat their own staff fairly and without bias relating to race, disability, religion, or sexual orientation. It would also simply seem sensible given the "war for talent" in many jobs and regions that opportunities should be open to all types of people, and that organisations should reward staff based on how well they do their jobs, not what they look like or believe in.

Like many professionals, procurement has traditionally been male dominated, although that is changing in many countries. There has also been some evidence that ethnic minorities are not well represented at senior levels in the profession, in the UK at least. So, there is much that many organisations can and should do internally to make their procurement and supply chain teams more diverse to address this.

Then there are actions that can be taken with suppliers. As in many of these issues, that can include simply talking to suppliers and persuading them that they should also follow inclusive policies internally. Or it might mean mandating certain actions (such as making sure bidders have an equalities policy if they want to compete for work) or even introducing direct bias into supplier selection to favour those firms taking strong actions here.

Which organisations should consider this issue?

This is something every organisation should be doing internally – probably for legal reasons and certainly for business reasons. Extending that to influencing the supply chain is particularly relevant for:

- Organisation that want to promote itself positively to current and potential staff, customers or investors as a good and concerned "corporate citizen" of the world.
- Organisations that have many customers/consumers who are from "minority groups" – ranging from different ethnicities to people with disabilities. (If your business is making stairlifts, you really do not want to be found discriminating against people with mobility issues!)

What can organisations do?

- Monitor the profile of their own staff and introduce policies that engage diversity and fairness in the workplace.
- Introduce specific programmes, e.g., mentoring for staff from diverse backgrounds.
- Ask potential suppliers to commit to equality and diversity policies as part of the qualification process and/or take organisations' approaches in this area into account when selecting suppliers.

What are the barriers and risks?

- t can be hard to gain awareness of unconscious bias or ways in which minority groups might be disadvantaged.
- Balancing the need to find the best staff with the desire to be inclusive and open (raising questions around the use of quotas, for instance).
- Verifying what suppliers / potential suppliers claim in terms of behaviour within their own organisations.

How do you measure success?

- Internal staff data on diversity.
- Number or % of suppliers committing to appropriate policies.
- Percentage of tenders or of contracted spend where diversity issues were incorporated into the supplier selection process or contracts.

SOCIAL – DIVERSITY IN THE SUPPLY BASE

Overview

This topic can be described at a high level but then has several different options in terms of how organisations implement supplier diversity programmes. At that high level, the principle is clear. Organisations can help themselves and support wider purpose by making sure their own supply base is diverse in terms of the types of businesses they buy from, particularly in terms of the size and the ownership of those firms. They can also persuade or even require larger suppliers to behave in the same way in terms of those firms' supply chains.

The benefit to the buyer comes from being open to new suppliers and those who may bring different perspectives and innovative approaches, rather than being stuck buying from the same old large suppliers for years on end. The wider benefit comes from supporting business owners and communities who are disadvantaged in some way.

The options here include support to smaller firms; female-owned businesses; minority-owned businesses (which might be based on ethnicity or sexual orientation); or military veteran-owned businesses. Often a relatively small amount of support from a few key customers early in the life of a small or minority-owned business can make a huge difference to its chance of surviving and prospering. So, the social return here can be considerable in return for a relatively painless investment from the buyer.

Which organisations should consider this issue?

- Being open to new suppliers, and avoiding accidental "barriers to entry" should be part of any procurement function's role. Every organisation should implement the key practices behind this approach.
- Supporting diversity can also support an organisation's customer base – so an organisation targeting female consumers may want to support female-owned businesses. Similar thinking could apply to a particular ethnic group, or those with a particular health or disability issue.
- Public sector organisations can link this to wider policy goals, e.g. supporting disabled people and helping them find work, or encouraging start-ups. That can be done through direct procurement from such firms or by encouraging major suppliers to follow desired approaches.

What can organisations do?

- Make processes friendly to all suppliers, particularly smaller or minority-owned firms.
- Introduce bias into the selection process to help the "target" group win contracts.
- Provide support outside the formal procurement process, e.g. "how to bid" workshops ".
- Encourage or even mandate first tier suppliers to use such firms.

What are the barriers and risks?

- Verifying that suppliers genuinely fall into the "target" areas of diversity.
- Finding diverse suppliers who are capable of meeting the needs of the buyer.
- Contract management – monitoring how and whether first-tier suppliers are meeting agreed commitments to open up their own supply chain.

How do you measure success?

- Number of suppliers or % of spend in specified target groups (SMEs, minority-owned, etc.)
- Number or % of first-tier suppliers who sign up to a diversity programme for their own supply chain.
- Positive narratives from diverse suppliers.

SOCIAL – SUPPORTING CHARITIES AND SOCIAL ENTERPRISES

Overview

Organisations can support charities and social enterprises primarily by buying goods and services from them. Buyers can also look to persuade (or even mandate in contracts) their major suppliers to direct some of their third-party spend towards such organisations. Many charities do not trade in a business-to-business supply sense, but some do and certainly many social enterprises target other businesses as customers.

Social enterprises tend to have individual goals and missions that often relate to supporting a particular group of people. So, some look to employ prisoners on release from prison, others employ people with disabilities or health issues. Some successful social enterprises have successfully focused on employing people on the autistic spectrum in technology roles. That plays to their strengths in areas such as attention to detail and pattern recognition.

There are various techniques for supporting this idea. A certain amount of spend can be set aside for social enterprises; or procurement might focus on making sure a charity or social enterprise is included wherever possible when it comes to supplier selection exercises, even if such organisations must compete on a level-playing-field basis.

Which organisations should consider this issue?

- Any organisation that supports a cause can support charities or social enterprises that work in that area. Organisations may choose issues which have resonance for their customers and staff e.g. a firm which works in the health sector might support social enterprises that help disabled people find appropriate jobs.
- In the public sector, organisations may focus on relevant areas. The Department for Work and Pensions in the UK (responsible for paying disability benefits), for instance, asked major suppliers to support specialist organisations employing disabled people, as well as perhaps employing more themselves directly.

What can organisations do?	What are the barriers and risks?
• Buy directly from these organisations. That can be done by setting aside spend, or by including organisations in selection processes. • Buyers can introduce a bias into the supplier selection process or ask that organisations compete on their own merits. • Buyers can also persuade or mandate major suppliers to do the same and offer support in their own supply chains. • Other support outside specific procurement processes can also be valuable, e.g. training or mentoring for staff in these organisations.	• Finding charities / social enterprises that can successfully supply what you actually need to buy. • Ensuring that organisations are genuine, well run, and effective in their mission. • Balancing the "doing good" with the inherent value for money of what is being bought. • It can be challenging to determine appropriate contract management for what may be "unconventional" businesses.

How do you measure success?
• Number of suppliers, amount, or percentage of external spend with suppliers of this type. • "Success stories", e.g. narratives around people whose lives have changed because of support.

SOCIAL – SUPPORTING LOCAL BUSINESS (AND COMMUNITIES)

Overview

Organisations can support local businesses and communities both directly (by buying from them, offering grants, donations, or employees' time, for instance) and indirectly through the supply chain. Buying goods and services from local firms helps them to prosper and grow, and keeps the money circulating in the local economy (the "multiplier effect").

It can also build resilience for the buyer, as opposed to relying on global supply chains that are more vulnerable, and can promote the positioning of the organisation as a good and concerned local "citizen".

Organisations can also help build the local economy by promoting the idea that key suppliers should have a strong local presence. That might mean encouragement to use the city or region as a wider base. Buyers can also encourage suppliers themselves to support the locality in different ways. Suppliers can be asked or required to spend money directly themselves in the locality, or through "social value"-type actions (described in earlier chapters).

In the UK, for example, suppliers to city or county councils have been encouraged to contribute to local educational initiatives, or provide support for local start-up businesses.

Which organisations should consider this issue?

- Any organisation that wants to promote itself positively as a good and concerned "local citizen".
- Organisations that want to gain positive PR, perhaps to counter perceived negatives that might affect their reputation in the local community.
- Organisations that are major local employers and want to be seen as a "good place to work" and attract the best people to their organisation.

What can organisations do?	What are the barriers and risks?
• Ensure supply opportunities are open and available for firms of different types and sizes, including smaller local businesses. • Buy directly from local organisations, by introducing bias into the selection process or reserving spend for local suppliers. • Encourage suppliers to spend money locally or to take other actions that help local communities or business.	• Questions about the economic "multiplier effect" and how measurable or real it is. • Danger of creating a protectionist situation (through buying local) with decisions that ultimately just prop up inefficient firms and benefit no one. • Risk of using suppliers that are not really fit for purpose purely because they are "local".

How do you measure success?

- Number of suppliers, amount spent or percentage of external spend with local suppliers.
- Wider local economic data (e.g. job creation).
- "Success stories", e.g. narratives around firms / people whose lives have changed thanks to these initiatives.

SOCIAL – HEALTH AND SAFETY

Overview

Many of the issues identified under the procurement with purpose banner are relatively new, at least in terms of the emphasis that procurement professionals are now giving to them. But some, such as "Health and Safety" (H&S), have been around for a long time, which can lead to them being perceived as a little old hat and perhaps less worthy of attention.

However, H&S continues to be an important issue for many organisations. We do of course have to pay attention to H&S issues within our own organisations; that is critical in certain industries such as construction, mining, energy or farming. But buyers also need to focus on making sure their suppliers are behaving in the right way, too. H&S failings in the supply chain can have serious ramifications, such as reputational risk for the customer firms.

There can also be an interaction with more contemporary issues. The tragic case of the 23 Chinese cockle pickers who were killed on a beach in Lancashire in 2004 combined human rights issues ("forced labour") with basic H&S failings. And somebody somewhere was buying the products those people collected, perhaps without asking too many questions of the owners of the business behind the tragedy. There have also been failings in many other supply markets, from garment manufacturing to mining.

Which organisations should consider this issue?

- Any organisation that buys products or services that have the potential to pose H&S issues for the suppliers' staff (or indeed for the buyer's own workforce).
- Particularly relevant for organisations that spend significant money in high-risk sectors, such as construction, and certain raw materials (oil and gas, metals, foodstuffs, etc.).
- Organisations that have a high profile in consumer markets and are aware of brand reputational risk that could arise from failings in this area.

What can organisations do?	**What are the barriers and risks?**
• Require suppliers to sign up to adherence of H&S laws and regulations, or a specific industry/firm code of conduct. • Monitor H&S performance through supplier audits or spot-checks, as well as robust contract management processes. • Work with strategic suppliers to address issues; be prepared at the extreme to sack suppliers who do not meet standards.	• Gaining enough understanding of what is going on in supply chains to make effective interventions. • Sometimes difficult to get behind the supplier "façade" to see what really goes on at working level (particularly for international businesses). • Balancing appropriate H&S actions with the danger of "gold-plating" and driving up costs unnecessarily.
How do you measure success? • Number of Health and Safety incidents in the supply chain / caused by suppliers. • Number or % of suppliers that sign up to a "Code of Conduct" or similar.	

SOCIAL – APPRENTICESHIPS

Overview

In many countries, apprenticeships provide a route into full-time employment that combines some academic study with practical on-the-job training. Traditionally, apprentices studied to become plumbers, jewellers, construction workers, or maybe car mechanics. Then, as more women came into the workforce, and the job market changed, occupations such as hairdressing or catering became common sources of apprenticeship opportunities. Even more recently, certainly in the UK, there are apprentice accountants, business managers or even golf greenkeepers.

Apprenticeships help young people gain valuable skills, increase the skill level of the nation generally, and reduce levels of unemployment. Organisations can obviously support this policy by taking on apprentices directly, and some have offered apprenticeships in the procurement and supply chain management area.

But it is also possible to encourage or drive suppliers into supporting apprenticeships. That can be an element in "social value" proposals made as part of bids in the public sector, or something that suppliers are encouraged to do through the bidding process or in the contract management phase of the contract.

Contracts in construction and related areas are often seen as appropriate when it comes to this procurement with purpose activity. And as the global economy enters a difficult period, this goal to develop local, regional or national employment and skills may receive more focus and priority.

Which organisations should consider this issue?

- Any organisation that wants to position itself as supporting the educational and career prospects of young people.
- Organisations for whom young people are a key target customer or consumer group and who want to be seen to support that age group.
- Public sector organisations where this is often a positive policy for elected representatives, and where "social value" approaches can support this issue.

<table>
<tr>
<td>

What can organisations do?

- Look at opportunities to offer apprenticeships themselves, including in the procurement area.
- Include apprenticeships as a priority area within public sector "social value" thinking.
- Encourage suppliers to take on apprentices by introducing bias into the selection process or mandating recruitment of apprentices as part of the bidding process.
- Encourage suppliers to support apprenticeships through the contract management phase.

</td>
<td>

What are the barriers and risks?

- Establishing whether your actions are really having an incremental effect (would the supplier have taken on apprentices anyway?).
- Checking up that any commitments from the supplier made in bid or contract are actually delivered.
- Can be seen a low-profile issue within the wider procurement with purpose agenda – do customers, staff or investors really care?

</td>
</tr>
<tr>
<td colspan="2">

How do you measure success?

- Number of apprentices taken on by suppliers.
- Number of apprentices from disadvantaged backgrounds, minority groups etc.

</td>
</tr>
</table>

SOCIAL – WAGE DISCRIMINATION

Overview

Not many procurement (or sustainability) professionals will have considered this as a key topic within the wider procurement with purpose agenda. But it is important at several different levels.

Most customers (whether business or final consumers) would not want the firms from which they buy to pay their staff differently depending on their sex, race, religion, or other factors unconnected with the job they do or their performance. Yet this has happened for many years, even in developed countries – women being paid less than men for doing similar jobs, for instance. Whilst legislation has helped improve matters, it can still be an issue.

In some countries, the farming and agricultural sector is still endemically discriminatory. Again, women may be the victims; or it may link to human rights and even modern slavery issues where a particular group is discriminated against.

Requiring suppliers to behave in the "right" way can therefore be included as part of the supplier selection and management process. This is an area where buyers tend to be binary, asking suppliers to sign up to a code of conduct or similar, rather than evaluating their actions as part of a scored supplier selection process. Buyers can also work with their supply chain to improve employment practices generally, something that firms like Unilever and Mars have done successfully with their growers and farmers in the developing world.

Which organisations should consider this issue?

- This issue has both general relevance and more specific risk and opportunity for certain buyers. So, it should be considered by:
- Every organisation, certainly as far as requiring suppliers to act legally in terms of non-discrimination.
- Organisations that buy from countries or sectors where there is more likelihood of wage discrimination issues being present.
- Any organisation where a key customer group might be shocked or annoyed about wage discrimination in the supply chain (a company selling cosmetics mainly to young women would presumably not want to find that key suppliers underpay young women in their factories).

What can organisations do?

- Include anti-discrimination clauses in supplier qualification documents and in standard contractual documents.
- Work with more strategic suppliers to address embedded issues of discrimination.
- Participate in wider industry or governmental initiatives.

What are the barriers and risks?

- Difficult to find out about issues, particularly if they are down the supply chain.
- May need a willingness to "interfere" in suppliers' business practices that some may find uncomfortable.
- Requires strong follow-through in contract management phase.

How do you measure success?

- Number of "incidents" in supply base (target to reduce towards zero).
- Number or % of suppliers signed up to code of conduct or similar.

SOCIAL – GDPR

Overview

It may seem at first sight that this topic has little to do with many other procurement with purpose issues, which deal with high-profile issues with wider societal impact, such as climate change or human rights in the supply chain. Yet GDPR (the General Data Protection Regulation) and data privacy generally do have some similarities with these other purpose-related topics. It was put in place to benefit the wider population, and to force organisations (public and private sectors) to behave in a responsible way. So, in a sense, it is not too different, for instance, from the legislation and policy drive to address modern slavery.

GDPR came into effect in Europe in 2016. It addresses data protection and privacy in the European Union and European Economic Area, but also applies to any business operating in those areas, as well as transfer of data outside those areas. "Controllers" and "processors" of personal data must put in place appropriate measures to implement the principles, such as ensuring that individuals' data is kept securely and can only be used in a manner that each individual is comfortable with.

There is also no doubt that the burden for much GDPR work falls on procurement and supply chain professionals. Many of the issues crop up in the supply chain: for example, marketing firms who hold customer data to access potential and actual customers, or outsourcers who handle payroll services. It can therefore be usefully considered as part of a procurement with purpose programme.

Which organisations should consider this issue?

- Virtually every organisation operating in Europe needs to consider GDPR – note that the provisions include organisations holding data about their own staff.
- But this is particularly relevant for organisations who hold data or require suppliers to hold data about customers or other key stakeholder groups, and even more so if that includes sensitive data.

<table>
<tr>
<td>What can organisations do?
• Require suppliers who hold relevant data to sign up contractually to adherence of GDPR rules.
• Monitor GDPR performance and processes by key suppliers as part of ongoing contract management.</td>
<td>What are the barriers and risks?
• Verifying and monitoring what suppliers say and agree to do in terms of their own processes and systems can be challenging.
• Constant vigilance is needed because of the threats from "hackers" and other malicious third parties that look to steal data.</td>
</tr>
<tr>
<td colspan="2">How do you measure success?
• Number or % of suppliers signed up to GDPR compliance policy or statement.
• Number and magnitude of any GDPR transgressions, data breaches etc.</td>
</tr>
</table>

ENVIRONMENTAL – CARBON EMISSIONS

Overview

Many would argue that this is the single most important issue of "purpose" discussed in this book, and it is covered in considerably more detail in earlier sections. Carbon emissions drive climate change (according to most scientists) and climate change is perhaps the greatest risk to the future of the human race. Again, it is intrinsically linked to other issues in this "environmental" section. Emissions drive climate, which drives species loss and other problems, whilst deforestation, plastic production and pollution contribute to the emissions crisis.

Many organisations rightly focus on their own emissions, in factories, offices or warehouses. They may also look at emissions generated by customers in using their products. But for many organisations, it is emissions coming from the various tiers of the supply chain that provide purchased goods and services which represent the biggest category of emissions. That is not just the obvious industries and sectors such as mining, agriculture, or manufacturing, but also in the energy used to run data centres, or emissions generated by lawyers and consultants flying around the world on a global strategy or M&A project.

So, most organisations are now looking for their suppliers to take steps to reduce emissions. Many of those steps can be done independently; but some initiatives will require collaborative working between buyer and supplier, or wider collaborative efforts at industry level. There is also an increased requirement for statutory reporting which is driving organisations to act, so the pressure from a whole range of stakeholders is growing for virtually every organisation.

Which organisations should consider this issue?

- This issue should be on the agenda for every organisation that has a desire to work in a purposeful and sustainable manner. Every organisation should be aware of the major sources of emissions in their own business and supply chain. But it is particularly applicable to:
- Organisations that are heavy users of goods (or services) which create significant emissions. That includes organisations buying transportation services, for instance, as well as many manufactured goods.
- Any organisation that is claiming to have a sense of purpose really needs to put this factor near the top of its priority list, given its overall importance and public profile.
- Publicly quoted businesses that are now required to report on emissions / climate change risk clearly need to focus on the issue.

What can organisations do?	What are the barriers and risks?
• Measure internal driven emissions and through the supply chain using the "scope" definitions. • Ask suppliers for their plans as part of supplier qualification / selection process. • Work with major suppliers collaboratively to explore options for reduction.	• It can be difficult to measure emissions, particularly through multitier supply chains. • Willingness of suppliers to act is variable and often driving change is difficult, e.g. growth in coal-powered power stations in China.

How do you measure success?

- Reduced emissions at the three different "scope" levels.
- Tracking emissions reduction from key suppliers or from specific initiatives. That can demonstrate more easily measurable improvement than the broader "scope" metrics.

ENVIRONMENTAL – DEFORESTATION AND HABITAT LOSS

Overview

Several of the issues discussed here under the "environmental" heading are connected. In the case of deforestation (the destruction of forests and woodland), and wider habitat loss (wetlands, rare heathlands, etc.) there are links to climate change, water conservation, and the threat to natural species.

The loss of rainforest is the major problem for the future of humanity, and is one of the greatest sustainability issues facing us today. Millions of acres of forest are being cleared every year, legally and illegally, and mainly for agricultural purposes, such as growing palm trees to produce oil, used in many food products as well as cosmetics and household products. In some countries, politicians support these activities because of the short-term apparent economic benefits, making measures to address the issue exceedingly difficult.

Deforestation and habitat loss generally have an impact on carbon emissions, as well as often leading to threats to plant or animal species. It can also lead to problems such as flooding or land erosion. All in all, there is an urgent need to address these problems, and firms can play their part by understanding supply chains and the impact that their suppliers (or suppliers' suppliers) might be having on the world's natural resources.

Which organisations should consider this issue?

- Any organisation that purchases products which could be grown in areas where rainforest or other vulnerable habitats are under threat. That includes timber; but also food-related crops such as palm oil, where growers are implicated in rainforest destruction.
- In particular, organisations with stakeholders who are likely to be interested in this sort of issue, and have strong brand values to protect, should take action to avoid accusations that they are complicit in deforestation and habitat loss.

What can organisations do?	What are the barriers and risks?
• Understand supply chains so (as far as possible) materials purchased can be traced back to source. • Include the issue as part of supplier qualification and selection, and work directly with strategic suppliers to ensure they follow sustainable approaches. • Work with industry bodies, charities, and others collaboratively to drive the right behaviours from governments, growers, and intermediaries. • Be prepared to avoid providers who do not operate in the right way.	• It can be difficult to trace materials back to their origin and truly understand what is going on through the supply chain. • Powerful forces that have a vested interest in destruction of the rainforest will oppose action – from Presidents to criminal gangs and less scrupulous agribusiness operators. • Consumers need educating to understand some complex issues here.
How do you measure success? • % of critical material (e.g. palm oil) bought from fully verified/certified sources. • Support to reforestation programmes, e.g. hectares of new forest planted. • Participation in collaborative/industry initiatives.	

ENVIRONMENTAL – PLASTICS

Overview

Plastic is material consisting of a wide range of synthetic or semi-synthetic organic compounds that are malleable and so can be moulded into solid objects. Whilst plastics are usually made from petrochemicals, they can be created from other base materials, such as corn or even cotton.

Plastics have brought huge benefits to humankind. They are flexible, relatively cheap to manufacture, and can reduce total energy consumption, as they are lighter than glass to transport. The weight of cars has decreased as more plastic has replaced metal in the manufacturing process, benefitting fuel consumption. They can offer valuable protection as packaging, from stopping physical damage to goods to extending the life of foodstuffs.

However, they are also increasingly seen as providing one of the world's greatest environmental challenges. They potentially also contribute to health issues which are not yet fully understood. Disposal of plastics is a key issue, and too much ends up in the ocean, from large items that can kill marine life (as shown memorably in The Blue Planet TV series) to micro-particles which today are even found in the soil and in drinking water.

Most responsible organisations are looking critically at their use of plastic, to see where that can be reduced, or where plastics can be used that are reusable, recyclable or even compostable. There have been many positive stories emerging in recent years, but the quantity of plastic produced still grows, and the pandemic may push this growth further (for instance, disposable aprons, more packaging to offer protection against the virus, and more plastic screens used in public places).

Which organisations should consider this issue?

- As a high-profile issue, and one that many consumers clearly care about, any organisation that presents itself as "purposeful" or "sustainable" should have this topic on its agenda.
- Any organisation involved in the production of plastics (the whole value chain from oil production through to finished products).
- Organisations that are major users of plastics in their processes, finished products, or packaging material.
- Organisations (e.g. food retailers) that sell a lot of plastic products or products using plastic packaging.

What can organisations do?

- Understand the role of plastics in their processes, products, packaging, and wider supply chain.
- Look to reduce use of plastic, e.g. through substitution, reducing unnecessary packaging or by reducing the weight of plastic packaging.
- Where possible when use cannot be avoided, look to use reusable, recyclable or compostable (biodegradable) plastics.
- Work with major suppliers and industry groups collaboratively to explore innovative options.

What are the barriers and risks?

- Plastics can be genuinely the "best" material for certain purposes, making substitution challenging.
- Some definitions of "recyclable" or "biodegradable" are questionable. Maybe accusations of greenwashing in areas such as declaring plastic to be "biodegradable" (over a 5000-year period…)
- Alternatives can be environmentally worse than plastic.

How do you measure success?

- Reduced use of plastic – by weight or spend.
- Use of more sustainable packaging (by quantity, percentage, spend).
- Percentage / volume of non-environmentally "friendly" plastics used.

ENVIRONMENTAL – SPECIES LOSS

Overview

This is another of the linked issues under the "environmental" heading. In the case of loss of natural species (animals primarily, but also fish, insects, plants etc.), deforestation and loss of habitat are clearly a causal factor. The destruction of the rainforest is leading to the threat of extinction for a large number of species, from orangutans to unique plants. But species loss can occur in any natural environment, not just the rainforest. Climate change is also an extinction threat; the warming oceans are affecting coral reefs, and increased temperatures bring changes to many food chains.

Closer to home, even building a new office or factory can have relevance here. Many countries now have laws to protect rare species – bats, birds, butterflies, or newts often feature in the UK – and construction work must take account of this. So, ensuring that suppliers are aware of their responsibilities in this area is important and provides a good example of a local procurement with purpose action. Most organisations can do something positive, even if fewer can contribute directly to saving the orangutans.

For firms that do buy products which are grown or sourced in areas where species risk is highest, the potential actions are similar to those described under the deforestation heading. Understanding the supply chain, and working with suppliers to ensure that they are acting properly is key. Buyers can introduce checks and verification within the supplier selection process and remain involved through the contract management period.

Which organisations should consider this issue?

- Any organisation that purchases products which are grown in areas with high species extinction risk.
- Organisations that commission or carry out major construction work – particularly on "greenfield sites".

What can organisations do?	What are the barriers and risks?
• Understand supply chains and suppliers to identify where species risk might be an issue. • Incorporate relevant questions – or develop a code of conduct for suppliers to sign up to – in order to bring this issue into the supplier qualification processes. • Work directly with strategic suppliers to look at ways in which this risk might be reduced.	• Sometimes difficult to understand exactly where the risks in the supply chain lie. • Monitoring supplier actions can be challenging, as is verifying any data and information they are providing. • This is one of the most difficult of all topics in terms of measuring success. It would be difficult, for instance, to relate the number of orangutans in Borneo to any particular corporate action! • Difficult to link outcomes to actions, so hard to get real "success stories".

How do you measure success?
• Number or % of suppliers signing up to code of conduct or similar. • Specific actions related to environment or species preservation (e.g. hectares of a particular habitat protected).

ENVIRONMENTAL – POLLUTION

Overview

Other topics here such as plastics and carbon emissions do have some overlap with "pollution", but there are other serious issues under this heading, including disposal of toxic waste, chemical discharges, pollution of waterways, and so on. Indeed, some of these issues have been huge events in the history of the environmental movement, such as major oil spills (from the Torrey Canyon back in 1967 to the Deepwater Horizon tragedy in 2010). Bhopal in India is still synonymous with the terrible gas leak in 1984 at the Union Carbide India Limited pesticide plant, which killed thousands of people.

So, these are serious issues and firms need to ensure their own activities are beyond reproach. But they should also assure themselves that key suppliers are not behaving in a manner that risks pollution incidents or accusations. The potential for reputational risk here is serious – serious issues do not come to light very often, unlike modern slavery transgressions, for instance, but when something does go wrong in terms of pollution, the issue is often extremely serious.

In most cases, buyers will mandate suppliers to behave in a certain manner, certainly obeying all the relevant laws and regulations, and perhaps going beyond that to meet a specific code of conduct or similar. Buyers may use inspections and audits to check up on suppliers, and where pollution issues are potentially serious, or difficult challenges are faced, collaborative work between the parties or even across entire sectors and industries can be useful.

Which organisations should consider this issue?

- Any organisation that is itself involved in processes that create pollution or pollution risks.
- Organisations that buy goods or materials where the production or distribution of those items creates some risk of pollution.
- Any organisation that positions itself or its brands as particularly environmentally sound, "green" or aligned with nature and the natural world. For such organisations, a major pollution event, even if caused by a supplier rather than directly, could have serious implications for the business.

What can organisations do?

- Understand the supply chain for any relevant material that is purchased.
- Implement standards, codes of conduct or similar and ensure all suppliers adhere to them.
- Include aspects of these topics in the supplier selection process.
- Consider specific initiatives with key or high-risk suppliers to improve behaviour in sensitive areas.

What are the barriers and risks?

- Identifying issues and keeping track of behaviour and actions in the supply chain can be challenging.
- Contract management must be robust to ensure suppliers meet their obligations and commitments. Suppliers may not readily own up to problems, for example.
- There may be additional costs in the supply chain to reduce the risks of pollution and pollution events.

How do you measure success?

- Percentage or number of suppliers signed up to code of conduct, standards, etc.
- Lack of pollution incidents and problems.
- Reduction in toxic waste or other polluting material produced in the supply chain.

ENVIRONMENTAL – WASTE

Overview

Management of waste materials and products is linked to other topics under the "environmental" heading, such as the circular economy, pollution, and plastics. This topic deals with non-pollutant waste materials and products that organisations produce as part of their operations, from wastepaper to industrial factory waste or unwanted outputs from construction processes. This set of issues is very problematic for humanity; the UK alone produced over 220 million tonnes of waste in 2016, with construction and demolition waste the largest component. Astonishingly, 350,000 tonnes of clothing go into landfill every year in the UK.

This is a topic where many organisations will focus more on their own performance rather than worrying about what suppliers are doing. Most organisations have looked to use recycled paper, for instance, and introduced a culture of reducing waste generally.

But there are positive steps that can be taken in terms of procurement, too. Buyers of construction services can look for suppliers who have an intelligent approach to waste. Clothing retailers have introduced innovative schemes – working with manufacturers – to recycle or reuse unwanted articles. Food retailers have worked with their supply chain to package "less than perfect" fruit and vegetables to offer to customers, rather than being wasted.

Buyers can stipulate the actions or behaviours they wish suppliers to follow, or can look for innovative ideas and assess those as part of supplier selection processes. As is often the case, robust contract and supplier management is then needed to ensure suppliers do deliver against their promises.

Which organisations should consider this issue?

- Any organisation can make an impact in this area both in terms of its own waste and through encouraging the right actions in the supply chain.
- Particularly relevant for those that produce a large quantity of waste, or whose suppliers do the same in providing goods or services to the organisation.
- Organisations that sell products to the consumer that can end up as waste – often the solutions here involve the wider supply chain rather than just the retailer.

What can organisations do?

- Understand its own waste profile and take appropriate action to reduce it.
- Look at where waste is generated by suppliers and in the supply chain and encourage or mandate suppliers to address this, including by taking action in the supplier qualification and selection processes.
- Look for innovative waste reduction ideas, working in conjunction with the supply chain.

What are the barriers and risks?

- Organisations may not be aware of waste in their supply chain, and it may be hard to obtain relevant information and data.
- This may not be seen as a high-profile or "sexy" topic compared to some under the procurement with purpose banner, so may not receive the focus it deserves.

How do you measure success?

- Reduced quantity of waste produced directly and/or in the supply chain.
- Examples of innovative programmes (recycling, reusing, alternative materials etc.)

ENVIRONMENTAL – RECYCLING AND CIRCULARITY

Overview

Circularity or the "circular economy" takes the concept of waste reduction and recycling to the ultimate and looks at a model where every material and product is used again in some way. Rather than ever coming to its "end of life", materials are looked at as "cradle to cradle", rather than "cradle to grave". It is therefore linked to other issues such as management of plastics and waste more generally.

Circularity means finding ways of reusing, recycling, or reprocessing everything that might previously have been thrown away, leading eventually to a "zero waste" society. Maybe that is unachievable, but there are many innovative and exciting developments, inventions, and initiatives underway that show how much can be done in this area.

This topic can have relevance both for how an organisation looks at its own products and how it works with its supply chain. Indeed, many of the interesting initiatives here involve collaboration between organisations at different levels of the supply chain. A retail organisation for instance, that sells clothing might work with their suppliers and even the original material producer to collect unwanted garments and reprocess them into basic fibres or cloth again.

As in so many of these topics, having a good understanding of the organisation's supply chain is a necessary condition for success. Organisations can then focus attention on areas of waste that might be addressed by circular economy-type actions.

<table>
<tr><td colspan="2">Which organisations should consider this issue?
• Almost any organisation can make an impact in this area, both in terms of its own waste and through encouraging the right actions in the supply chain. But these concepts will be most relevant to firms that produce goods rather than services.
• Particularly relevant for those that produce a large quantity of waste that could be considered as part of a circularity initiative, or whose suppliers do the same in providing goods or services to the organisation.</td></tr>
<tr><td>What can organisations do?
• Understand their own waste profile and take appropriate action to consider where there could be circularity opportunities.
• Look at where waste is generated by suppliers and in the supply chain and encourage / mandate suppliers to address this in a similar manner.
• Look for innovative ideas working in conjunction with the supply chain.</td><td>What are the barriers and risks?
• Organisations may not be aware of waste in their supply chain, and it may be hard to obtain relevant information and data.
• Looking at issues from a circular economy perspective requires some imagination and innovation at times. There is not always an off-the-shelf, simple or clearly defined solution.
• Some of the solutions may be technologically advanced and therefore expensive.</td></tr>
<tr><td colspan="2">How do you measure success?
• Reduced quantity of waste produced directly and in the supply chain.
• Examples of innovative circularity programmes.</td></tr>
</table>

ENVIRONMENTAL – FOOD PROVENANCE AND ANIMAL WELFARE

Overview

This includes some of the most emotive and at times controversial issues across the entire universe of purposeful topic areas. The challenges around loss of natural species are covered as another heading, but this topic includes the treatment of farmed animals – or wild animals that are hunted or captured – as well as wider food provenance issues which can include animals, fish, fruit or vegetables.

There is a greater desire now amongst consumers to understand where the food they eat comes from, and the growth in vegan and vegetarian preferences has been significant in recent years. Equally, firms that buy significant quantities of edible raw materials or finished products – from broad beans to beef, from mangos to mackerel – increasingly want to understand where they have come from, who has grown or handled them, and how the "product" has been treated throughout its supply chain.

A lack of regard for animal welfare, traceability or hygiene has caused scandals in many industries, including the European horsemeat scandal of 2013 and regular exposés of terrible conditions for hens, pigs and other animals in the food supply chain. Indeed, those events may explain in part the growth in veganism.

Buyers who want to address these issues need to work with suppliers to make sure that they minimise the reputational risk that can come from failures in these areas. On the positive side, some firms have made management of these supply chains a factor that forms a central element of their marketing approach. Of course, in taking those actions, wider value beyond each business should emerge, as the quality of products and the welfare of animals increase over time.

Which organisations should consider this issue?

- Any organisation that buys raw materials with an animal origin and/or are used in food and drink products, or that sells food products to the consumer (including retail and leisure sectors).
- Particularly relevant for those who seek to produce or sell quality, branded products where reputational and brand risk is highest.

What can organisations do?	What are the barriers and risks?
• Understand the supply chain for any relevant material that is purchased. • Implement standards, codes of conduct or similar (in areas such as the welfare of farmed animals) and ensure all suppliers adhere to them. • Include aspects of these topics in the supplier qualification and selection process. • Consider specific initiatives with key or high-risk suppliers to improve behaviour in sensitive areas.	• Even tracing supply back to original growers or farmers can be difficult, particularly when sourced from inaccessible or underdeveloped areas. • Verifying claims made by different players in (often complex) supply chains can be difficult. • Additional costs may be incurred by suppliers which may be passed on to buyers, e.g. for organic crops or free-range animal products.

How do you measure success?

- Quantity or percentage of material bought from accredited and verified sources.
- Quantity or percentage of organic / free-range / premium quality materials bought.
- Examples of innovative programmes working with the supply chain to improve standards and quality.

ENVIRONMENTAL – WATER CONSERVATION AND MANAGEMENT

Overview

Water is taken for granted in the developed world. For drinking or washing at home, watering the garden or the golf course, or playing critical roles in many manufacturing processes, the tap is turned and out it will come. But as humanity uses more and more water every year, problems are building up. Drought is a key issue in many areas, whilst the building of dams is causing geopolitical tensions between different countries through which the same river flows – for example, recent issues connected with Ethiopia's new Nile dam which has affected the relationship with Sudan and Egypt.

Organisations which use a large amount of water themselves can look for initiatives that will reduce that – and suppliers may be involved in supporting such developments. In terms of sustainable procurement, this is clearly most relevant where key suppliers are major users of water. That ranges from organisations that buy large quantities of agricultural products, where crop irrigation is key, to those using chemicals that require large amounts of water to manufacture.

As in many of these issues, there are different approaches that can be taken, ranging from the relatively light touch to strong collaborative approaches. Innovation has featured strongly here, too, with new processes designed to dramatically reduce water use, for example, by recycling and reusing water in manufacturing processes.

So, while this will not be a top priority for many (public sector procurement, for instance, does not tend to worry too much about this issue), for a percentage of firms and industries it can and should be very significant.

<table>
<tr><td colspan="2">

Which organisations should consider this issue?

- Any organisation that purchases products which require large amounts of water to manufacture.
- Organisations that are based in countries or areas that suffer from water shortages and want to be seen to be supporting wider initiatives and programmes.

</td></tr>
<tr><td>

What can organisations do?

- Understand supply chains and suppliers to identify where water use is significant.
- Incorporate questions about water use – or develop a code of conduct for suppliers to sign up to – in order to bring this issue into the supplier qualification processes.
- Work directly with strategic suppliers to look at ways in which water usage might be reduced through the supply chain.

</td><td>

What are the barriers and risks?

- Difficult to understand sometimes exactly what water use is through the supply chain.
- Monitoring supplier actions is challenging, as is verifying any data and information they are providing.
- Sometimes simply little in the way of realistic alternatives to water use in certain processes.

</td></tr>
<tr><td colspan="2">

How do you measure success?

- Reduction in direct water use in the supply chain.
- Number or % of suppliers signing up to code of conduct or similar.

</td></tr>
</table>

ENVIRONMENTAL – LOCAL ENVIRONMENTAL ISSUES

Overview

Some of the issues discussed here are truly amongst the biggest and most pressing that humanity is facing. Climate change, deforestation, human rights, and diversity... these are hugely challenging and massively important topics. Yet, for most people, local issues matter more on a day-to-day basis. Concerns over local transport or traffic, noisy neighbours, vandalism, or antisocial behaviour can affect individuals more than these huge global issues.

On that basis, procurement with purpose approaches that focus more on these local issues can be important and positive. For instance, if a firm outsources logistics to a large transport firm, how does that provider manage traffic around their depots, so they are not keeping local residents awake all night? How do firms act as good local citizens in terms of issues such as noise, traffic, waste, or even litter?

These issues may be more relevant in terms of how organisations manage their own behaviour and actions. But at times, as in the example of the transport supplier, it can be appropriate for buyers to ask or require suppliers to behave in certain ways. There may be crossover here, as some issues might relate to the buyer's local issues but be facilitated by suppliers. So, a firm might work with its logistics provider in terms of vehicles coming to the buyer's own factories, in order to avoid upsetting local residents.

As in many of the topics, that can be done by requiring or mandating suppliers to behave in a certain manner if they want to win contracts; it can be included as an element in the supplier selection process; and it can be based on collaborative work with a supplier once the contract is up and running.

Which organisations should consider this issue?

- Any organisation that wants to demonstrate it is a good local citizen.
- Organisations that identify major suppliers who are in danger of alienating people through their action, and fear the reputational risk from that behaviour.

What can organisations do?	What are the barriers and risks?
• Understand where issues may lie both internally and through the supply chain. • Implement standards, codes of conduct or similar and ensure relevant suppliers adhere to them. Include aspects of these topics in the supplier selection process. • Consider specific initiatives with key or high-risk suppliers to improve behaviour in sensitive areas.	• Identifying issues and keeping track of behaviour and actions in the supply chain can be challenging. • Contract management must be robust to ensure suppliers meet their obligations and commitments.
How do you measure success? • Percentage or number of suppliers signed up to code of conduct, standards, etc. • Lack of negative "local issue" reports.	

ECONOMIC – TREATMENT OF SUPPLIERS

Overview

This subject differs from most of the others featured here, because the prime responsibility for action sits firmly with the buyer. For most of the topics, buyers are persuading or mandating suppliers to take action, or working together with suppliers. But in terms of how organisations treat their own suppliers, the onus is of course very much on the buyer. However, the buyer may also want to persuade suppliers to pursue a similar approach down the supply chain, and is interested in how first-tier providers treat their own suppliers – and so on.

Too often firms "talk the talk" about ethical or sustainable business, but then do not back that up with action in terms of how they treat suppliers. At the first sign of economic trouble, supplier invoices are ignored, payment terms are unilaterally extended, or price reductions, discounts and rebates are demanded. Whilst there is a fine dividing line between acceptable but tough commercial behaviour and unethical action, the line can and should be drawn.

There is nothing wrong with firms using supply chain finance, for instance – offering buyers accelerated payment in return for a small fee. But if that is based on standard payment terms of 120 days or more, it becomes onerous and less acceptable. Similarly, a negotiated payment from a supplier to share the costs of in-store promotion is fine, but demanding retrospective rebates after the event by threatening to cut off further business is not.

Unusually again, this topic applies to any organisation, large or small, in whatever sector. It is a fundamental building block for all who want to consider that they work in an ethical, sustainable, and purposeful manner. And it is not just about "doing the right thing" – there are business benefits to being seen as a "customer of choice". Equally, acting unethically with suppliers will in the long term damage supplier relationships, affect the organisation's reputation, and is unlikely to be a sustainable route to success.

Which organisations should consider this issue?

- Literally every organisation – it is hard to see why any respectable organisation would consciously wish to behave unethically towards their suppliers.
- Organisations that particularly position themselves as "caring", ethical, or purposeful should be aware of reputational dangers in this area if they do not subscribe to these principles.

What can organisations do?

- Implement standards, codes of conduct or similar (within the organisation) that lay down how suppliers will be treated. Ensure all staff are aware of the standards and work to them at all times.
- Persuade or mandate their own suppliers to behave in a particular manner with their suppliers. (Paying suppliers promptly is often a central element of this initiative).

What are the barriers and risks?

- There are difficult "grey areas", such as payment terms where the difference between unethical approaches and simply a tough negotiation stance can be blurred.
- When times get tough, it is tempting to take simplistic approaches such as demanding price reduction or extending payment terms.

How do you measure success?

- Prompt payment statistics (average days paid, overdue payments, etc.).
- Supplier surveys can be a useful tool to gauge supplier views of the customer organisation.
- Absence of negative media comments.

ECONOMIC – FRAUD, CORRUPTION AND SANCTIONS

Overview

This is another topic that might cause surprise in terms of being included under the procurement with purpose heading. But these topics have the issue of legality (or illegality) in common and clearly relate to how organisations relate to their suppliers (and customers) and how they can contribute to society in that wider sense beyond short-term profits.

Procurement is a major source of fraud and corruption, because so much of any organisation's money flows through the purchase of goods and services from external parties. Whilst fraud is often thought to be driven usually by the sales side of the equation (the brown paper envelope being offered to a buyer in return for a contract), it takes two for that sort of corruption to happen. And there are many types of corruption and fraud, ranging from the simple to the extremely complex. Unfortunately, those within organisations who control budgets are often the instigators of fraud, and sometimes suppliers are dragged into that, willingly or perhaps reluctantly.

So organisations need to have processes in place that guard against fraud and corruption, and policies that make it clear what will happen to anyone who conducts themselves in an inappropriate manner. Those "rules" should be communicated to suppliers, too, in terms of how they behave, and can be built into supplier selection processes and contract terms.

Sanctions issues relate to countries, sectors, or firms that global bodies such as the UN or individual countries have decided should not be allowed to sell certain goods. Embargoes on selling arms is a common example, or it may be restricting the export of minerals from a war-torn region. In any case, it is essential that buyers are aware of any sanction regimes in place that may affect their procurement, and work within the regulations.

<table>
<tr><td colspan="2">Which organisations should consider this issue?
• Every organisation should guard against fraud and corruption – that should hardly need saying. Some will be more vulnerable than others depending on the profile of their business (both supply and buy side) but the basic precautions and processes should be in place everywhere.
• In terms of sanctions, clearly those organisations that buy (or sell) materials from countries that are covered by sanctions regulations should pay particular attention to this issue.</td></tr>
<tr><td>What can organisations do?
• Put clear processes and policies in place that make fraud and corruption difficult to execute and be willing to take action if staff do transgress.
• Understand any relevant sanctions regimes in place that might affect potential procurement decisions.
• Communicate appropriate policies to suppliers and require sign-up contractually or through codes of conduct or similar.</td><td>What are the barriers and risks?
• By their very nature, these incidents and issues are usually well concealed and not easy to uncover.
• Even if there is evidence, organisations may wish to keep their response low-profile to avoid bad publicity, which means perpetrators escape lightly and good practice is not shared.</td></tr>
<tr><td colspan="2">How do you measure success?
• Measurement is mainly through things NOT happening – a lack of fraud and corruption cases, or sanctions infringements.</td></tr>
</table>

ECONOMIC – FAIR WAGES

Overview

For many of these purpose-related topics, it is easy to understand what is "right" and what is "wrong". There may be some nuances, but virtually everyone would agree that polluting the oceans, or driving orangutans into extinction, or holding workers in slavery conditions, are not good things to be doing. However, the issue of "fair wages" takes us into more difficult moral and ethical areas.

Many countries have implemented minimum wage policies and regulations. In those cases, buyers can and should make sure that suppliers are working within those rules, and that requirement can be covered in the supplier selection process and in the contract if that seems appropriate. There may also be initiatives such as the "London Living Wage", which goes above and beyond the legal minimum, and has been implemented by many firms in that city.

The difficulty comes when we look at employment in the developing world. What is a "fair" or "living" wage in Benin, where half of the population lives on less than $1.90 a day? If a large multinational firm pays $5 a day to local workers, is it being very generous, or is it exploiting workers?

These are difficult issues, and apply both to firms' own employment practices, and through key supply chains. Some firms have implemented approaches where suppliers are asked or required to pay "fair wages", but the difficulty comes in defining the right level. However, that does not mean buyers should ignore this issue. The reputational risk is considerable where firms have significant numbers of very poorly paid workers in their supply chain.

Which organisations should consider this issue?

- Any organisation that either directly or through key suppliers is a major employer of relatively unskilled/low-paid workers in the developing world.
- Organisations that buy from supply chains that have endemic issues even in more developed countries (e.g. clothing manufacturing in the UK).
- Organisations that particularly position themselves as "caring" and concerned should be aware of reputational dangers in this area.

What can organisations do?

- Understand key supply chains and where issues of fair wages might emerge within them.
- Implement standards, codes of conduct or similar (based on legislation or voluntary codes) and ensure all suppliers adhere to them.
- Include aspects of these topics in the supplier selection process.
- Consider specific initiatives with key or high-risk suppliers to improve behaviour in sensitive areas.

What are the barriers and risks?

- The ethical judgements particularly in the developing world can be tricky.
- It can be exceedingly difficult to establish what is happening through the supply chain in terms of wages and employment conditions.
- "Perverse outcomes" are a risk – force a supplier to increase wages and they may close operations in that country or go out of business.

How do you measure success?

- Percentage or number of suppliers signed up to codes of conduct, etc.
- Absence of negative media stories.

ECONOMIC – PAYING TAXES

Overview

This topic moves the discussions into contentious territory. Taxation is an economic, political, and moral issue. Some fervently believe that taxes should be minimised and the government should provide only the most basic of public services, leaving citizens free to spend as much of their money as possible in the manner they see fit. Others will argue for high taxation, so governments can provide more services for the public good – health, education, defence, social services, and so on.

Almost everybody will agree that business should pay their "fair share" in terms of taxation. The problem comes both with defining what is "fair", and then in the detailed mechanisms and regulations that relate to taxation. Businesses have a responsibility to shareholders not to pay tax they do not have to. And one person's definition of "tax evasion" (which is illegal) might be another's "tax avoidance" (which is perfectly legal). Most people avoid tax in legitimate fashion – paying into a pension scheme, offsetting losses against capital gains, or investing as a business in plant and machinery.

Governments have tried to use public procurement to some extent to drive good behaviour by firms, or at least to avoid awarding contracts to firms that are not paying taxes as they should. The UK government, for instance, asks firms to state in bid documents whether they have convictions for tax issues, but the barriers for exclusion are high. In Spain, however, 37 municipalities have publicly committed not to work with companies that operate in tax havens – this includes the major cities of Madrid, Barcelona, Seville and Zaragoza. But what is the definition of a "tax haven"?

Generally, private sector buyers have not followed the lead of government. Few firms consider their potential suppliers' tax affairs in the supplier selection process. That is understandable – this is primarily an issue for governments, both in terms of protecting their tax revenues, and to be seen by voters to take a strong line against those who are perceived as not paying their fair share.

Which organisations should consider this issue?

- This is primarily an issue for public sector organisations, particularly central and local government entities, who have a strong interest in tax revenues and in fair taxation approaches.
- Any public organisation that is led by elected representatives may want to be seen to take appropriate action against tax evasion, including by suppliers and potential suppliers.

What can organisations do?

- Implement laws, standards, codes of conduct or similar that define how suppliers should act and behave in terms of their tax approaches and payments.
- Do not allow firms that fail to meet standards to bid for or deliver contracts.
- Work with key suppliers who may have issues to resolve those before banning them.

What are the barriers and risks?

- Defining "tax evasion" or "tax havens" is not always straightforward.
- Identifying bad behaviour in terms of tax is also not easy in many cases.
- A stringent approach might eliminate a lot of otherwise good suppliers from the market.

How do you measure success?

- Absence of suppliers with "tax problems".

ECONOMIC – PROMOTING SUPPLIER INNOVATION

Overview

Why is this topic included under the "procurement with purpose" heading? Most executives now recognise that innovation is vital for organisations and that capturing innovation from suppliers is a key element of that, because much potential innovation will come from suppliers and supply markets, rather than purely from inside the firm. Making use of such innovation has become a key objective for most of the better procurement functions around the world in recent years.

But does it really link to "purpose" and "sustainability"? The argument is perhaps a little tenuous. It certainly is not such a clear linkage as in topics such as climate change or human rights. However, it is included here for two principal reasons.

Firstly, innovation drives economic performance, at global, national and local level. Whilst there are arguments about trickle-down economic theories, generally innovation is what has improved the lot of humankind over the centuries, from invention of basic agricultural tools to the discovery of vaccines and life-saving drugs.

Secondly, many of the other "core" procurement with purpose issues rely strongly on innovation to address the serious issues faced in areas such as plastics or sustainable energy approaches. Look at the way large firms such as Unilever have worked with packaging suppliers to develop more environmentally friendly plastics, or the manner in which wind and solar energy technologies have become price-competitive with traditional means of power generation. Innovation is driving success in many of these key "purpose" topics, as well as contributing to general economic well-being, so it seems reasonable to include it on the list here.

Which organisations should consider this issue?

- Most organisations should be encouraging innovation from their own suppliers and supply chain as a matter of course. Whether it is formally considered as part of a procurement with purpose programme does depend really on where attention is being focused in terms of that innovation.
- But organisations whose success depends on innovation, and that includes most businesses in most sectors, should have some sort of strategy for addressing identification and capture of innovation in the supply chain.

What can organisations do?

- Organisations should be open to innovation from any supplier or potential supplier, across everything and anything they buy. That is an attitude of mind as much as anything.
- Consider which spend areas and which suppliers (current or potential) could be included in a formal "supplier innovation" initiative.
- Such programmes should be structured, based on benefit sharing, with relevant tools and technology used to support them.

What are the barriers and risks?

- "Innovation" is not something that can be stipulated contractually in most cases. It depends on a range of factors – from choosing the right suppliers, to knowing how to work in a collaborative manner.
- Many organisations struggle with concepts such as sharing benefits with suppliers. Capturing innovation from the supply chain requires a range of skills, knowledge, and behaviours that many "traditional" procurement organisations do not possess.

How do you measure success?

- Number of "innovation ideas" from suppliers.
- Some firms go further and have targets for % of revenue from products introduced in the last (say) 3 years – and how much of that comes from supply market innovation.

ECONOMIC – PROMOTING EMPLOYMENT

Overview

This overlaps with the "Social" category of initiatives, particularly when considering public sector bodies that want suppliers to employ a particular type of person – which could mean local people, those with disabilities, apprentices, long-term unemployed, or other disadvantaged groups.

Of course, spending money with suppliers is part of the basic economic life, and always promotes employment in some way. But it is possible to go further and persuade or even mandate suppliers to take certain actions that focus on employment. That can be achieved by different mechanisms; so potential suppliers might be asked to guarantee a certain number of new "local jobs" in a tender for a public construction contract in a town or city.

Or different proposals could be sought from potential suppliers, and the different options evaluated and the social value of each assessed and compared, which might include employment of disadvantaged groups, or guaranteeing a number of apprenticeships.

It is fair to say that generally it has been the public sector which has pursued this sort of option. Most private firms do not consider that employment through the supply chain is particularly relevant to their decision-making, other than ensuring it is done in a manner consistent with legislation and human rights. It is also apparent that these commitments from suppliers are often not really monitored once the contract is up and running, making it questionable as to how effective this approach has proved to date.

Which organisations should consider this issue?

- It has mainly been public sector bodies, particularly those with a "local" focus such as councils (local authorities) that have looked at using this approach.
- However, any organisation that positions itself as having a local focus (or perhaps a particularly local customer base) might want to consider how it can use procurement in this way to drive local employment.
- The same could apply if, for instance, a firm's customer base was skewed towards people with disabilities – encouraging employment of similar people in the supply chain might be an appropriate approach.

<table>
<tr>
<td>What can organisations do?
• Encourage suppliers or even mandate certain numbers or types of employment linked to the contract.
• Include the issue in the supplier selection process and ask bidders for their proposals.
• Manage the contract and supplier to ensure commitments are honoured.</td>
<td>What are the barriers and risks?
• Private sector organisations may feel this is intruding too far into how their suppliers run their own businesses.
• It is difficult to verify information provided by suppliers in terms of job creation.
• It may be hard to establish whether supplier actions are really linked to the buyer – e.g. would these jobs have been created anyway?</td>
</tr>
<tr>
<td colspan="2">How do you measure success?
• Number of new jobs created, or jobs sustained, potentially broken down by groups, e.g. disabled people, apprentices.
• Number or percentage of suppliers signing up to some sort of code of conduct or charter relating to job creation.</td>
</tr>
</table>

A Final Word

We hope you've enjoyed this book, found it interesting and informative, useful, and perhaps inspiring in some sense.

It's clear that procurement with purpose is a huge topic. Each of the issues covered in Section 3 deserves and indeed has inspired many books in its own right. In fact, there are subsets of subsets that have generated entire books – a topic such as human rights has many aspects, and each aspect can be considered in different ways or in different countries, for instance.

But the purpose here has been to help executives think about how they and their organisations might become advocates for the procurement with purpose approach. To that end, we hope you are convinced that there are benefits to be gained here, both for society and for your organisation itself. There are also benefits for executives in procurement and sustainability teams, as well as for other sponsors of these purposeful approaches within the organisation. There are encouraging stories of procurement increasing its profile and perceived importance in large businesses as it embraces what is seen today as a highly important and strategic agenda.

It is important to note, too, that adopting procurement goals that focus on wider purpose should not be seen as something that is going to cost the organisation a lot of money. Indeed, these initiatives can often actually deliver better value for money (in the traditional sense) as well as contributing towards wider societal benefits.

However, it is important to think carefully about how the organisation embraces these ideas. It is easy to waste time and effort if you don't think strategically about what you're trying to do. No one can address every procurement with purpose issue fully and meaningfully, so organisations need to focus and have a clear strategy. Then implementation needs to be carefully planned and professionally executed to deliver real benefits and outputs.

It is also important to understand the pitfalls, such as being accused of "greenwashing", or the dangers of awarding contracts for the wrong reasons. There have been examples of unintended and negative consequences after firms or public bodies implemented well-intentioned ideas about helping certain types of supplier.

But the positives that have been seen in areas as diverse as protecting the rainforest, helping minority-owned businesses, or improving working conditions in the developing world, make procurement with purpose a very hot topic and one which has much further to run. Much more can and should be achieved, and the urgency of addressing many of these issues should not be forgotten. As Sir David Attenborough, Greta Thunberg and many others have reminded us, we need to take action now – not over the next decade, not even next year, but now. Time is running out.

We hope this book will help people and organisations as they make this journey towards purposeful business in general – and procurement with purpose in particular.

INDEX